Crohn-ly get better

The Memoirs of the Crohnically Fabulous

Sarah Donnelly

Contents

Introduction

They say the road to hell is paved with good intentions, which brings me to begin writing my memoirs, aged 25 factually, 65 physically, and 17 mentally. From the end of 2017 and all of 2018, I struggle to find the words to describe both the physical and mental endurance my body has been put through. All from a small 5 lettered word, called "Crohn's" (formally known as Crohn's disease). It is hard to believe this time a year ago, I thought the answer to my problems would be to continue "treating" it in my own fashion, consisting of numerous imodem tablets, naps, pain relief, and it would all be fine, after years of misdiagnoses. Alas, my sorry logic was as massively flawed as putting a feather in the ground and thinking it would grow a chicken.

I have promised myself I would sit down with my thoughts and feelings in a bid to help even one other person with this illness (or person in general), especially in a moment of darkness where they can hopefully not feel so alone. But like all things, "I'll do it another day."Part of the issue is the dreaded; where do I start?! How candid can I be? Who would actually want to read this? And will I actually show this to anyone by the end? Barely 250 words in, and I'm already doubting whether I will finish this. But if 2018 has taught me anything, the unimaginable is possible. My world feels permanently full of doubt and 90% of the time full of pain and disappointment, but if this is how I feel, how the hell is everyone else feeling. So, in this moment of compassion or my sleep-deprived steroid-induced state, I begin shovelling the concrete.

I've learned so much about myself and grown as a person this past year, and I think it is also important to take a moment to document it. They say everyone is fighting an internal battle daily, and I am a firm believer in this; a problem to one person may seem completely trivial to another. No person's problem is trivial when you haven't experienced first-hand their problem or the range of emotions that have led them to feel that way. Apart from that expression "I'm dying from the cold", as a chronic illness sufferer, that now fucks me off big time.

I began attempting to write this in November 2018 when suffering insomnia due to Prednisolone. As soon as I was off it, I, of course, stopped writing again. Now it is the end of February 2019, and I begin to write again. I'll be honest and say it terrifies me, as suffering from Crohn's, I've become very used to my small comfort zone. I'm supposed to be a 25-year-old woman, yet I feel like a scared, lonely 5-year-old girl that can't relate or be understood anymore. I think due to the daily facade of smiling, being friendly, and pretending like it all doesn't get to me, it has been working. I'm regularly asked, "how have you not had a breakdown yet?", told "you're so brave" and "I've so much respect for you". Comments I usually laugh off and tell people they'd do the same in my shoes. Crohn's has consumed my life now for over 5 years, albeit I was undiagnosed the first 4. So unfortunately for myself and the millions of other sufferers around the world, surgeries, medication, pain, fatigue, and most importantly, shitting (if you can call brown water and undigested food shit) is all in a day's work.

I'm not sure where to begin, to be honest, they say at the beginning, but I get the fear, and part of me doesn't want to relive it. Part of me also feels like I forget how bad it was. However, I will try, as it surely can't be as bad the second time around...

Is it something you ate?

Symptoms started around September 2013. I was approaching 20, in the second year of my law degree, and had just moved in with friends. I knew something was wrong, but I kept ignoring it. My morning coffee, which I had been drinking every morning since the first year of secondary school (with no side effects except waking me up slightly), was now sending me to the toilet urgently about 5 times in a row within having a mouthful. I was vomiting my stomach lining or breakfast most mornings and, on occasion running out of lectures to get to a toilet. I put it down to starting the pill again after reading the side effect of nausea and hearing a few others say the same thing. I was not ready to admit to myself something was wrong and especially the whole toilet aspect. I also thought maybe I was starting to suffer really brutal hangovers now I was 20 and ancient (if only I thought 20 was ancient now). I kind of knew it wasn't the hangovers, though, as symptoms were actually worse when sober. It was mainly a morning thing, but on a bad day, I could be sick at any point of the day, and the sight of undigested food like lettuce or tomatoes in the toilet bowl was horrifying me. I should have done something, but I was young and embarrassed. This continued and worsened for about 2 years.

When I began working, getting the bus every morning was my real-life worse nightmare. Mornings were now nearly impossible, and I was still trying to pretend there was nothing wrong with me. I felt violently sick with nausea and what I now realise was anxiety. I would spend the whole journey internally screaming in my head, "OMG, I need a fucking toilet, what if I shit myself? I feel so sick", all while sitting casually looking at my phone. I realise now I did slightly move or twitch as the anxiety grew and probably looked like a massive weirdo to those near me on the bus. I had lost about a stone of weight over the final year of uni, but it was put down to stress. Thinking back, I was so tiny but never thought I was; I must have been closer to 7 stone, but as I am petite and around 5'1, my weight was still in a healthy range of "underweight" on the BMI scale. At this point, the bleeding started when I went to the toilet, and I only went to a doctor after being on a night out and doubling over in pain with my stomach visibly spasming through my dress. I was staying at my boyfriend, Conor, family's house that night as we had both moved home after uni, and I remember crying in front of his mum as my stomach continued to ache and spasm. I was mortified the next day, especially as I sobered up, but I was scared and in a lot of pain. I had now admitted to people about the bleeding when going to the toilet, but I knew that everyone's main concern was"is she pregnant" due to my age and how healthy I looked. Especially with nausea, stomach pain, bleeding, and vomiting. Now I'm no medical expert, but I was bleeding out the wrong hole to be pregnant, so that was off the cards. The next day I phoned the out-of-hours doctor, who definitely thought the same as she made me do a pregnancy test. She felt my stomach, and when I said where the pain was, she asked if I was having toilet trouble as it was my bowel that was in agony. So, of course, I lied through my fucking teeth and told her no, everything is alright. She continued to ask, she was really good thinking back actually and properly probed me, but of course, I continued to lie. I wish I hadn't. So, I was prescribed some buscopan, and off I went.

Conor and I were going to Iceland in less than a week, and I was unbelievably excited about this, so nothing was getting in the way of it. Of course, with an early morning flight, the inevitable happened, and shortly before our flight was to board, my bowels went. I went to the toilet, mortified if anyone could hear in these public bathrooms, also aware of the time and mentally and physically now shitting myself. Conor didn't know what was going on, and my phone started going when in the toilets, with shouting texts asking where the fuck was I and to hurry up, or we'll miss our flight. When I finally left the bathroom, I was greeted to this due to his lack of understanding and already feeling like shit, I tried brushing it off, saying my bowels were bad. I got the standard, "You can hold it like everyone else", but unfortunately, that is not a luxury people with any form of bowel disease have. Especially an undiagnosed/ not controlled form. I told him, no, it was really bad, and I was dreading the flight. This was something I was right to dread, and I still feel sorry for the poor woman in the aisle seat trying to sleep, I must've woke her about 10 times. What I now know to be called a flare-up was happening big time, and I apologised to the flight staff and told them I had been told something was up with my bowel by the doctor and was on tablets, mortifying. Thankfully, the staff on that EasyJet flight were super lovely and understanding and made me feel great. They told me not to worry at all and whatever I needed to do not to worry as long as I was ok and if there was anything they could do to help, just let them know. This helped a lot, and still to this day, even now diagnosed; I wish people could be this understanding and kind. The guy flight attendant was really funny and even made a joke about if I needed to shit go for it; I laughed and lightened my mood.

Having finally made it to Iceland, which is undoubtedly one if not the most beautiful country I've seen, Crohn's went back to being its standard, mostly bad in the morning until flying back, and it flared a bit worse. I vividly remember nearly shitting myself at the check-in and running to the toilets after. I've now learnt stress is a major trigger for me, and the stress of travelling and not knowing where the nearest toilet is and the what if I shit myself or vomit in public panic. It's probably strange for those without IBD to imagine, but it is quite literally the main thought on my mind at all times. The taboo topic for most of going to the toilet is mine, and other IBD suffers life 90% of the time. Although it's something that we can hide most of the time, it also means not many really see how much those with IBD suffer. When he is teaching medical students about it, my consultant said, think of having your worst case of gastroenteritis and then think, not knowing when it will stop. He said most couldn't get their heads around it, which I find quite amusing as I am so accustomed to it. But then again, you can't imagine something you've never experienced, so in a way, mildly envy them.

Fast forward a few months, and again, symptoms got progressively worse. Especially with the bleeding, and at this point, I had given up being in denial. I phoned the GP for an emergency appointment one morning and mortified told the reception my symptoms. I was also walking into work, so I was really trying to keep my voice down. No one needs to hear, "I'm shitting blood!" at 8.55 am. My normal GP couldn't see me as she was on holiday, and I was booked in with another doctor covering, who basically laughed at me when I told her my symptoms. "You're far too young and too healthy-looking to have anything seriously wrong with you" was what I was told. The shitting blood symptom was shockingly dismissed as "normal" and "not concerning" as it was "probably piles". My diet and allergies were blamed as the most likely causes as she actually continued laughing and smiling, explaining this, but a precautionary blood test was arranged. It was honestly not very nice when I was already embarrassed about going to the doctors and trying to tell them what was wrong. It was nearly as bad as when telling some people, I had to be careful with tea/coffee as it can make me unwell (already embarrassed as people literally live for caffeine), and their response being a funny look and saying, "it's all in your head". There weren't many of these assholes, but there was a few.

After blood tests, my inflammation levels (ESR and CRP) came back raised, so I was asked to give a faecal calprotectin sample. In layman's terms, a sample of my shit. I have to say doing that was not pleasant. It turns out the water in the toilet bowl actually traps a lot of the smell (unbelievable, I know), and starting my day by shitting into an old Chinese carton then using the little shovel on the vile they give to scrape it in at 7 am is not the one. I thought I was going to vomit. A couple of years later, alas, I've done this so many times it doesn't really bother me now. The things you get used to, eh (I say that, but the smell always gets you, boke). Those test results came back, and my GP phoned me at 7 pm one evening saying my levels are raised, and they suspect an inflamed bowel, so I was being referred to gastro. My mum and dad were growing concerned too at this point, so my mum, through her works private health insurance, took me to who was considered "the best" for further testing. He told me my levels were very raised, and due to this, he would only need to do a flexible sigmoidoscopy, which is basically a tube shoved up your bum that looks at the first third of your large intestine. It's as pleasant as it sounds. He also said that this smaller scope should only be needed due to my high inflammation levels, as he should see the inflammation as soon as he goes in.

Apprehensive but also excited to hopefully have an answer, I began researching inflamed bowels myself. I learned about Crohn's disease and Ulcerative Colitis and how they were both the main forms of Inflammatory Bowel Disease (IBD), and also about IBS. Crohn's affects your whole/any part of your digestive system, depending on the person, causing inflammation and ulceration, whereas Ulcerative Colitis only affects your large bowel. After reading the symptoms, I remember thinking I don't think I have IBS; mine seem more like IBD. I knew that they could treat this, although there was no cure, and I didn't mind this as I thought I would get better. I thought it would be like taking antibiotics; you get better for a while, and if it flares up, take more medication, and repeat as necessary. Whereas there isn't much, you can do with IBS except watch your diet. I love food far too much to be watching what I eat all the time, and life's far too short not to enjoy the small things. Get fucked IBS, I remember thinking, medication is a much better answer to extreme diet change. Thinking back, although I still agree with some of this logic, I forgot how young and naive I was, now 22. I thought there was going to be light at the end of the tunnel soon; little did I know this was just the beginning.

The day of my flexible sigmoidoscopy came, and I remember having to fast from 12 the night before, but my appointment wasn't until after 3 pm. I had done a half-day in work and could barely concentrate. I was so hungry and wanting the latter half of the afternoon to be over when I would hopefully have some answers. I have to say that's one of the worst things about those tests, the hunger. I'm a starvo at the best of times, but there's something about having to fast that's 10 times worse. I suppose being told you're not allowed to do anything makes you want to do it more, but closer to 24 hours of fasting is not ok. I genuinely worried if I was going to do it or not as I tend to go weak and dizzy when hungry, never mind the hanger. I learned it came in waves of intense hunger, then passed again before repeating back to hunger and thought of the starving children in Africa. How do they do it? How do you get used to this? Fucking hell, it's inhumane. It really is a cruel world.

My mum took me to the appointment, and it was in the Ulster Independent. Fuck me, it's nice. Felt like I was in a weird medical hotel and learned to wish all my hospital stays were there. It had felt like the longest day already between waiting and fasting, but I was nearly there. I was put in my gown and told they needed to use an enema to "clear me out". Yes, they are as delightful as they sound. I remembered a gay friend saying a lot of gay guys would use them before sex and thinking, fuck me, you heroes. I would not be ok with that clear out method every time I wanted my hole. The argument for choosing to be gay and not being born that way really goes out the window if you've ever experienced one. Also, as a firm believer, you are born gay, and those who don't believe this are ignorant cunts, so my sadistic side also hoped someday they too would experience an enema. I mean, I have no idea if the enema gay guys' use is the same as this medical one for a scope up your ass, but either way, not pleasant. The nurse looking after me was super lovely and put me at as much ease as she could. I mean, fair play to her; it was difficult given the circumstances of just meeting and asking me to put my knees to my chest and lie on my side so she could squeeze some liquid up my ass. She gave me a real mum/granny kind of caring vibe, and with hindsight, I'm really glad I had her.

I was told to hold it for 15 minutes if I could, and if I needed anything to press the buzzer, and the nurses would be right in. Unfortunately, the remote with the button was right where my elbow was, so approximately 5 minutes in, when the burning medicated liquid that had been squeezed up my ass was getting a bit much, I jumped up, elbowing the buzzer. Low and behold, two nurses came running in (they weren't lying) and were asking if I was ok. At this point, I was standing outside the en suite, backless gown open, clenching like fuck, saying I was going to pace to see if it helped with the sensation (lies, but at 5 mins in, I was desperate). Of course, they didn't believe me and said back into bed and hold a bit longer. I returned to bed but, of course, waited until they left the room to run to the en suite again, absolutely elated to see a toilet. The burn. Jesus fucking Christ, the burn. They don't tell you about that! As I exploded out the burning blue liquid, this was where I stayed for quite some time. The sensation left you feeling like there was always more coming, which isn't anything new with Crohn's, but this time, it was burning my insides and the skin on the way out. I was not excited about this scope. Apart from all that, my room was lovely and had a proper bed with proper bed sheets, a tv, wifi, and en suite. I could've got used to it, minus the enema.

It was time for the scope, and I can't remember at what point I had the cannula put in (the needle into your vein that allows the medicine to go into your system), as I was 100% taking the sedation. Nobody likes a martyr when there are free drugs going. I got wheeled in on my big bed to the room and saw my consultant, where I was given sedation, and without much warning, it started. I remember being alarmed they had an oxygen mask on me and kept being told my blood pressure was very low (but that isn't new for me; it's usually low, also unsurprising as I hadn't eaten in closer to 24 hours). The scope itself, I remember being painful; the sedation they used is actually a medicine they use to make you forget. So, at the time, I remembered it all so clearly but afterwards was foggy. In essence, I was roofied by a doctor. Although he could've given me something stronger, the stingy fuck. The scopes consist of blowing you up with air which is uncomfortable considering it's meant to come out, not in. I watched as I could see my intestines on the screen and thought, I'm no doctor, but this looks clear. The biopsies being taken were more alarming as bits of my insides were cut at, and I could see them bleeding on the screen.

When they got to the last bit of the scope, I heard him say I need to take a picture, and that's it. Thank fuck I thought. He then pulled the scope back down, and the words, "you never took a picture", were said. WTF, I thought. Some nurse or doctor, whatever they were, then replied, "I didn't know", so he went back up again, this time full speed and full force and apologised. Christ, that hurt, but at least that's it, I thought. However, I've never been a lucky person, and the next thing I heard was, "you didn't put the flash on". No. fucking. Way. So, again, he went at full speed and full force, and this time, it hurt even more. SOMEHOW this happened yet another time, and by the THIRD ramming of my insides, I learned over to the nurse who was by my side, grabbed her by her collar and screamed, "MAKE IT STOP!!!".

Half sedated and in pain do not mix. They said to the consultant no more, and she took my hand and laughed, saying, don't worry if we hurt you, you get to hurt us. I felt really bad, she was really nice, and I never meant to hurt her, but she knew it was an accident, thankfully, and I was in a lot of pain. I think that's the one and only time in my life I've grabbed someone by their collar and screamed in their face. After this, I heard the consultant say, "Sarah, we couldn't find anything, just a few polyps we have biopsied." I chose to ignore him as I was soo gutted. How the fuck couldn't they find anything?! I'm shitting 5-10 times a day, bleeding and in agony. Fuck you too, Dr, fuck you. It all didn't seem worth it, and I just wanted to pretend I was half asleep as I lay there wallowing in my own self-pity.

I was brought into recovery and remember being told to fart loads to get the wind they had just blew up me out, as if I don't, it'll get trapped and be really painful. Scundered! But I did as they said and got it out; however, with the burning of the enema still lingering every fart felt like I was going to shit myself. So naturally apprehensive of their advice. It was thankfully all good, though, and I got some tea and toast in my room. I have to say, although it wasn't cooked to my liking, it went down well (I prefer my toast on the more well-done side, lol, also kept forgetting this place wasn't some sort of hotel). I was so hungry they brought me extra biscuits too, amazing. I knew I wasn't going to get this treatment at home. The consultant had told my mum the news and had said he didn't think I heard it as I was out of it with sedation. I remembered thinking, Nah mate, I was just ignoring you. We went home, and I was exhausted.

Conor came down to visit me but poor him as I slept on my couch all evening. Of course, he understood, though. I ate half a fish pie and remembered thinking tomorrow's BM's (bowel movements) shouldn't be too bad due to how little I've eaten today. How wrong was I? I hadn't learned yet that, unfortunately, when flared, it doesn't matter what you eat; your body will still make you shit like fuck at all times. As Crohn's is auto-immune, it attacks all healthy tissue and bacteria, including the fluid that's naturally there in your body. The next morning going to work was still a nightmare. I probably should've had the day off, but money was an issue when where I currently worked didn't pay sick leave and was on minimum wage; missing a day seemed too much.

I went back to the standard routine of needing the toilet as soon as I woke up or the need waking me. The bleeding continued, fatigue was getting worse, meaning being permanently tired and napping most days for at least 2 hours after work. I had begun vomiting my stomach lining every morning too. I had a follow-up appointment with the consultant who misdiagnosed me and was told the biopsies came back clear, and he was surprised, but I had IBS. I was told to watch my diet, and due to eating anywhere between 1-3 takeaways at the weekend depending on how hungover I was (sue me, I like food), my parents believed my problem was poor diet. I told them repeatedly it didn't matter how healthy or unhealthy I ate; the effects were the same, but nobody listens when a consultant has told you otherwise. I was advised to try probiotics too. I gave them a go for over a year and found they sometimes help as a bulking agent. But when things were bad, no amount of probiotics would really help, and I found them pointless. I actually haven't taken them since being diagnosed, as they're not particularly effective when in a flare apparently. You're telling me.

At this point, I had become very open and firmly believed I had Crohn's disease. Due to that first third of my large intestine being clear, I had a feeling it wasn't colitis. I knew I had been misdiagnosed, and it became the running joke how many times I could shit in a day. I had been suffering both mentally and physically now for closer to 3 years now, and when I needed the toilet, I couldn't hide it any longer. I was no longer ashamed or embarrassed; I was frustrated. I mean, I was mildly embarrassed, but I was so desperate for help and an answer; frustration was the winning emotion. I know friends and family were probably bored stupid hearing about my BM's or how much blood there was, but I honestly didn't care. It was my life this was affecting, and I knew something was wrong. If they were in the same situation or experiencing what I was, they would probably be the same, if not worse. I kept being told by my parents and boyfriend I didn't have Crohn's because it's "so bad and serious", and I'd really know about it if I did have it. I know they weren't being horrible; it was just a lack of understanding. I often thought maybe if you had to wipe my ass for me every time I went to the toilet, it would be a different story.

About a year later, I got a call from another consultant; my GP gastro referral from the year before was now being looked at. I was shocked at the NHS waiting time. Image having some kind of gastro cancer?! How the fuck can those people wait that long, it's quite literally asking for them to die. But again, I knew waiting times for most services on the NHS were ridiculously long, really very shameful. Fuck you, Tories, fuck you.

I never met this consultant; it was all telephone consultations, and he sent me for an endoscopy (scope down your throat to look at your stomach and top of the small intestine) and a barium meal x-ray (fucking rotten, a radioactive drink that outlines your small intestines when put under an x-ray). At this point, though, I had discovered imodem. OMG imodem. I thought it was sent from the heavens, and I'm not a religious person. At this point, I thought I could "cure" Crohn's myself, not realising it was an inflammatory disease that was causing your intestines to erode away and form ulcers in place of healthy normal tissue. I thought if I just keep taking a couple of these a day, it'll keep the flare up's to just the morning. At this point, it wasn't just mainly morning time anymore, and it was starting to happen most of the evenings too. I was suffering more and more, and mouth ulcers were also becoming very common, usually about 10 at a time. They weren't like normal mouth ulcers, as in they just appeared; these were different. I could feel these little burning, painful lumps starting to rise in my mouth, all across the front of my gums. They started small and continued to grow until full size. They usually lasted 3 weeks, and once they left about a week later, the process started all over again. I knew it was a Crohn's symptom and was actively telling people I had undiagnosed Crohn's disease at this stage. I had just moved jobs as well and was now a paralegal in another firm (where I still am) and had even put on HR question sheets when starting, I had suspected Crohn's in the illness/disability part. I was again excited and apprehensive about my upcoming tests.

I went for the barium x-ray first, and as it was a morning appointment, on the way over the standard, "fucking mornings" thought was running through my head again and, of course, continued to need the hospital toilet. I was embarrassed when this happened in public. However, as I thought, the other patients waiting in the waiting area noticed how often I was getting up to use the toilet. I didn't overly care in a needs must aspect, but I was also paranoid about being watched. I got called by the nurse and was brought round into a room. I was told I had 15 minutes to drink the Barium meal. It was really rotten. It tasted like creamy Sambuca. Fucking rank; I hate that liquorice taste. It was about a pint, maybe less, but it didn't taste great and was heavy. The thick creamy white paste stuck to my mouth, and no amount of rubbing or wiping would get it off. I had been warned of this though, as when the nurse was leaving me to my room, we walked past a patient who was in front of me getting the same test. He said it tasted like liquorice, and I wondered why he hadn't wiped the white paste off his mouth. I originally thought, does he not realise, or is he just a stinking guy who's not bothering to clean it off (soz lads but a good few of you's are stinkers). I got the drink down me but thought I was going to boke numerous times, as again I had been fasting, and a thick radioactive Sambuca tasting drink at approximately 9 am is not the one.

When I went for the first x-ray, though, the lady was lovely and said, don't worry, it doesn't come off without water and a paper towel, and got me one. Stubborn shit it was. I was optimistic though, and thought today I would get the answers I needed. They took you into the x-ray room periodically to see how fast your body was digesting it, so they would know when it hit your small bowel. Mine digested quickly, and I actually overtook the guy who was in front of me. He was really nice, and we had a few more conversations when passing in the hall, telling each other why we were here and what was going on in our life's/how the test was going. Both suspected Crohn's but having great difficulty with diagnoses. I saw him about a month later in Castlecourt, and we said hi, walking past, both remembering each other. I wondered how he was and if he ever got sorted. I always enjoyed these experiences, talking to people and learning about them and their lives. It also made me realise just how many people are suffering from some sort of illness or problem and again how massively underfunded the NHS is. I've never particularly like politicians, but I can fully say I despise them now. Their disgusting attitudes to petty problems leaving an already suffering country without a government. A disgrace and embarrassment, I honestly don't know how they live with themselves. But I suppose their ignorance is bliss, and if it's not affecting them directly, they really don't care. Fuck you, Arlene and Michelle, a disgrace to all women in a position of power that should be taken away from you. I swear I'm so close to forming a coup.

When I went in for my final x-ray, as the Barium meal had reached my small bowel, I was made lie down on an x-ray bed. The bed then lifted high into the air, and an x-ray came down close on top of my stomach. It was so weird as I was literally in bed in the sky, looking down at the staff doing the imaging. I could see my intestines on the screen, and as stupid as it sounds, I was alarmed to see them moving. Even when I was told to hold my breath, my insides were still moving. Ewwww, I'm alive! I saw the white liquid move through my insides on the black and white screen with my pulsating insides and wished I knew what it meant. If only I was a doctor or x-ray person for a day, God damn it. Then I saw it. I remember thinking, "Oh wait, what's that I see in the middle-lower part of my intestines, omg it's a weird black circle! Is that Crohn's? It looks weird, it's like a perfect circle, what the hell is that?!" I then realised it was the metal button on my jeans the x-ray was showing up...lol. I guess I'm not a trained medic then. They then needed to get the Barium meal to a certain part of my intestines, and it wasn't moving fast enough, so I was asked to down a pint of water. I had been fasting from the night before and hadn't been allowed water either, so this was very welcome. The guy doing the imagining made a joke about it as well as I had downed the pint, and he knew I had obviously been fasting. I hate water too, showing how much it was needed. I watched the water run through me in what was less than 20 seconds. I was really amazed and thought, Christ, no wonder you piss loads on a night out; liquid runs right through you. I also began to struggle with the theory of if it's so good to drink loads of water, what's the point if it just makes you piss in 5 minutes.

Shortly after the test finished, the table I was on went all futuristic and lowered me down, then put itself upright so I'd be standing getting off. How fancy. I was now ready for my results and was thinking, what have they seen. I asked the x-ray man what he had seen, and he said apprehensively, "mostly normal", however, the nurse standing there interrupted him and said, no, away you go, time to go home. What?! I was so shocked and taken back. Not by the nurse or anything she said; I had really liked her. She was older and gave me the caring but takes no shit vibe, my mum is like that, and it's something I've definitely inherited, so it was absolutely nothing to do with her or the imager. They both passed the sound test. My thought process had been, surely they saw what they needed to, and someone could give me the results! This was the day I was supposed to be diagnosed at long last; what was happening?! All I was told was that the radioactive substance tends to constipate people, and don't be alarmed when my shit is white. I thought, chance would be a fine thing and no sweat man, I'm sure that'll not be alarming at all. I left holding back the tears and returned to the cubical room where my belongings were. I grabbed my things and phoned my mum to come to get me, as she had been sent away as the tests were going on. I must have been hysterical on the phone, and she was very concerned.

We left the City hospital, and I was still very upset and couldn't understand why I wasn't told what was happening. My mum then explained to me the man taking the x-ray was only a technician, and the video was to go to the consultant to read, then I'd get the results. Phewww. I calmed myself down, knowing that wasn't it. I had been getting progressively worse, and one of my mum's colleagues who is in his 40's has had Crohn's disease since his teens. We took my dog for a walk around the park, and she said he had said my symptoms sounded like Crohn's, which helped me feel like I wasn't mad but also frustrated I couldn't get an answer. By the time we got home, it was about 12 pm, and I was starving, so we made lunch, and I thought I could probably make it to work for 2 pm. I had just started my new job the week before, so I wasn't getting paid for my day off and again wanted to be paid. However, Crohn's ugly head crept up, and as soon as I went to start eating my lunch, I was like, oh fuck I need a toilet right now! As I had thought, the Barium meal did not do the norm of constipating me and, for the remainder of the day, continued to reproduce the white liquid as if I was vomiting it, only out the other end. Unfortunately, it was also as hard to remove from all areas of skin no matter where on your anatomy, meaning showers after each toilet trip. I phoned the hospital to see if this was normal and was told that it's fine if that was my norm. Also, as it was radioactive, they would rather it out than in. Thank fuck I didn't go to work. They were right about everything coming out white, though, and that continued for a few days.

I had worked myself up so much though my mum had suggested

I go to Farmar Health on Lisburn Road as it tests for allergies and all sorts. I had booked the appointment for a Saturday a few weeks later when walking around the park with her. I went to the appointment, and the woman taking the test was super nice. She asked questions, and I explained, suspected IBD etc. She said many people who got tested were usually in for something similar, and my symptoms sounded like it. The machine basically put like a metal pen to your thumb, and different vials went in the machine. If it screeched, that was bad; if it didn't, that was good. She said a lot of people with IBD can't tolerate dairy, which I have now learned is a very common thing as Crohn's most commonly affects the last part of your small intestine where dairy etc., is absorbed. Due to inflammation, it cannot complete this process, so, therefore, it is poorly digested. She also said wheat is a real trigger, but hopefully, I wouldn't have both. Dairy, no surprise, let out a wail of a sound, but thankfully, I was all good with wheat. I wasn't surprised as I thought back to anytime in recent years if I drank anything with milk in it; I knew about it quite quickly. My diet was basically meat and carbs, so I also wasn't surprised wheat didn't annoy me. However, tomatoes, oranges, peppers, and potatoes, basically anything with a skin my body did not like. I got told to look up the nightshade family, which are basically those foods, and they're known for being inflammatory. A lot of people without IBD apparently cannot digest them either. The list was shocking, and I actually stuck to my new dairy-free diet for a while. However, it wasn't a life-changer, and it only reduced some bloating, as I had been eternally bloated for I couldn't tell you how long. Every time the diet didn't work though, and I said to someone, I got the standard, "you need to give it a few weeks; all the other stuff is probably coming out of your body" crap. I knew it wasn't that but more that no diet was going to fix me totally.

In July 2017, I was sent to the Matter hospital for their Sunday clinic of endoscopies about two months later. I was really nervous about this one and had to fast from 10 the night before. I remember being raging because Conor and some of my friends were going on a night out, and I had to go home to my family house at 10 pm on a Saturday and miss it. I again thought I better get some fucking results from this, impacting my social life fs. It was another early morning appointment, and I had to be at the hospital at 7 am. Again this was not ideal, and I continued using the disabled toilet in the waiting area. I recalled how much shit I had threw down my fat gullet the evening before I had to fast. Conor and I had also been on a date day, and after visiting Castleward, we also went for dinner and drinks. None of my previous day's decisions were helping me in the present.

My name was called, and my mum actually had to bang the door to try to get me out, but I was not for moving. When I eventually came out, I was brought in for the pre-assessment questions and said I wanted sedation when asked. The nurse was weird and repeatedly told me it made no difference, and they sprayed my throat with numbing spray, and it's all I needed. Me taking sedation would only mean she had to look after me longer in recovery...thanks bitch. I didn't listen to her as I was already very nervous, and from my last scope, I remembered being awake even with sedation, which scared me. I repeatedly told her I was taking the sedation, and she repeatedly tried talking me out of it. The weirdest part was when I was in recovery, she wasn't one of the nurses on the ward. I do not know what her issue was, and she wasn't anywhere to be seen post-pre-examination questioning. She was not compassionate, and her strange agenda baffled me. She also told me if I took the sedation, I couldn't go to work the next day as another measure of trying to get me not to take it. Again not the case as I was given it before 9 am meaning it was out of my system in 24 hours, all explained in recovery. I'm glad I stuck to my gut, as I was so nervous at this point when I was waiting, and when having the cannula put in for the sedation, I was getting teary. I don't know why I was so nervous, I think it was the fear of the unknown and the last one being so horrible, although it was in the opposite end. I didn't let anyone see this, I would have been mortified and kept a brave face for the doctors and nurses.

The doctor performing the scope was lovely, and all the nurses in the room were also lovely. They sprayed my throat with the numbing spray, and I remember it being a weird sensation, I can't remember exactly how it felt, but it was weird, like I couldn't feel swallowing. I was then given the sedation and given a plastic thing for my mouth to bite on, to keep it open. I lay on my side, and as the camera went down, I remember nothing. This sedation was way better! It was probably no different, but I closed my eyes and had a mini sleep when I lay down. They even biopsied, and I have no recollection and seen nothing on the screen. When they began pulling the tube back up again, my body thought I was vomiting, so I went to sit up to be sick whilst half asleep. I remember hearing a few nurses saying no, Sarah and holding me back down as I was gagging. I was still pretty much unconscious, so I wasn't really aware of what my body was trying to do. It was all over very quickly, and the experience was fine. I had built it up much worse in my head but was very glad of the sedation as I feel it was what made it ok. I was put in recovery and was allowed to leave an hour later. I just felt massively stoned; this sedation was great. I went home, had breakfast and chilled out with Conor the rest of the day. Overall, it was a good day as we also got a beloved takeaway, a lot of munchies and ice cream for my "ordeal" that morning; yay me!

I got a letter in October saying I would have my telephone consultation with results in a week or so, and it was near the end of October 2017. I had seen my GP for a repeat prescription the week before and asked her if there was any information on the biopsy or test results on her system. The labs had written they found inflammation in my duodenum (lower part of the stomach that joins the stomach to the small intestine), and I was ecstatic. I actually exclaimed, "I'm finally going to be diagnosed with Crohn's disease!" and she laughed. She probably thought, what sort of weird 23/24-year-old wants a chronic illness. I was so desperate at this point and just wanted an answer. I waited patiently and excitedly for the next few weeks for my telephone call. At this point, the mouth ulcers were getting really bad, and my mum was also convinced I had Crohn's, for the first time ever. Another colleague of her's had a sister with Crohn's, and all my symptoms were matching, especially the mouth ulcers. They were really painful, burning all the time, and my mouth/gums were bright red constantly. Imodem was also no longer helping. Come home time, it was also a nightmare trying to get a bus. Before they took off, I was on buses and sprinting off them and back into my office/public buildings to the nearest toilet. I was growing more and more depressed also as this was completely taking over my life, and I could get no answer. I had to miss a night out for my friend Mark's birthday, which is something I normally never do, because I came home hysterically crying after a bad flare up when trying to get home from work, and missed a few buses as I couldn't leave the office. I remember sobbing, "I can't even get a fucking bus anymore", beyond consolable. My parents were really worried at this point, especially as they could now see how this heavily impacted my mental health too.

I got the phone call from the consultant a few weeks later, thinking this is it, I finally get my answer. Of course, it wasn't that simple. He came on the phone to tell me all good news, nothing found from both tests, and I had IBS. I was so gutted, but of course, I never let this show. He asked how I was, and I said the same as normal, never mentioning the ulcers or how symptoms were getting worse. I said I was taking probiotics and imodem and thought they helped a bit, but I still passed undigested food. Very alarmingly, he told me that's normal in IBS, and I seemed to have a good handle on it.

The phone call ended, and I returned to my desk in the office, silent. The other paralegals I sat beside knew I was awaiting a call from the hospital, and I had been excited before the call and then came back with a face like a slapped arse. I was trying so hard not to cry, so I had to sit in silence until I calmed myself down. How could there be nothing wrong?! This was not normal and only getting worse! I was never like this before, I still remember what it was like not to have all this FS. I couldn't even phone my parents or text Conor as I knew I couldn't control my emotions if I was to say anything. I calmed myself down and spoke to my colleagues when I knew I was composed enough to speak, and I could tell they felt sorry for me. I told my parents and Conor later and again more sympathy. I was beginning to feel crazy. What if this was normal and all in my head? I was really struggling to cope. I wasn't even finding jokes about it funny anymore, and I was always the first to make jokes about my dodgy bowels.

About a week later, after the telephone call and being discharged from that doctor's care, I had a similar experience when trying to get a bus home. I left the office, and when getting on the bus home, I bumped into an old school friend. We were chatting, and my stomach went, and oh my God, the agony. Stomach pain is a massive symptom of Crohn's, but I had constant stomach pain for years; I didn't really mention it as it had become so normal. There are different types of stomach pain as well, so it always varied. I knew I needed a toilet then and there, and the likelihood of me making it home was slim. But as I had been doing for years, I clenched for dear life and tried taking an imodem discretely from my handbag mid-conversation. I could barely concentrate; I needed to vomit as well. We reached the bus stop outside the Waterfront, and I apologised and said I'm so sorry. I'm getting tested for Crohn's, and I need a bathroom, or I'll vomit everywhere. I was so embarrassed. He was, of course, polite and said no problem, and I ran off the bus, saying I'd message him later. Thankfully I knew him well enough to do this. I ran into the Hilton hotel as I knew from work functions where their bathroom was. That was me for the next half an hour, shitting, vomiting, sweating and shaking. This was a bad flare-up. I was so unwell I could barely move and felt so sick.

I phoned Conor, who I was now living with, and two of our friends, Michael and Ryan. He wasn't exactly compassionate at this point. I asked him if possible, could he come and get me. I was really unwell and couldn't leave and was too scared to wait to get the next bus. He said no because of traffic, and I'd be fine. Thanks a lot you cunt, I thought. I was beyond distraught at this point. I know it wasn't out of malice, and he didn't understand or realise how bad it was, but I was really done. Also, my mum was in Australia visiting my auntie, so I couldn't even phone her and my dad was working.

After about an hour sitting by myself in the Hilton bathrooms, I mustered up the courage to walk somewhere. I didn't know where, but I wasn't going home. I was distraught, I was sobbing as I walked, probably looking like a right weirdo, but I didn't care anymore. As I walked over the bridge beside the central station in rush hour traffic, surrounded by many people also walking home, I remember wishing they weren't there because I wanted to jump into the Lagan, the fucking filthy disgusting river. I can't swim either, so it's pretty obvious where my thoughts were at. I wanted to die. I didn't want to do this any longer. How could this all still be happening?! I take imodem daily, probiotics and watch my diet, yet this still happens! What the fuck was wrong with me. I was really inconsolable and very depressed. If it hadn't been for the crowds, I think I would have jumped. It probably wouldn't have taken long to die between how filthy the river was, the fact I can't really swim, and it was a freezing start to November. I had changed into trainers and had a warm puffy coat on, I wouldn't take long to drown. I remember thinking do I jump in with my handbag or not because I kind of wanted to die with my stuff. I also thought as the wall over the bridge is so small that maybe I could jump really quickly, and no one would notice. But I couldn't bear the thought of being stopped or caught and having to explain myself. So gurning to myself, I continue to walk in a lost, zoned out state. I just kept walking with no purpose.

At this point, Conor was trying to phone me to see where I was; I wouldn't answer the calls or WhatsApp. I eventually answered as I had made my way over somewhere near Cregagh road. I wouldn't speak, and he was begging to know where I was. I told him to leave me alone I wanted to be by myself, but he wouldn't back down. After continuing to walk practically in circles for another half an hour, barely speaking, I finally told him where I roughly was, but I kept walking. He left me when I needed him and could fucking figure out where I was for himself. He eventually found me, and we spoke in the car for another while; it was probably closer to 8 pm by the time we made it back to the flat, and I was still upset. I remember walking up the outside stairs to our flat, and our housemate Michael was on the balcony. Michael's extremely funny and welcomed us with a joke. However, I was so upset I didn't even hear him speak. I went inside and straight to our room, continuing to cry. Conor stayed down with Mike and told him what happened. When I eventually came downstairs for dinner, although not hungry, Mick asked if I was ok and said he knew something was wrong when I didn't laugh or say something in response to his joke, like I normally would. I messaged my old school friend explaining what happened and that I'd been getting tested for Crohn's and unfortunately wasn't well when I saw him. He was really nice and understanding and hoped I was ok. Mike and Conor cheered me up a bit too; I really loved living in that flat, it was constant jokes and laughing, and nothing could really be serious for more than 5 minutes. I was still saddened by all this but did what I always did and pretended like I was fine.

Since about August/September, I had also been having this pain on and off that was making walking, coughing, sneezing or basically any sort of movement really painful. It felt like my insides wanted to explode and also a sharp shooting pain at the same time. All, of course, coming from the waist down to my back side. I somehow never clicked this could be related to all my ongoing problems; I was just really baffled as to what this pain was, which was getting progressively worse and now affecting my walking. Whenever I tried describing this huge pressure pain like my insides wanted to come exploding out, the usual response was maybe it's haemorrhoids. I, unfortunately, didn't know what haemorrhoids were, and although I would consider myself the queen of googling symptoms, I never bothered. I think I was passed it. I've since learned that they are blood vessels that come out of you, and if you had them, you would know about it. I did not have them. Of course, I had already bought anything going that might help, and of course, it didn't work.

Stranger things in a stranger place

My morning routine was now Conor would leave me into town on his way across town to work, so I was in my office between 8.00-8.30am every day, traffic dependant. It was Monday 6th November 2017, and I had been up most of the night with the pain. Conor had said he noticed I was awake most of the night and was I sure I should be going into work because I really didn't look well. I said I was fine, and it would probably pass; it usually does. Unfortunately this time, it didn't. I was in so much pain I phoned my mum who was still in Australia and awake. It was nighttime in Australia, and I was in my work bathrooms trying not to cry with the pain. A colleague had heard me on the phone and when I came out of the cubicle asked me how I was as I didn't even sound well. I explained at my desk what was happening, and the pain was so bad I began crying. She was super lovely and said not to worry and go straight to the hospital or home and rest. She had thought I maybe had a kidney infection or something, and we have since laughed about it, as I said how mortified I was but was in so much pain I literally couldn't hold back tears.

I knew I needed to go to the hospital as it was getting worse and when I had phoned my mum, who was staying with my auntie Anna-Marie, who is also a nurse, they were both very concerned this was Crohn's related. I could barely walk at this point but made my way down to the office manager and asked to speak to her, again holding back tears. She was also super lovely, and I explained what was going on. She told me not to worry about work at all and either go to the hospital or home and rest. I quickly emailed my two bosses to say I was sick before leaving and would hopefully be back soon. They're both gents and were also very understanding. I never said what was wrong, but when I returned, they responded to my quick email, one ordering me to get straight home and chill with Netflix's and not come back until I was better and the other saying not to worry at all and hoped I was ok. I've been so lucky in my current workplace. I've always worked with the most genuinely nice people.

I got a taxi to the Royal, and as I hadn't been to A&E since I was a child/teenager, I was quite alarmed as I originally thought it would be the City hospital I would go to. Apparently, its A&E had been closed for years. I went in in agony, trying to hold myself together as I told the receptionist my details. I began the routine of casualty that I didn't realise I was going to become extremely familiar with. I was triaged and asked for symptoms, blood pressure and temperature etc., taken, then sent back out to the waiting room before being called back for bloods, urine samples etc. I remember the nurse being really lovely; all nurses I've dealt with in A&E have been lovely and really compassionate. I began the few hour wait and began talking to a lady who wasn't well and had been repeatedly in hospital, and they didn't know what was wrong with her either. I was telling her I had suspected Crohn's, and the pain I had been having was becoming unbearable. She said something that I had begun to hear a lot from family members included, "you don't want it to be Crohn's disease you have, it's awful." It was strange, as the thing I knew I had and was desperate to be diagnosed with so I could finally get sorted was so terrible to others who had never experienced it. I knew it was thought of as that terrible incurable shitting disease, but at this point, I was jealous of those diagnosed as I wanted an answer so bad. People can't empathise with what they haven't experienced, and I know it was out of niceness people hoped I didn't have it. I personally didn't care; I just wanted an answer.

I was called when my blood results were ready by a junior doctor, who I firmly believe is the definition of an arrogant prick. I don't even think he was trying overly to be a dick, he just was one; it was everything from his tone of voice to his hair. He questioned me on bowel movements etc., and looked at previous test results. He agreed my symptoms pointed to Crohn's, and when he looked at my blood results, the inflammation levels were raised as per. He simply told me, "there's obviously something going on, but I'm not a consultant. Here's some buscopan and go home. Come back if it gets worse, though."

I heard him shout at a nurse to get me buscopan, and I really didn't like how he spoke to her. He was probably only a few years older than me what made me hate his behaviour even more. I also notice a wedding ring and thought his wife is probably a stuck up prick too. He gave me posh boy Methody vibes, and I was honestly affronted in my weak state. He looked like Steve Harrington out of Stranger Things. It was definitely the hair, but I couldn't take it seriously. He was honestly more interested in my occupation. I had never been sick as a child and literally got a cold once a year.

I never even had chickenpox's I'd been that healthy. I was now coming to hospital years later, and my occupation was still listed as a schoolgirl. At 24, I was probably pushing it trying to still crack that one, so I told him I was a paralegal when he asked so he could update my details. He was interested in this, and I surmised it was because he was an arrogant young doctor who probably thought this was nearly at this level, having completed my law degree and working in the legal industry. Maybe he thought I too was a pretentious prick, but unfortunately not Steve. I actually get embarrassed when I tell people I have a law degree or work as a paralegal due to the connotations/assumptions made about it. It was so unfortunate that my wave of pain had dulled down by the time I saw him, so I couldn't even show how much pain I was really in most of the time. Typical. I also thought about how long it had been since I had been to A&E and how I used to never be sick until the last few years.

Since having undiagnosed Crohn's, only then in my life, did I start to catch everything going. Always having colds or infections, like if I was a little bit too dehydrated/run down, I would get a kidney/UTI infection and usually need antibiotics. I even caught the flu for the first time ever, and from how bad it was in comparison to a cold, I've never been able to take people who say they have the flu when they actually have a cold seriously ever again. I phoned Conor, and he left work to come and collect me from the Royal. In pain and deflated, I left with the buscopan, knowing it would do fuck all. I remember taking one and then stopping. I had taken these loads in the past, and I always found that they dried out my skin after a few days and made me feel worse. I wasn't sure if it was the buscopan or not, but it happened every time. However, I have learned that it is actually a side effect and happens to other people. No thank you.

I went back to our flat and slept for a few hours after not sleeping the night before. The pain was easing even more, and I was back to thinking, is this all in my head. Of course, I spoke too soon; that night, it was the worst it had ever been when I was trying to sleep. I was shivering and trying not to pass out with the pain. Conor was holding me as I was yelping and shivering, and he was saying we needed to go to the hospital now. I was in so much pain I said only if he called an ambulance because I physically couldn't move. Conor had called Michael at this point too, because they were trying to find any form of painkillers in the flat as the shop beside us was now shut. I had also smoked some grass about an hour previous for pain relief before the real pain kicked in. I normally find it a great pain killer and sedative, but it wasn't helping at all when this new wave of extreme pain started. When Michael came upstairs, I tried joking, pretending I was fine, but he obviously seen right through it as I lay unable to move on the bed, whimpering pathetically whilst putting on a fake laugh in my really poor attempt at a brave face. Michael was concerned and told me at a later date, never to pretend I'm ok when I'm really not. I think he may have had a point.

I put off going back to the hospital, although I should have/regretted not going and just lay there shivering in pain the rest of the night, no sleep again. I told Conor and my dad to go to work the next day when they said about taking me to hospital, as they wouldn't get paid if they weren't in, and I wasn't getting paid being off work either. I needed Conor still earning for our rent/bills as I didn't know what was currently happening. My mum phoned from Australia and said to phone my auntie Sharon and get her to take me to hospital as she was off. I felt bad, though, as Sharon had cancer and probably didn't want to spend time in hospital. She was lucky and was fine at the time and to date still is. However, due to how advanced her stomach cancer was and having 80% of her stomach removed, it will come back at some point; they just don't know when. I phoned, and she had no problem taking me so off we went, another long wait in the Royal. It was averaging around at least 4 hours of waiting every time, and I was bored of it already.

It was a different junior doctor today, and she was really nice. She did definitely think I was pregnant and lying though. Another theme I noticed being a young woman complaining of stomach pain. So I gave a pee sample, and of course it was clear, just traces of blood. Although I was also bleeding from Crohn's when I went to the toilet, so I had a feeling it was trace blood that got into it. Due to how the pain felt like my insides wanted to explode out of me, she said she needed to do an examination. Little did I know these examinations would become pretty routine, and the gloves and lube went on, and her finger went up my bum. Noiceee. This is people's job. She said I had a few small piles down and wrote it on my notes, and I remember thinking there is no way the pain I'm in is from piles. They're probably only down because of how often I also need the toilet as well. I said again about the pain, and she asked if my blood had been taken that day, as they normally don't take it two days in a row because blood shouldn't really change in 24 hours. I said no, and she proceeded with taking more blood, and I waited another few long hours with my auntie. When I was eventually called back in, she said something is wrong, as my blood inflammation levels had increased in 24 hours, and I was to see the Gastro team at 9 am the following day and that I could have proctitis or something. Of course, I Googled that and was like, yeah, that's what I got proctitis (inflammation of your bum basically, usually linked with IBD).

I stayed in my auntie's house that night as she was closer to the Royal ahead of my morning appointment. It was strange not being in my flat as I had got so used to it being my new home, I missed it already. We went in the morning, and the pain was again really unbearable; as it moved, it was also beginning to feel like something was crawling around inside me, gross. I was sitting waiting until after 12 pm before seeing the doctors and had taken some of my auntie's strong co-codamol to try to numb the pain. They were prescribed cancer level pain relief, so they did help make the pain more bearable when they kicked in. I was annoyed, though, that when I was sitting withering in agony, the nurses there couldn't have given less of a shit. They actually just watched me crying in pain. My auntie was also baffled, and when she asked for water so I could take the pain relief as I was obviously in a lot of pain, it took them a seriously long time to do that. Another theme I've noticed, medical professionals are either really good at their jobs or really bad. However, you get this in all workplaces, but you tend to expect a level of care at a hospital, not sure why really...

I eventually was called into a room with the main doctor and about 3-4 junior doctors. I gathered he scared them as when one of them was asked to read out my notes, and he done it in the timidest, quietest manner I think I had ever seen. I felt really bad for the kid, he was so obviously shitting himself, and I couldn't hear a word he was saying as he was almost whispering as he spoke. After my short encounter with the head doctor, I understood the poor junior doctor's position. He was rude and arrogant. My auntie began asking about colonoscopies and pill cams, which Annie had told us to ask about. The answer to the colonoscopy was we don't like doing them because of the chance of perforation of the bowel...which I even knew then was a pile of shite. It's like a 1 in 1000 chance of happening, it's just because they didn't want to do it. Pill cam was also dismissed. I said about the pain I was experiencing, and he read my notes and blamed it on piles. Fucking idiot hadn't even examined me. He told me they wanted to do another faecal calprotectin sample to check inflammation levels and to do it before leaving the hospital, as my previous from years before had been 400 and something, but anything over 500 tends to be a definite for showing IBD. I told him I'd try, and his response was, "you did say you were having loose bowel movement", with a face basically accusing me of lying. Aye mate, because I just come to the hospital for the craic and just tell people I shit close to 10 times a day when there's really no issue, no sweat. He left the room without saying anything more, and the junior doctors also followed in silence. It was really uncomfortable as Sharon and I just sat there and said, "What next?" Whilst looking at each other confused. A few minutes later, one of the junior doctors came back in to ask us to leave and tell us where to go next. He was really nice and really fit, I must add (muscles popping through his shirt, yum); I was also with him the next few days, oh nooo...

I was brought to the nurses, and they gave me the stuff needed for the sample. I saw the familiar vial with the scooper on it and thought, hello my old friend. Now for the process that I shouldn't find hard began. Of course, the one time I needed to give a sample on demand, I couldn't. I sat in the disabled toilets for over an hour trying, drinking coffee, the works and nothing. For fucks sake. I remembered even trying to sit in different positions as I had to get enough for two samples, but thankfully, the nurse explained they only need a tiny amount to examine.

I thought back to the first one I ever gave at the GP. Oh fuck. I filled that bad boy to the top. Poor lab person, lol. Eventually, I managed to go enough and left my, what I considered, pathetically small samples in. I worried it wouldn't be enough, especially as these test results take weeks, closer to a month, to come back. I went back to my flat and rested; I felt so unwell and was starting to burn up. I now know it's the fever that comes with a bad Crohn's flare/fistula/abscess. These burn-ups continued for months, I actually started worrying people could see how red my face was, but I was always told I just looked very pale any time I said I was burning up.

I got worse during the night and was in extreme pain, and I was also starting to go to the toilet A LOT more. But it wasn't normal, it was like stomach lining. The next few days, I went between 20-30 times a day. Even I was amazed and knew something wasn't right at all. I wasn't sure if I had brought this on myself as the day before, after the hospital, Sharon had brought me back to hers before Conor picked me up. I was saying about the horrible exploding feeling inside, and in a bid to help, she gave me some prune juice. 1. Not nice 2. I did not know it was a laxative. Later that evening, when back in the flat, I learned the hard way. Not pleasant, and it did not help the internal pain or burn; it only aggravated it. The next day my mum phoned and said I needed to go to the GP to see if they could help. She was also not happy with the prune juice story, and her and Annie were raging. I had drunk it, unaware of the consequences and how it would not have helped my insides. I got an emergency appointment with my regular GP, who had known me since I was a baby and knew I was going through these tests. My dad came with me but waited outside, and when I went into her room, I burst out crying. I was so embarrassed but in so much pain. I really like Doctor Keane, and she was very concerned; she knew this wasn't normal behaviour for me. She brought it up the next time I saw her and said I was in a bad way that day. Mortified, but she was right. She printed out my blood results and wrote a letter to the hospital, and she even circled the results like a school teacher to outline there was obviously something very wrong. She said I needed emergency medical treatment, most likely steroids, and I was to go straight back to the hospital. 4 days in a row, whoo...

My dad brought me up, but I told him to go back to work, and Sharon was going to come over and wait with me. Conor's friend, Conal, who is a doctor in Scotland, was home for the week and had messaged when he heard what was happening. I always loved him, he's one of the nicest people ever, and I regularly joke that I wish I could hire him as my own personal doctor. He asked me did he want me to come up to the hospital, and I told him not to worry. I'm sure he spends enough time in one. He also told me what I needed to emphasise to the doctors but to obviously not say a doctor had told me to say it. When I described my symptoms, he said what looked like stomach lining is mucous (yum) and needed to really tell them that. My auntie came up a couple of hours later, and I was very thankful as I kept needing the toilet and was worried my name would be called and I wasn't there. I had to ask others sitting waiting to let the nurses/doctors know I was in the toilet if they called my name, cringe. Of course, this happened a few times, and annoyingly could hear my name being called from the disabled toilet. They wanted to admit me this time, so I waited for more hours in the major triage bit, telling Conor to bring me up a bag of my stuff after work. I was waiting a long time, hoping to get a bed ASAP as the smell was terrible and the place was full of old people lying in hospital beds. It was like a cattle market, it was so busy. It was quite shocking to see first-hand the rows of elderly lying there without a proper place to stay; I felt so bad for them and hoped they got a ward/proper place to stay soon. I was waiting so long I was brought a "lovely" hospital dinner. There are always a few options, so it's a matter of choosing what sounds the least risky/most appetising. This is honestly a conundrum when you're unsure of the outcome. I remember it being fine, I think I got chicken, gravy and mash, but hospital mash should honestly be illegal; it tastes like cardboard. Pro-tip is to pour basically all your salt and pepper sachets on them to try to disguise the taste (thank me later x). I was also scared about staying over in the hospital by myself for the first time; I thought I probably wouldn't sleep.

I looked around to continue people watching, there wasn't much else to do and a lot of people. I remember a couple in their 40's-50's approximately, sitting opposite me, and I think it was the woman that was being admitted. They just sat holding each other's hand, occasionally reassuringly smiling at the other or having a brief conversation. There was something really lovely about it, and I couldn't stop watching them. Sharon had noticed them too. I think it was watching genuine love between 2 people who were surrounded by chaos. After hours and hours of waiting, I was called into a cubicle by a junior doctor who told me gastro wanted to see me in the morning and to go home and come back again at 9 am. The place was so busy that there wasn't a proper place or bed to go to apart from behind this curtain in the empty cubicle. I could tell this annoyed her as she couldn't examine my stomach properly. She also told me I was lucky to be getting home because hospital is not a nice place, and I really didn't want to be here. I concurred.

So I went home with Conor and went back to the hospital in the morning. I was back waiting where I had been on Wednesday, and the hot junior doctor was in tow. He said they wanted to do a flexible sigmoidoscopy, but as the asshole, sorry more senior doctor I had been with on Wednesday had swapped over (whatever way they do their shifts), he needed to get approval from the new doctor in charge on who was currently at the City hospital. I was dreading it as I knew it wouldn't show anything and the pain of it. I waited for hours and was told to stop eating. Sharon had come up to the hospital to wait with me, but I knew I'd be there for hours between waiting for my slot and recovery, so I told her to go home, and she said she would pick me up later.

She jumped at this and was definitely as bored as I was. I was brought around for the usual pre-procedure questioning, and although I looked like a stinker with no makeup on and really rough because I was getting progressively sicker, the young, fit doctor told me I looked good (like 'at do yeeee). He also said he wanted to see the procedure if he was free as he wanted to know what was going on. All I was thinking was he probably just wants to check out my ass, which I knew would be on show the entire process. Of course I made this joke to my friends when relaying the story as well. He said depending on what they found, I could be admitted to hospital, which I began to panic about as Conor, for my birthday, which had been a few weeks before, had booked us the Galgorm for the following week. I had never been and really wanted to go. I put it out of my head in the meantime though, just hoping I wouldn't be admitted.

The nurse who was looking after me was so nice, I really liked her. We had chatted away, and she had said she was also frustrated at hearing doctors continuously tell people they have IBS when there's obviously more going on; she probably saw it regular. She brought me around to the endoscopy unit once the questions were done and gave me my gown to change into. This was a BIG difference from my sweet private room at the Ulster Independent. It was a standard clinical looking ward that just had the standard curtains to pull around your bed area. I changed, and then it was enema time. What had I done to deserve this, as if I wasn't in enough pain?

I really dreaded this, but alas, I soldiered on. Unfortunately, I looked up and could see the lovely nurse's face and the concentration in it as she tried to make sure all the liquid was squeezed up there. I don't think it's a face I'll ever forget. I remembered it burned your insides, but this time, the pain was worse. I ran across to the toilet cubicle on the ward, I don't think I even held it for 3 minutes, it was too painful. I was just told to hold it as long as possible, and the nurse said I would no doubt be running soon. She wasn't wrong. There was blood and everything coming out, and it really really hurt the internal burn. I remember sitting and shaking with the pain, trying not to yelp as I wanted the pain to stop.

Whenever I left the cubicle, I said to another one of the nurses on the ward about the bleeding, and she asked if I was being tested for Crohn's or colitis, and I replied yes. She said this was sometimes the norm due to internal bleeding and would hopefully get sorted after the scope. I was becoming more hopeful I may get diagnosed if the bleeding was a sign, and hopefully this ordeal would come to an end. I had forgotten how much the enema makes you think you need the toilet from the internal burning also, very uncomfortable. As I waited, a guy probably similar in age to me was wheeled down from a ward. I heard them question him as he lay beside me; and he had ulcerative colitis and was going to the toilet with the shits 4 times a day, and that was his normal. I remember lying there thinking, fuck, if he's admitted with that little symptoms, Christ knows what they'll do with me at currently closer to 30. He was wheeled in, and when he was out after the procedure, I heard them tell him he was still badly inflamed and was brought back to his ward. I wondered if he was on steroids as he was a big looking guy, and thinking back now, he would've had to have been to be the size he was and flared. I was the last person there, and a student nurse was cleaning everything down at this point, using those wipes that look like baby wipes but are apparently full of alcohol and actually kill germs (I'm sceptical). I was scared thinking back as I lay there waiting alone in a silent eerie ward, and then when I think about it, I've always been scared before anything that's happened. I've never shown it though, I know I have to get on with it and push the fear to the back of my mind like it's not really there.

My doctors/nurses came through double doors and introduced themselves before a few more questions. They were two women, and I remember them being really nice and funny. One of them was really purposefully sarcastic, which I enjoyed. They wheeled me down the corridor and into a room for the procedure where I asked about sedation, but they told me that they only gave gas and air due to how quickly this should be over. WTF does that do?! I pondered and was told it makes you feel as if you're a bit drunk and works well. What a fucking lie. I was told to breathe in the gas and air, but it had begun without any time to kick in. It was painful, especially as they blew you up full of air. The enema hadn't done as good a job as the last time at clearing everything out, and I remember being turned looking at bits of liquidy shit on my intestines on the screen. Fucking gross man, but not surprising as I didn't hold it for half as long. I was at this point heavily breathing in the gas and air for pain relief, and it gave me a woozy head; that was it. The nurses laughed when I lay back and stopped breathing it in as it had gone straight to my head; I think they thought I was off my tits. Little did they know about the high doses of grass I had been smoking recently to try to combat my pain.

Well, it probably wasn't "high doses", but fuck, this gas and air was shite. I'd have much rather had a smoke as I think it would've been way more effective. I couldn't believe they give this useless excuse for pain relief to women in labour, they might as well do it with nothing! I was too aware during this, and as they took biopsies, I could see my insides bleeding and was actually turned. Especially as I thought about the risk of infection as I could literally see shit so close to the bleeding cuts. I was hoping it would be over soon due to the pain and blood, and I also couldn't see anything that looked like inflammation. I knew they weren't going to find anything, and all this was for nothing. The flexible sigmoidoscopy ended, and the doctor announced it all looked normal and took biopsies to check for microscopic colitis. I was wheeled out and told to get ready to go home, not before loudly announcing to the room full of medical staff I felt like I was going to shit myself, then remembering and also being told it'll be all the wind they blew up me coming back.

I was wheeled back into recovery and began to get changed. However, the most disgusting thing had happened as the scope was pulled out. Body fluid mixed with medical fluid had also come out; I was nearly sick. I thankfully had tissues and wipes in my handbag and also spare dog shit bags I had forgotten to take out. It turns out it was lucky I didn't. So I proceeded to wipe up the residue mess I had seen got on the tops of my legs (it was mostly on the hospital gown, thank fuck) and shove it in the dog shit bag. It was the smell more than anything that was getting to me. I can't describe the smell, and it actually very surprisingly didn't smell like shit but just some kind of a foul body fluid smell. I got changed before going to the bathroom cubicle again to clean up more and dispose of the disgusting bag. I was also needing to pass the wind and blood that was coming out after the biopsies. I was so upset and holding back tears as I knew nothing was to be done now, and I was to go home still with no answers.

Once I mustered up the courage to leave the cubicle, I went to leave and wait for Sharon, who was on her way, but a nurse sat me down to give me the leaflet explaining what was happening next. She was horrible; I was fighting tears and asked about biopsy results, which she told me would take a few weeks and would probably get a letter and that they found nothing in the meantime. I asked her what to do next, and she said to go home and wait, at which point, due to the pain and humiliation I was feeling, I started crying. I could not hold back the tears any longer. She proceeded to tell me I should consider myself very lucky that they didn't find anything more sinister and asked if I had been to gynaecology, as that's the area that's probably wrong and where I need to go next. Fucking clueless cunt. It wasn't even what she said, it was her tone. She also then proceeded to tell me the reason I was crying was from the gas and air. She didn't have a clue about anything, yet thought she could say this. I just wanted to go home and curl into a ball and cry. It had been the longest week, stuck in hospital, being in more and more pain and nothing happening. My opinion of some medical staff and the NHS, in general, was getting lower by the second. Probably because they are very much human and are as flawed as anyone else, but in a supposed caring environment, some of the staff just openly don't give a shit.

My auntie arrived, and I went to leave, but she wanted to speak to the nurse. I told her to leave it as they hadn't found anything, but she wanted to keep asking. I wasn't in the mood and couldn't speak, trying to fight the tears, so I walked out. I probably looked rude and dramatic but really didn't give a fuck at this point; I was distraught and in agony, also trying to keep my composure in public. She gave me a lift home and asked if I wanted to stay with her as she could see how upset I was, but I just wanted to get into my flat and be alone. I went straight to my bedroom and cried, feeling hopeless and alone. I still felt really sick too, and the procedure hadn't helped. Very unfortunately, I hadn't got all the wind out, and the warning about it being very painful was right. Conor was home soon after, and I gave him the honour of burping me whilst also lying in every position going to try and get rid of the severely trapped wind for the next few hours. I remember being so uncomfortable and sore and wishing I had actually got everything out in hospital as I paced about and lay in more weird positions on the floor. Our flat was also full that night. Ryan was back from London and had friends around, and so did Conor. I chatted for a bit and went to bed, exhausted but also still couldn't sleep as I was still in so much pain. Conal, Conor's doctor friend, was around as well, and as we had known each other for years, he confirmed I looked awful and was definitely sick. I thought of my fit doctor friend, who on the contrary, thought I looked good (or more likely lied through his teeth) and realised he must have been too busy to get to view my scope/hoop. My only regret, I never caught his name x.

The exploding pain thankfully dulled a bit, but Crohn's symptoms were getting worse, and my right-hand side was permanently sore and sore to touch. I was bleeding a lot as well, and I was literally going to the toilet just to pass blood. The mouth ulcers that I had thought were bad before were nothing compared to what happened next. Over 20 appeared, so many I couldn't count properly, and they all joined together to form massive clusters. I don't think there was a part of my gums that didn't have something. I had to phone my GP, and she arranged a prescription for a lot of different treatments that thankfully did help. Especially that igloo gel, which I was regularly smearing over them, as it hurt to eat and talk. Thankfully, I got on my Galgorm trip and loved it, but of course I wasn't well during it as my mouth was interfering with fully enjoying the class food, and I was up during the night being sick. I still had a great time, though. I had also convinced myself at this time, I probably had microscopic colitis or Crohn's and was hoping for some sort of answer soon.

The journey to diagnosis

Maybe 2 weeks later, the bleeding was so bad at work, I phoned my GP for advice and was booked in for an emergency appointment with another doctor that day. I left work early and went to the appointment. What I now know to be fatigue, was also really bad and I was sleeping closer to 15 hours a day. The GP was super lovely; I explained what was happening, my symptoms and that I was also waiting for biopsy and faecal calprotectin results. Dr McKegney checked, and there were no biopsies results yet; she then checked for the calprotectin one. What came next, I was not expecting. She said my results from 2017 were there. They were over 400 then, which I remembered and thought to myself, hopefully these new ones are over 500, as that shitty doctor in hospital had said, so that I can get sorted ASAP.

I could tell by her face something was up, but what I heard next nearly had me fall off my seat. "1800 and ..." I couldn't hear past 1800 as I was in disbelief. Oh my fucking God. I'm not a doctor, but I knew that was insane. Dr McKegney was great and said I needed an urgent colonoscopy as I definitely had Crohn's; they just needed to identify where so I could get on treatment. She even printed off the results sheet, as I said, I couldn't believe it was 1800, and she said no, it's 1800 and something, closer to 1900. I was shocked and amazed as I left and phoned my parents and Conor to let them know. My housemate Michael was at his parents' house, which was a street over from the doctors, and couldn't believe it when I told him on our way back to the flat. "You have Crohn's mate", I remember him saying. Indeed I did Mike, indeed I did.

My mum had spoken on the phone to Dr McKegney a few days later, and she had been really good and was chasing the Royal for them to progress with me. My mum had asked her honestly what she thought was wrong with me and Dr McKegney told her I definitely had Crohn's; it was just they needed to see where in my intestines and to what extent. She's so lovely and said to me on the phone one day after I was diagnosed that the hospital really owed me an apology for how I was treated. They did, but I was never getting that. The pain on the right-hand side of my stomach was getting worse, and I got told on a Sunday when I was shopping with my mum and granny by an out of hour's doctor I had phoned, that I needed to go to A&E. I felt bad as my granny was down from the country to visit for the day, but my mum was really concerned and basically forced me to go. We went to A&E for the hours and hours-long wait, and as it was a Sunday, it was mostly busy with stupid drunken accidents. I also heard some man come in and say he had been experiencing an ache somewhere in his body that hadn't gone away in a few weeks… go to your fucking GP then dick. He also got fed up waiting so went home before being seen by a doctor, so obviously wasn't that bad. The same thing as before happened, they wanted to "admit me" due to my symptoms and tender stomach, but as the GI team needed to see me, I was to come back the following day at 9 am. I told my mum they were always late, so we'd be best just going down at 11 or something, which did not go down well if you know my mother.

We arrived at 9 am and waited. I was so tired I began snoozing in the chair I was waiting in, but the consultant was around early that day, so if I hadn't listened to my mum, we probably would have missed him. This consultant, Dr Turner, became my permanent consultant and still is. He was really nice first impression (still is) and felt my stomach, agreeing when I said that's where the pain was. I now know it's because they're trained to feel for inflammation etc. He said I needed an urgent colonoscopy, and as he also worked in the City hospital, I'd have it there in just under 2 weeks. I knew I needed it really badly but also was dreading it. I was given a prescription to collect the colonoscopy prep from the hospital pharmacy, which I did and was on my way.

The following week I went to my appointment in the City to collect the pre colonoscopy information; I didn't realise the different hospitals have different notes and files on you. The nurse called me into a room and looked at my very small City hospital file, and it included nothing of the past few weeks. All it had was the tests I had done in the City that had misdiagnosed me by the previous consultant, who had discharged me a month earlier. She quite rudely questioned why I was there, and I had to explain the previous few weeks and how I'd been misdiagnosed and need an urgent colonoscopy now. She became more understanding and empathised. I think this consultant who misdiagnosed me was called Ryan Scott, which reminded me of the character, Michael Scott, from the American Office. I wondered if he was of similar intellect.

The nurse explained the laxative wasn't pleasant and that it will be very painful on my backside. I had heard this from numerous people who had all had it done, and the term "shitting water" was also a recurring theme. I said this to the nurse, and she agreed and told me about the nurse guinea pig who said that you are raw by the end and to put Vaseline on. I could hardly wait. She went to give me another packet of the prep, but I explained I already had it at home. I took my leaflets and went. It was my work department Christmas dinner that afternoon, and I had a really great night. I thankfully was feeling fine that day and could stay out the whole evening. I had been feeling ok in the weeks in between, with no massive improvements or downfalls, just coasting by. I was asked did I know how they treated Crohn's by a few colleagues, and I was unfortunately very naïve, not at all in the know then. I told them steroids, and I should be better.

If only that was the case.

I had the dentist the week before my colonoscopy, and the mouth ulcers were starting to heal. Thankfully a lot of them had gone away, but still some lingered, and there were marks all over my mouth. My dentist couldn't believe it when she saw my mouth and tried writing down for her records how many I had, but she said there were too many of them to all be recorded. They had also temporarily scared my mouth. She confirmed from what she saw it looked like Crohn's and wished me well. I was so close to a diagnosis and just wanted sorted.

The day of the colonoscopy prep came, and I just wanted it over with. It had been Conor's birthday the day before, and it had been a late night. I was really tired. Unfortunately, I couldn't drink the night before, but I had been surrounded by a lot of steaming people when I was sick, tired, and unable to drink. Not ideal. Also, I can't imagine drinking 4 litres of laxatives on a hangover would be great for you. It was another occasion I felt I was missing out on due to Crohn's and not yet diagnosed. Dr Turner had also joked and warned me about not drinking alcohol before the procedure, to stay hydrated with clear fluids but no G&T's. I remember thinking I don't even like gin and tonic, so we're safe there. I was also fed up with not being able to drink blackcurrant juice (I live off diluent juice, hate water) due to the dietary requirements to be followed for 2 days prior to the procedure. As the leaflet said, I ate my last meal at 1 pm to start the prep at 3 pm. It was Klean prep I had been prescribed, but as the Crohns was bad, I had already been to the toilet about 8 times before starting, so I wondered if there was actually much left. I realised I didn't have a litre jug to mix it with, so I proceeded to use a big coke bottle and measure it that way. Of course, bits of the powder fell out, and I wouldn't recommend it as a jug substitute, especially for mixing it as I violently shook the bottle, but it done the job.

I went to my bedroom, as Conor and I had a bathroom just outside our room that was practically an en suite, with the prep in tow and began pouring it into a pint glass so I could try to finish this first litre in the recommended time. I think it was an hour, and then you get an hour break before starting the next litre. It tasted not great, not the worst thing in the world but definitely not nice. It was kind of salty and medicated all in one. I was surprised at how well I was doing and nearly had the litre down in the hour. Then I really started not to feel well, the side effects said intense nausea, but I couldn't remember the last time I felt this sick. It was really, really horrible, I had to sprint into the bathroom, and projectile vomited the first litre into the toilet. My lunch made a reappearance too.

I felt much better after that but had to keep going and was concerned that I vomited the first litre up.

Of course, I googled this, and it had happened to a lot of people. This happened again, and the remainder of the food in my stomach came up. It was like the laxative was tearing anything in its way out. I was concerned now I had vomited a bit of the second litre too. I also wasn't making great progress now and I was still drinking during the supposed "break" time. It was getting more and more difficult to get down, and I was worried it wasn't working as it was now a couple of hours in, and I hadn't been to the toilet yet. I shouldn't have worried though, as once it started, I sat there for the next 5 hours. It hurt sitting for so long, and everything I was warned about was worse when actually experiencing it. It wasn't just shitting water, the water was like acid. It was flushing your insides out so burned as it came out. Wiping hurt, even with baby wipes, but I was lucky it was clear water quite quickly. I made it through 2.9 litres, I couldn't even finish the tiny bit left in the 3rd litre.

When Conor came home from work, he sat in the bathroom with me for a while. He was trying to encourage me to keep drinking, but me and my body were very aware it was like poison, and every mouthful was brutal, especially as I knew the outcome. It was a really long, painful day; I thought it would be fine because I'd be sitting, but sitting for that long, it turns out actually hurts. The painful burn of my poor raw ass also hurt, and I was really starving. It completely empty's you out. It was a real distinct hunger too, because you feel empty. I was worried I wouldn't be able to make it home to my family house as my appointment was at 8 in the morning and my mum was coming to pick me up to bring me home. I told her to put something down in the car in case of a watery accident, which she did, but I was thankfully fine. She collected me at around 9 pm, and I hated leaving the flat as I viewed it as my home now but knew it was just for the night. I went back to my family house, and there was still water coming; it was never-ending. I tried to go to sleep but didn't sleep well due to apprehension for the morning and also worried about relaxing and more water coming out. I was also STARV-ING. Conor, Michael and Ryan also got a takeaway, which was our routine on a Thursday, as when Ryan flew home from London, he had his expenses still from his work, so we used the allow-ance for the flats "Take Away Thursday". We regularly reinforced the fact it was the food we really looked forward to and not him actually coming back. They kindly never told me about it this week until after the procedure; they knew it would be cruel. They were right.

The morning came, and I got up and got ready. I showered and had to be careful as my skin was still so raw, and I was still need-ing the toilet, but was passing the same yellow bile/stomach lin-ing looking crap. I knew something wasn't right as I shouldn't be passing anything. It was snowing, meaning the traffic was bad and people lose the ability to drive. Also it was my office's main Christmas do, and I was raging I was missing it, and kind of hoped the snow meant it was postponed. Fuck you yet again, Crohn's. I got told later it wasn't great though, and the week before was much better, which made me a little bit happier. We made it to the City hospital, and I was really scared.

I had to bring slippers and a nightgown, and I was also dosed with a cold and cough, which I was trying to hide in case this meant I wasn't allowed sedation. My consultant had said he would give me some before, 2 weeks ago at the prior appointment, and it would make me nice and sleepy. Mum and I waited until we were called and were brought into a very, very small room. Every time I let out a muffled cough or sneeze, my mum shoved me to try to shut me up; this procedure was happening. I changed, done the pre-procedure questions, and as I asked for sedation, they put the cannula in, which from being dehydrated and having shit veins was difficult. It went in though, and I was told there was one lady in front of me, and once they were done with her, I was next. I was so scared, I was fighting back the tears. My poor mum was trying to calm me down and tell me it was fine, I'd be sedated. The nurse then saw this and was super lovely and asked if I was ok. She was so nice throughout. My mum explained it's just a lot for a 24-year-old to go through, and the nurse agreed. It wasn't even that I was scared of. What if they didn't find anything? What would this mean? I was also mildly traumatised from the flexible sigmoidoscopy the month before due to its pain. I knew this was longer and even more invasive, and what if the sedation was shit. There was a lot going through my head, and I was really quite terrified.

They called my name, and I brought my stuff with me, and it was placed under my hospital bed, and I was wheeled into the room. My consultant was listening to music and was very relaxed. So strange that this is someone's job, like they actively choose to do this. I'd rather not be sticking cameras up someone's bum for a living, to be honest, but I guess someone's gotta do it, and it comes with the job description. The sedation was put in my cannula, and quite quickly, I felt woozy. This stuff was much better; I was out of it but awake, as if you are really drunk. I also couldn't feel a thing. I knew if I closed my eyes, I'd sleep, but I had been waiting for this moment for years. I couldn't sleep now, I needed to see if I had Crohn's or not and what was going on. I vaguely remember chatting away during it to my consultant and the surrounding nurses, not a care in the world talking shite. I was also definitely asked should I not be sleeping. Medicine did interest me, so I must have been asking questions, as I remember my consultant showing me the biopsier. He said, look how tiny it is in person, but it looks so big on the screen, and he was right. I remembered them asking me to move and change positions and the nurse coming over to help me, but of course, I had already spun myself around.

I was so pain-free that when they first blew the air up at the start and I was forewarned, I could barely feel it. It was just a mild sensation in my stomach. We then got to the Crohn's. As I looked on the screen, I could spot it, it was very discoloured compared to the rest of the healthy colon. As we got to the last bit of the small intestines, there was loads of that yellow looking goo stuff. I now know what I had been passing for the past few weeks and that morning, was ulcers. There was bleeding, inflammation, and everything.

Me, as a sedated none medical professional, knew this was Crohn's disease. I said to my consultant, "is that Crohns?" and he agreed. FINALLY!!!! I KNEW IT!!!!! I WAS SOOOO HAPPY!!!!! I honestly don't think you could wipe the smile off my face. Biopsies were taken to confirm, and when the tube was on the way back around, at the very start bit/first part of the large intestine near your ass, there was inflammation starting. My consultant took biopsies as he had seen my scope from the few weeks before and said it wasn't inflamed previously. I remembered this as well, and this area was now slightly inflamed compared to the main Crohns area. The nurse at the end told me I done brilliantly and was amazing during it. I must have been talking some shite. I got wheeled back around to recovery one happy diagnosed girl.

When in recovery, I was too excited to sleep, it was a busy ward too, and I was easily the youngest there by approximately 30-40 years. I asked the nurse if she could get me my phone from my belongings that were under the hospital bed as I was bored and couldn't wait to tell my nearest and dearest after years of harping on saying I have Crohn's, I was, in fact, right. I had a few messages wishing me luck, and I responded and let others know. I couldn't wait to get out of recovery to see the next step. I remember the nurses telling me they wished all their patients were as cheerful and nice as me; they probably get some nightmares. When I told a few I had good news and was diagnosed with Crohn's disease, they were quite shocked at my reaction. I explained it was a long time coming, and they understood, but I could tell they thought this is very serious, and she doesn't realise. I don't think I've ever appreciated how severe it is as an illness as I live it every day, and it's just my life.

My mum arrived, I got changed after leaving recovery, and we waited to see my consultant. I was given the standard tea and toast to eat, which always tastes amazing after not eating in nearly 24 hours. I saw my consultant, and he confirmed I had Crohn's in both my large and small intestines, affecting the last part of the small intestine (terminal ileum), and the start of the large bowel, which turns out to be the most common type of Crohn's. It was frustrating as I should have been checked for this years ago, but it was done now, and I thought this would be me on the mend. I got told the treatment would start with steroids, and if they didn't work stronger steroids, then if that failed key-hole surgery. It seemed really positive, and I got told I needed an emergency prescription from my GP to start the steroids that day. Budesonide 9mg I was put on and consisted of 3 tablets every morning about 30 minutes before eating. I was also put on bone tablets due to steroids thinning your bones and being at risk of osteoporosis. Also, Cholestagel tablets, primarily for cholesterol but also absorb bile salts. Due to the area of my small intestine that has Crohn's/was inflamed, absorption doesn't happen properly. These are to do the job for it. I was also given some helpful information about the Crohns and Colitis website and the IBD helpline, then away we went, ecstatic and elated. I saw my file before leaving, and pictures had been taken from the colonoscopy, and I asked to see them to show my mum. The nurse happily showed us, and I remember my mum being a bit horrified at all the ulcers and bleeding; I think I said something cheeky like told you I wasn't making it up.

I got my script from the GP and started the steroids that day. I went home and slept but couldn't wait to get back to my flat that evening and be back with my boyfriend and friends. I missed takeaway Thursday, and after today, I knew I'd be in charge of ordering whatever I wanted as well; a real bonus to top off a weirdly great day.

I thought getting diagnosed was the hard part?

I thought I was feeling better the next few days because of the steroids, though my cold and cough got 10 times worse, and I couldn't make it in to work on Monday. The pain I was having that I was going to the hospital for seemed to be going, so I thought everything was working. Even though I was told the steroids I was on took a few weeks to really kick in. They release in the gut compared to prednisolone, which is systemic, meaning there should be fewer side effects. I had convinced myself that I wouldn't get any side effects, and I'd shortly be in remission. I know now I am not that lucky and never have been, so I don't know where I get this stupid, constantly positive attitude from. I should have realised I was going to get bad side effects when on Sunday, 2 days after I was diagnosed, I think the steroids brought on a really weird bout of depression. Conor was out drinking and watching the football with mates, and I was sitting by myself in our room watching TV. I was very content, and all of a sudden, I felt like a cloud had surrounded me, sucking me into it, and I was now extremely upset and down. I was hysterically crying and felt stupid and alone. I was thinking to myself, why did I think I was so grown up and brave and could handle this when as a matter of fact, I was a clueless, stupid bitch who had no idea what she was up against.

I went on the Crohns and Colitis app I had downloaded and posted, asking had the steroids I was on ever made anyone feel really down. I got told by those who responded no, and it could be me coming to terms with my diagnoses. Part of me wondered if it was a subconscious element, but all I could think was how happy I was when finally diagnosed. It was a horrible feeling like I was trapped in this cloud and couldn't get out no matter how much I talked myself down. I messaged Conor and said what was happening, and he said he'd be back after the football, but if I really needed him, he'd come back. He'd had a few drinks and was enjoying himself, so I wasn't going to ask him to come back; I just couldn't wait until he did. I'm not one to ask for help, and as per usual, I was just hoping he could read my mind and come be by my side until this passed. I had even phoned my mum, and she was really concerned and wanted me to come home. I didn't want to leave my flat and just wanted Conor to hurry up. She kept phoning and asking, but I kept saying no. Ryan had found me downstairs weeping as well when I had gone down to get a drink, and I told him not to worry. But being a typical boy, he just saw the tears and had a mini freak out, which actually made me laugh a bit. He didn't know what to do and began looking for Michael or anyone/anything that might take him out of the situation. I laughed through the tears and said not to worry, I think the steroids were just fucking with me, and I was fine. Hours later, Conor arrived back, and the weird cloud of depression had already started lifting. It was really strange, and I do think it was from the medication. I felt cried out but more rational as it passed; maybe years of tears and emotion came out. Who knows? I just wished he had come back earlier, but I don't think he realised how bad it was; nobody does unless they have experienced it.

It was the run-up to Christmas over the next few weeks, and I began noticing on Christmas Eve the shape of my face changing. The moon face was coming. The Crohn's also wasn't getting any better, and I actually didn't feel that much better, but I was still trying to wait the full four weeks for the steroids to fully kick in; it was also an 8-week course. As we went into 2018, my health was still getting worse. Of course, I tried convincing myself I was getting better though. I bought a diary and made to-do lists in it every day to feel super productive. It's something I actually still do and really sadly enjoy ticking off my to-do list for the day. I was coming home from work, and to stop myself from passing out, I was deep cleaning our bedroom or en suite and hating myself pretty much as soon as I started as I had no energy. Conor questioned WTF I was doing, and I told him I was just being productive. One day I tried exercising as I wanted to be in good shape for being a bridesmaid in June and thought I could start my exercise regime now. I tried doing a star jump and nearly fainted. Conor proceeded to tell me to sit the fuck down and stop exercising. I did after only a little bit of resistance.

This attempt at convincing myself I was getting better, when in reality I was getting worse, soon stopped as the fatigue that had been bad for years was at its worst ever. I was sleeping as soon as I came home from work for 3 hours, getting up only to have some dinner and passing out again. I would get up exhausted going to work, be exhausted in work, come home, sleep, and then repeat the process the next day, not much else in between. I was also in a weird low mood most of the time and was starting to struggle with the concept of this being a lifelong illness. I knew a lot of cancer patients with better health/outcomes than my illness (obviously depending on the type of cancer) however, when someone hears the "cancer" word, they shit themselves, although most are a lot more treatable/not as long term as IBD. I think a lot of my mindset at the time was from the steroids as it all correlated, and a known side effect is depression.

My bloods had been taken, and I was also low in iron, meaning anaemia, which was not helping the fatigue. I was still urgently and suddenly needing the toilet and still disgustingly passing undigested food. I was definitely getting worse, not better. It impacted my relationship with Conor as well; he didn't get it, and I needed a lot of emotional support, but I wasn't asking for it. I was hoping he would just be there instead of arguing with every emotion I told him I felt. Phrases like, "You don't feel like that" or "You're not that bad" were regularly heard. He likes to get out at least once a week for drinking and would tell you himself he gets antsy if he doesn't. On the other hand, I was sleeping at least 15 hours a day, still exhausted, and my whole body felt heavy, like I was dragging it around all the time kind of heavy. Our normal life and going out was currently far away for me.

The exploding pain had also come back a lot worse, and I had noticed between my front and back passage (polite wording) or "my gooch", as I like to call it, a lump was forming as if there was something under the skin. I had asked Conor to take a look, and he said my left-hand side was swollen compared to the right. I told my auntie Anna-Marie, and she suspected I had a fistula. So, of course, I googled it, and it matched what I was feeling. I had no idea at this point what it meant but was seeing my consultant in mid-January, so I would tell him then. Thinking back, I don't know how I was at work, but as I don't get paid when off, I had to drag myself in. I was also growing silently upset too when I heard ones whinging about having colds and taking days off for them. Then when they were getting better, going on about how they were "feeling like myself again" and were absolutely delighted. Here I was dragging myself in whilst getting progressively sicker with an incurable, lifelong illness. Coooool.

One of the worst days/nights was when I was really unwell and couldn't make it into work one Friday, but it was my friend Neil's birthday, who I'm extremely fond of and he was heading out that night. I knew I wouldn't be able to head out, but I made an effort to go around to his house beforehand. I was experiencing the guilt I've learned all IBD patients have felt, having to cancel plans but not wanting to let people down and still trying to pretend you're ok but dying inside. I put on a full face of make-up and dressed up to do my standard of keeping up appearances. Just because I was very internally sick, I didn't want the world to see. When we were to get the taxi around from our flat on

Ravenhill to Stranmillis, I was so full of dread for that journey in case I needed the toilet. Any journey filled me with anxiety, but I couldn't wait for the less than 10-minute taxi to be over as I had been so bad that day. So many times, travelling, it has been like mental torture/endurance. At this point, I was also so tired and sick I couldn't follow any conversations that were happening; I also couldn't wait to go home. I kept being told I looked amazing even with everything going on and how anyone who knew someone else with anaemia looked a really funny colour, but I looked good. It was all makeup, but I was still very pale and had an ever-growing moon face I was insanely conscious about, telling everyone I had one so they wouldn't stare at my deformed face. I really wanted Conor to come back with me, I was feeling so unwell and vulnerable, but he was getting drunk and said he was going out. He had actually begun annoying me before we got in the taxis, as everyone was finishing their drinks. I had been sipping on a bottle of Smirnoff ice (I'm normally a rosé or vodka kind of person, Smirnoff ice is just a 10/10 on flavour), and he took my bottle and poured his Buckfast into it and tried getting everyone, including me, to drink it. I was not amused at having my drink stolen to be contaminated with disgusting Bucky and shared around a room. He was at least tipsy at this point, and when I said I was annoyed, I got told to wise up and asked why was I actually annoyed. There was no point discussing.

The taxi left them at Lavery's, and I went on home. He told me he'd be back when the bars shut at 1 am, so I arrived back to the empty flat but was so upset, and in so much pain I couldn't sleep. My stomach was so painful, and I knew I needed a smoke to try ease the pain, but I didn't have a lighter, so I needed to wait until Conor was back. There also wasn't much to eat in the flat, and it gives me a massive appetite, so I knew I should probably text him to see what food he wanted, and order something. People assume people with Crohn's don't like to eat or can't eat, but it's very dehumanising as everybody/everything has to eat in some form. I've also always been a massive foody, so it's been a very cruel disease to get, and when you're in a flare-up, it doesn't matter what you eat; nothing is getting digested. So, I was eating what I wanted, apart from things high in fibre, as I was still on a low residue diet. I patiently waited until 1 am, thinking he would arrive home soon, but I hadn't been getting much response.

I continued to wait, but now it was closer to 2 am, and I was really starving and exhausted, so I began phoning; I hated doing it, but he said he'd be home about an hour before. He was really drunk now and told me to work away as he didn't know when he'd be home. I was so upset at this, I really needed him. I was already gutted I was missing another night out with my friends and one of their birthdays and was alone and isolated yet again. Conor is very good at being able to turn anything around on you, like it's your fault when it was actually him. I've commended him on it many a time, and he has agreed. We got into a huge fight on the phone when I told him I thought he'd be back and had been waiting for him. He was really drunk and started shouting back, turning it around on me, and saying he didn't know what he was doing and was staying out. I was so upset that I began crying so much and packing my bag; I was fed up and not dealing with this shit, but I also really didn't want to go home. He now wouldn't answer his phone, so I had to phone Michael to get him. Mick said he was really drunk, and I knew what he's like when he's in a state. I agreed and explained to Michael where I was coming from, and he understood and said he would try to talk Conor down. I was an emotional, exhausted, steroid altered wreck, and I didn't feel like myself at all.

Angry and upset, I began throwing my belongings around the room whilst screaming. I wanted to damage something really badly as I screamed and uncontrollably sobbed. I got the scissor from downstairs and began tearing up a pillowcase. It didn't make me feel better as I wanted to actually smash something, so I began the ritual of packing and unpacking my bag, hoping he would come home and see this and maybe wise up. I kept the scissors in the drawer beside my bed and thought about using them to hurt myself. What was the fucking point in all of this and the shitty life I was living? I even tried cutting myself with the scissor but didn't press too hard because I knew if I cut myself too much and began to regret it, I'd probably bleed out pretty quickly and would be fucked as there was no one in the flat. I was really tempted though and was extremely angry at this point, so kept the scissor in the table beside my bed for the next while. It must have been closer to 4 am when they arrived back, and I was still distressed and exhausted. There was a pizza in the freezer we found, and after a smoke, I managed to eat it and pass out. I think we made up the next day, but as you can tell, I didn't forget. I never disclosed the fact about the scissors or the cut-up pillowcase and had tidied the room/my belongings again. This was the start of me realising how alone I really was.

When I saw my consultant, he asked me about symptoms, and I told him. He said straight away the steroids weren't working, and I told him about the suspected fistula. After being examined, he confirmed he thought the same, and I was to get an emergency small bowel MRI and pelvic MRI. I wouldn't have been waiting any longer than a week as this was an emergency, but my mum had private health care through her work, and she said she could get it sorted ASAP. Dr Turner hoped we could get it done ASAP on the NHS, but it was fine as we didn't have to pay anyway through insurance cover. When he felt my stomach, he said he could still feel the ulcers as they felt "squishy" (I honestly thought it was just fat). The next plan of action was no longer steroids, and they wanted me on infliximab, an IV infusion. My friend Michelle at work who's brother has Crohn's, said he was on it and responding well. I had heard a few others talk about it too after my diagnosis and said I should suggest it to my doctor. It turns out there was no need as it was the next step anyway. My consultant also checked my blood as I needed to be checked for chickenpox immunity. I had never had them as a kid, neither had my sister and a few cousins on both sides of my family (which seemed to be a girl thing), so I had hoped there was some natural genetic immunity. As I was going to be put on infliximab, a serious long-term chemo level, immune suppressor, if I were to contract chickenpox, I would end up in intensive care or potentially die. It turned out I had a mild immunity, that as a kid, must have been strong enough to protect me but not enough for someone with no immune system. It was arranged I was to get the chickenpox vaccination (I never knew it was a thing) with my GP the following week.

The next week on Monday, we got the two MRI's sorted at the Ulster Independent hospital. I was quite glad as it was so nice it didn't feel like a hospital. Even the nurses' uniforms were nicer and different, kind of old school pinafores. I was very apprehensive, though, as I had read in my pre-procedure letter, the contrast I was to drink for the small bowel MRI had a "mild laxative effect". Considering a mouthful of coffee could have me on the toilet for the next 3 hours, I already knew there would be nothing mild about it. I drank the contrast over the 45 minutes and actually liked its taste, it just tasted like sweet water. Much better than that normal shite. I did all the pre-MRI questions and went to get changed into my gown before it. Of course, then I felt my stomach go; even the imodem I had taken earlier to try and help wasn't even remotely effective. Also annoying as it was another test I had to fast for and was starving. From drinking the litre of contrast, I also learned that when people tell you to drink more water when hungry as it could be thirst, and it never worked, it was because to feel full, you need to drink about a litre of water in a short space of time. It also only subsides actual hunger for a while. On top of my bowels going, of course, the amount I needed to pee was a lot too. I was hoping that as I had gone to the toilet before the MRI, that would be it. How wrong I was.

I went into the MRI room and had the cannula put in, as they needed to put in different dyes and other stuff at different points of the scan. I had to be strapped in, and different layers of things were put on top of me for the small bowel MRI. They gave me headphones for the noise and a button to push if I needed to talk to them. I wasn't strapped in 2 seconds, and I had the buzzer pushed. Fucking laxative contrast and fucking Crohn's. I apologised and ran to the toilet and remember actually saying aloud to the nurses, "fucking Crohn's". It was like the colonoscopy prep, mostly just water and I hoped I was getting most of it out.

When I returned, the nurse was concerned it might have passed through me, so I was made to drink another cup of the contrast. I can't remember if this MRI last 20 or 30 minutes, but it felt incredibly long when fully concentrating on not shitting myself in a million-pound machine. It was noisy with a lot of beeping sounds and the nurses telling me through the headphones when to breathe, hold my breath, exhale etc. When it was over, the pelvic MRI only lasted about 5-10 minutes, but again as I was panicking, I wanted it over ASAP. I never found it overly claustrophobic as I was put in on my stomach, feet first, so my head was poking out. When it was over, the nurse came in to let me out and asked how I was. I told her I was fine but dying to pee, and she laughed and said, yes, she could see my bladder was full from the MRI. I sneakily said to her, I know you can't tell me anything but was there anything there. She confirmed she couldn't say but left me with, is it on your left-hand side, to which I agreed, and she smiled. It was very kind of her and helped put my mind at ease; there was something up.

I knew something extra was wrong at this point because I had started passing more weird yellow stuff every day. The abscess was now so painful it hurt to walk, cough, sneeze, sit, and basically be alive. When I got out of the room, I ran straight to the toilet to essentially pee out of both holes; I probably went in between scans too, but I can't remember. I'll just safely assume, though. I was shocked it was still going, but then again really shouldn't have been, and I didn't realise how unwell I was. I got changed and went out to get my mum, but also needed the toilet again and felt really bad as she was waiting over half an hour. The laxative wouldn't stop, and like the colonoscopy prep, it also burned like a bitch. When I eventually got out, I told her we need to be quick back to my flat and, in case, put a towel down on the car seat. I was thankfully fine, and I always have been extremely lucky that I've been able to hold it or get to a toilet quick enough. I did however sprint into my flat and push past my housemates for a toilet, telling them I'd be down in a minute to explain, as they asked how the MRI went.

The MRI's had been on a Monday, but the next day I of course, impatiently chased up my GP's office to see if I could get a copy of the MRI results. The doctor I spoke to on the phone left a copy of the letter out and confirmed they couldn't really read the results as they're not specialists in the area. When I read it, I didn't blame them as it was an entirely different language. I gathered I had 7mm or cm (can't remember) of ulcerated and inflamed small bowel and it had been damaged, affecting how it worked, but the rest looked fine. There was also a couple of fistulas and an abscess. So I guess for all these months that had been the pain. I wondered what the next step was but didn't have long to find out. I got a phone call from my consultant on Friday saying I was in for emergency surgery on Monday. Fuck, that's quick, I thought, not appreciating anything that was really going on. I remembered naively thinking, "how is the NHS so drained if they can do this for me right away?" not appreciating I was, in fact, like he said, an emergency. He asked how I was, and I replied, not great. He said they'd get me better really soon and if over the weekend I felt worse, or any shivering or fevers set in straight to the hospital. He had said this at my last appointment too, really stressing shivering, fevers etc. I now know this is because I was at high risk of sepsis, and that would have in fact been symptoms of me dying, whoo...

I had my chickenpox's vaccination that Friday afternoon too, so let my work know that I'd be having the surgery on Monday and would probably be back in a few days as they were draining the abscess. HR was more clued in than me, though, and said not to be rushing back and may well be longer. They were very right. I got a phone call from the City hospital soon after Dr Turner's call, telling me where to go on Monday in case the pre-op letter didn't arrive on time. Unfortunately, I was in such a fluster that I forgot what hospital they said, so I didn't know if I was in the Royal or the City. I was so flustered when I phoned my mum saying I was having surgery on the Monday, that when she asked what hospital, I responded with a very blank, "I don't know". I remembered I needed to be at the Day of Surgery unit at 7 am, and the guy had described where to go in the hospital, so I tried figuring it out from the description. My mum told me in both hospitals you go past the shop to get to where you need to go, so I may get phoning to see where I am. She wasn't wrong; I knew that and didn't have a notion. It was all a lot of very sudden information to take on, and I hadn't been writing any of it down. I phoned my GP and the hospitals to see if they knew, and a receptionist in the GP came back to me to confirm it was the City hospital. I thought it would be the Royal because I had my appointments there but thankfully phoned; otherwise, I'd have been very wrong. The letter came anyway the next day, and I was shocked to read I couldn't wear nail polish/fake nails or even have moisturiser on. I said to my mum, and she said it's because your nails change colour and they need to see everything clearly, especially if something were to go wrong and you were to die. Not where my head was at, but there you go.

I had my chickenpox's injection, and it was fine, just a bit sore as it had to be administered a different way than most injections. I think the fluid had to go under the muscle rather than into it, but I remember it being sorer than other one's, just due to how it was administered and kind of felt a burn. I chilled out that weekend just having a few drinks in the flat with my housemates, not really thinking much about the coming Monday. I think it was good though, I didn't have time to think about it. I was more dreading the fasting, and because my Crohn's wasn't good, how much I'd need the toilet that early in the morning. Standard. Mornings are something all people tend to hate, but with Crohn's, it's for a whole other reason. I hadn't realised either that my mum and auntie Annie had been chatting and she was very concerned. My mum had sent her my MRI letter, and she had read it, saying to my mum I was getting emergency surgery as I was on immune suppressors, already sick, and I had an abscess which is basically a pocket of infection.

She then explained all the shivering warnings from my consultant and how I was at high risk of sepsis. I had never actually heard of it before but learned that it was an infection getting into your blood system, and if it was to get in there, there is a high chance of dying, whether healthy or unhealthy. My mortality rate was not good with everything going on and no immune system. Basically, what was happening was the new yellow crap I was passing was the abscess bursting and passing out through the fistula. Absolutely delightful. Infection was already getting out of where it should be contained, passing into my system.

The pain I was in all the time was horrible. The abscess tended to fill up all day, meaning any sort of normal body function or movement, e.g., walking, was agony. I hated when I had to get up or walk around, especially when at work. I felt like such a dick as I had a weird slow walk with a slight limb as my insides were so permanently painful, all whilst trying to pretend like there was nothing wrong. If I had to cough or sneeze and Conor was around in the flat, he used to try to hold my stomach in place to stop the pain a little. He could see the pain I was in as I grabbed something, doubled over or winced, then took a few seconds to recover if I had a general body function. It was much less painful when it passed, and I got a few hours of a bit more comfort. However, as it began filling before bursting again, the pain was really horrible.

I was most excited about getting time off to sleep. Fatigue was so bad, and I was continuing to struggle to follow conversations and pretending like I was in group settings. It was really embarrassing when caught out, however. I looked like an idiot but didn't have the energy to explain. I felt like I was drowning. Everything was foggy, unclear and muffled. My body felt permanently heavy, like I was dragging it around; everything almost felt like it was in slow motion with the weird drowning effect. It was all fatigue. Crohn's toilet symptoms were so bad; I was grossly doing my make up on the toilet as I got ready before work so Conor wouldn't be late. I felt really bad, and I always had him late when he was supposed to start at half 8. I was still bleeding and at times was still running to the toilet just to pass blood or vomit my stomach lining. Really embarrassingly, on a client conference call with my boss Tomás, I knew I was going to be sick and mouthed this at him before running out of the room. I went straight to the disabled toilets to vomit and then pass some blood. I apologised when I returned, and he said not to worry and look concerned and a bit alarmed. He probably thought I had the shits, standard Crohns, and probably shouldn't be in work, but this was all so normal to me now.

My steroid-induced moon face was in full swing, and people had actually kept saying how well I looked as I no longer looked so gaunt. I just had a fat face and resembled a 3-year-old; it was so depressing I hated myself and especially my face. I was wearing hats, mostly those baker boy hats, as they have a flat cap to hide more of my facial deformity. For some reason, it was mostly boys who felt the need to comment on my new fashion accessory, saying I was probably drawing more attention to myself with the hats. Desperate times called for desperate measures, and further comments on my appearance were not helping how I felt at all. I also really learned about how easy it is to catch everything going whilst on immune suppressors. Colds and coughs would not shift and were 10 times worse.

I also somehow got a really aggressive form of conjunctivitis. After not responding to a strong dose of eye drops prescribed by a GP, I got sent by Boots pharmacy to eye casualty one day to check it wasn't Crohn's related. It turns out Crohn's has loads of extra ways to manifest in your body, and eye inflammation is one. This reminded me of before I had been diagnosed, and the year before, I had some kind of dermatitis break out on my face that took ages to treat and go away. I now know this was a Crohn's skin manifestation. Thankfully, it was just a bad infection though when checked out, and I was moved onto an eye gel numerous times a day for a week. I must have looked wiped out when I returned to work after eye casualty. They put some drops in your eye when being initially seen, and I couldn't see a thing. It was really disorientating the feeling of temporary half blindness, but the lingering after-effect was the huge pupils. The sensation and large pupils lasted hours, and I still couldn't see properly when back at work. I also couldn't wear eye makeup for a week as I needed to keep putting the gel in, again further looking like a cretin whilst trying hard to pretend everything was fine. That infection was so bad I had to get another tube of the gel and use it for two weeks. With hindsight, imagine trying to fight off something actually super serious with a suppressed immune system, not really worth thinking about.

That Monday morning, I got up, and my mum and I headed over to the City. We found the place where to go, and it was full of men and women all with family members, and we all had packed bags with us in case we were to stay. The room was cramped with all the people and suitcases/bags. Of course, I repeatedly needed the toilet and kept coming in and out of the room as the cubicle was down the corridor. I was also thinking at this point, what if I shit myself during surgery? Is that a thing? Can it happen? Christ, that'd be embarrassing, like they know I have Crohn's but still.

At about half seven, the men got called into one ward down the hall, and the women were called into the other. We went into our wards with our names and consultants' names above the bed, so you knew where to go.

Dr Tan was my surgeon, I hadn't met him yet, but he seemed to be friends with my consultant Dr Turner. There was 3 other women and me, and I was again the youngest. However, there was a young woman opposite me who couldn't have even been 40 who was by herself. The rest of us had family who were told to say their goodbyes and leave; I felt bad she was by herself. There was also an older lady whose husband, God love him, was crying leaving her; it was very cute. I said goodbye to my mum and said I'd see her after. I didn't realise how busy it would be the morning before surgery. We all had to pee in metal cups to ensure we weren't pregnant (some of the older post-menopause ladies laughed hysterically at this), weight etc., was taken, and different rounds of questions from the nurses, doctors, surgeon and anaesthetist. In one of my rounds of questions, I got warned that if I was on any contraceptive pill, the anaesthetic would wipe it. I confirmed I had to come off it as I was on that much medication affecting it. My doctors were lovely, but I really embarrassingly had to ask them all the same question. My mum and Conor had forewarned me that before surgery, you have to let them know if you have taken any form of drugs in the last two years as it can affect anaesthetic. I really cringely asked this to the doctors who told me to say to the next doctor (I don't think they actually had a clue) and felt like a dick needing to explain myself and say, I occasionally smoke grass for pain relief due to the Crohns. I really didn't want them thinking I was some kind of addict, but I may have come across as one when one of the junior doctors said it should be fine but as long as you haven't in probably the last 48 hours. I lied and agreed, thinking, mate, my last smoke was less than 24 hours ago, so I could eat an amazing last supper before I fasted, and my stomach's far too sore to be doing that sober.

The anaesthetist came in, and when doing her questions, I said to her. She was not approving; I got a lecture on how much better pain relief there is out there but with no suggestions as to what. I really wasn't in the mood for arguing as Crohn's was not her speciality; trying not to kill me while putting me to sleep was hers. I had never once been offered pain relief for Crohn's pain, and I actually don't think there is one; otherwise, everyone would be on it who had it. My friend Conal, the doctor, had also said he didn't think there was anything you could take for the pain. Morphine is probably what they could give, but that's not prescribed for the craic. In all the other questions, I had been asked if I had any metal plates etc., in my mouth, as I hadn't realised when you're unconscious, a tube is doing your breathing for you. I have a permanent retainer behind my top 4 teeth since I was 14, and when I told her, she said she would try not to hit it but can't promise anything, yet every other doctor had said it was fine. I kind of felt with how she said it she was going to purposely try to hit it because of where it is. Although it's kinda hard to actually hit, I can only feel it with my tongue if I purposely rub it; it's tiny. She struck me as a doctor with delusions of grandeur, which is all too common in most "respectable" professions. I honestly have more respect for bin men or others considered to be in "low" jobs, compared to people thinking they're something they're not. Don't come at me with your profession if you've got no manners.

She left, and my surgeon came round, Dr Tan. He was super lovely, and explained they were going to drain the abscess and hoped that would be it, but because of the nature of Crohn's, it may come back again. Nah, that'll not happen to me, I thought... if only I knew. He, of course, needed to examine me so he could see what he was doing prior to surgery and apologised, as I knew the inevitable, "we needa stick a finger up your bum," but in polite doctor chat was coming. Low and behold, it did, and I always found it amusing they used what they called "cold jelly", a.k.a. lube, before shoving their finger up there. I think this was maybe the 4th stranger's finger up my ass over the last few months, and the novelty was really wearing off. Jokes aside, it certainly wasn't great, but I was getting slightly immune to it. Well, as immune as you can be, I think it was just coming to the point of not caring as much. All I could think of was Conor, and how I had told him, I'm not half as forthcoming when he asked compared to a doctor and to try not to get jealous. We had joked about it, and now I had to stop myself from laughing at the memory as I was examined. I told Dr Tan it was to the left to see if that helped, and he confirmed he felt it and knew where to go. I'm nothing if not helpful.

It was so busy getting everything organised, even the nurses looking after me agreed. They said I was an emergency, and even on Friday, when preparing, it was all a rush. I noticed some of my notes and sticky labels that should have been printed were hand wrote due to the rush. They were super lovely, and I really liked them. Thinking back, they are my all-time favourite nurses. I got changed into my surgical gown and had surgical stockings to put on, which I also hadn't realised was a thing. A couple of nurses rushed around me because I was to go into theatre very shortly, and a lady maybe in her late 60's in the bed beside me obviously thought I was getting more attention than her and piped up. She started calling over one of my nurses who was trying to help me with the stockings (they're REALLY hard to get on, super tight) and started asking her what she was doing and what was happening with her and generally just being a whiny dick. You could tell the nurse was internally annoyed but was so lovely and kept her calm composure and explained that I was having a different operation than her and I was going into surgery now and needed to get ready. The old bitch clearly wasn't happy, and I thought, Christ, this is why people in the NHS deserve medals and why I could never be a nurse. Like seriously, what the fuck is wrong with people. The rudeness and self-entitlement just really got to me, especially interrupting people trying to do their job.

Shortly after, I was wheeled out of the ward and brought down to the operating table. I was getting nervous now, and it was mostly because I was worried my Crohns would be bad whilst unconscious, and I didn't know if that was a thing, but I also didn't want to ask. They put the cannula in my hand and said before the anaesthetic, I'd be given pain relief and diazepam to calm the nerves. I think it was anyway, and it was basically a mixture of drugs to make me relax. They got the cannula in, and in went the drugs. Within seconds I was woozy and thinking, this is great. I totally get pain relief addicts, this was great and fun in these circumstances. I wasn't nervous anymore; I was calm and sleepy. I got wheeled over beside the operating table, which I was surprised to see was a thin leather log looking thing. It wasn't a big table like I assumed, it was small and skinny, and I wondered would I fit onto it. Although I'm only 5 foot 1 approximately and was puffy from steroids but still skinny, I was genuinely concerned I wouldn't fit. I wondered if they needed a bigger table for bigger or fatter people; again, I never asked I just did what I was told and rolled over onto it. They put the pre-anaesthetic mask thing on that I think also helps knock you out, and I was told I'd be under soon. Seconds later, the anaesthetic was put in, and as I felt myself go under, I half laughed to the doctor or nurse beside me and said, "that's me going now, isn't it", she laughed and said, "yes, it is." And like that, I was gone.

Then I woke up. Well jumped up instead, and think I actually startled the nurse that was near me. I had no idea how long I had been asleep; one second I had been put under, and the next, I was awake, nothingness in between. It was like an even more extreme version of when you wake up disorientated from a nap, except I was more relaxed and drowsier with everything in my system. Unfortunately, upon waking up, that's when the pain kicks in. I felt like a hot rod had been shoved up me but was apparently getting more pain relief through my IV. It was not working. I also really needed to pee, and apparently, that's from all the fluids put through you during surgery. I was covered in wires and tubes and couldn't really move but wanted to get back to recovery ASAP. The nurse I had was lovely, and after a while, I really needed to pee, but wasn't allowed to leave the hospital bed, so was told I'd have to use a bedpan. I also noticed there was no toilet on the ward, and it has to be for keeping you in bed purposes. What I learned from my next experience is that old people are fucking heroes. I was given a bedpan and tried peeing while lying down. This, I learned, is impossible as you need gravity, confirmed by the nurse. I remember thinking when people piss themselves, it must really be an accident.

In my post-op woozy state, I decided I needed to sit up to do this, again nearly impossible as I kept going to fall back and couldn't get myself up properly. There were too many tubes and wires, so I thought I'd just take off a few so I could help myself up. Unfortunately, this meant I no longer had a heart rate, and the machines started going mental. I heard the nurse shout, "Are you ok, Sarah?" from behind the curtain she had pulled around me so I could piss in private. I sheepishly said yea, as I tried reattaching my wires and do the impossible, kneel in a bed and piss. I was also bandaged up and noticed a lot more blood than I was expecting. Of course, in my head, I thought it would be like a movie, and I'd wake up not covered in iodine and blood.

I managed to pee, and the nurse was actually impressed. The weirdest thing is they measure the output for their records, eww. I remember her being shocked at how much I did go; I mean, I wasn't lying, I thought I was going to wet myself, I needed to go that bad. Afterwards, when collecting the bedpan, the nurse with the biggest wad of tissues gave me a quick pat as the equivalent to a wipe. God love her, I thought, that's her and many others job. Although she never actually touched me, it was quite literally a pat from a huge wad of tissues, and she didn't blink an eye. Definitely not a job I could get used to.

I shortly after went back to recovery and waited there, eating tea and toast and talking to the old lady across the way from me whose husband had been crying, and she hadn't been for her surgery yet. She was saying she was getting a double mastectomy, and it was meant to be in the morning, but now she has to wait until the afternoon and was starving as she had been fasting from the night before. I felt her pain. I realised the younger lady, who was definitely no more than 40, had gone in for her surgery, and she had the same surgeon's name as the older lady waiting. I assumed she was having a similar/same op and really felt for her, especially being here by herself and so young for such an operation. My mum arrived, and the annoying old lady who had questioned my nurses prior to my surgery was being wheeled back in and still half out of it. I heard the nurses say she had requested more pain relief and basically everything going and was now refusing to wake up for them. I gathered they thought she was annoying, and my mum picked up the same. She refused to wake up or cooperate when asked repeatedly, and my mum said, "She's a pain in the arse, isn't she". I concurred.

I was a wee bit shocked at how much pain I was in. I was given strong co-codamol when asked what my normal pain relief was, and I also was noticing how painful my throat was getting. My mum said it was from the tube they put down your throat, and I then remembered the anaesthetist saying about it and trying not to hit my teeth. She mustn't have; my teeth and permanent retainer were intact. It also put my mind at ease as I had initially really badly thought, "Was I fucking violated by a doctor in my sleep?!" I knew it was highly unlikely, but I initially couldn't understand why my throat hurt. As I was lying there under the fluorescent clinical bright lights of the ward, I opened my phone and went onto Snapchat, getting the never flattering face camera, and couldn't believe my eyes. I had a fucking moustache. A little prepubescent boy moustache!! I said to my mum, and she said, yeah, there was one coming in, and it would be the steroids. I was fucking raging, moon face and a moustache, come at me boys! I couldn't wait to get off the steroids, and it was nearly the end of the course too. Shortly after, I got changed and got to go home, glad I didn't have to stay. I was put on antibiotics, ciprofloxacin and metronidazole for the next few weeks to clear any infection. Little did I know what was about to happen.

I was very tired and sore after the op but thankfully got back to my flat that evening. I had been going to the toilet A LOT more and felt extremely sick. Every time I stood up, everything went white and dizzy, and I kept nearly fainting. I was up during the night too being sick and apparently didn't look a great colour. I remember being so tired I never wanted to wake up but put it down to the antibiotics. By Wednesday, I was getting progressively worse, and my auntie had phoned my mum from Oz to tell her I needed to phone the doctors. I phoned the GP for a callback, and when I was called back and listed my symptoms of going to the toilet 3-4 times an hour, including during the night for the past 2 days (which when asked what it was like, I confirmed, "black water"), having no energy, very nauseous and dizzy, I got told I needed to come in. I was so tired, and I just wanted anti-sickness tablets, which I had initially phoned for and to sleep. I knew I couldn't sleep yet as I was waiting for my appointment shortly. I called my mum, and she left work to come get me, she was probably concerned at this point, but I was that out of it I didn't really appreciate what was going on. Conor and my housemates had been at work, so I had just been crawling in and out of bed to be sick then trying to sleep again.

I got called into the GP's office, and she was a really nice young lady; I had never seen her before in the practice. I told her my symptoms, and she took my blood pressure and heart rate etc. I wasn't expecting what she said next. "You need to go to hospital now, your symptoms aren't good, and I don't think it's the anti-biotics. Your heart is also racing, and you've barely been moving, and you're extremely pale." Well that escalated quickly. She phoned the IBD nurses to confirm and said they had said the same, so she wrote me a letter and said it would be highly unsafe if she were to send me home. I think my mum was delighted I was to go to the hospital to be properly looked after, but I was not. I couldn't be bothered with all the waiting, especially when I was so tired and needing the toilet so much. I was also still bleeding from either the op or a bad Crohn's flare. Another joy of Crohn's, when you're sick, you never really know if it is Crohn's illness or something else.

There's no place like home

Off we went to the Royal and began the tedious waiting game. Standard bloods, obs etc., taken and was brought round to the major's triage bit, waiting to see the surgeons, as they needed to decide if I was unwell from surgery or a bad flare-up. I was soo tired, and just wanted to sleep, but the noise and bright fluorescent lights of the hospital stopped that. I was asked if I could give a stool sample, and that was absolutely no problem. Unfortunately, bloody too, so I felt even worse than normal handing that one over. I was given a bed as I waited for the surgeons to come around; the doctors were worried that the abscess had already come back. They put up fluids, and I was given them through the IV. The poor nurse had to change my fluid bag from being attached to the bed to one of those movable poles because I kept needing the toilet so much. She was really lovely and was really understanding as I was initially embarrassed. Another thing with Crohn's is you're embarrassed about asking for a toilet, even when you desperately need one out of no fault of your own. I think it's a denial thing, like maybe it'll not happen if I try not to think about it. Unfortunately, that couldn't be further from the truth.

We were waiting for hours, it must have been closer to a 12-hour wait in total. The staff even changed over at half 8, and the surgeons hadn't come back from theatre yet, and they had no idea when they'd be back as it was emergency surgeries they were doing. A junior doctor, whom I met when in hospital the Sunday before I met my consultant and the colonoscopy was arranged, recognised me. He was another F1 fitty, so I obv recognised him too. He asked me how I was, and I said I was finally diagnosed with Crohn's but unfortunately had just had surgery for an abscess due to fistulas, so I was waiting to get on infliximab. He said to me, "oh, you're going on the big boys". I hadn't understood what intense treatment biologics were prior to receiving them, and as he was fit, all I was thinking was, "I'd like a go on you big boy", but unfortunately couldn't say that. I was really embarrassed about my moon face and current facial hair status, as my eyebrows were also now growing in from my forehead. So, I proceeded to inform the sexy doctor of this, in case he just thought I got really stinking looking or something since he last saw me. I was actually surprised he recognised me, I at least had makeup on the previous time, and my face was a lot skinnier; now I was like a chubby makeup-less Chewbacca. He laughed at my, "all the steroids gave me is moon face and a moustache" comment. However, upon our first meeting, I remembered my mum shouting at him, saying how badly I needed sorted and if it were him in my situation, his mother would be the exact same, to which he agreed. There was a strong possibility it was, in fact, her, he remembered.

Hours past and I got to know the people around me. The guy to my right was here with his partner and had to wait until his cast dried before he could go home, and was growing exhausted and impatient. It turned out he had been at the City hospital that morning for an appointment for another health condition he had, which possibly may have given him brittle bones, as he slipped on someone else's blood that he didn't see on the floor, fell, breaking his arm and banging his head...what a claim. You'd be so raging like, I could understand his frustration and longing to go home. The guy to my left was also waiting for the surgeons; they thought he had appendicitis and needed emergency surgery, so he had been given blood thinners and an IV with fluids attached. But as he had been waiting so long, his blood was now dripping out of the IV and onto the floor... another claim? Another patient the whole of the major's triage area got to know, was asked to come behind one of the cubicle curtains with a doctor, and the doctor was heard loudly saying he was fine and he could go home. The man must have proceeded to show the doctor something as the next statement was, "yes, that's your herpes, but I'm not concerned with that." My mum and I burst out laughing; that was not expected. Shortly after, an old man and his wife/partner of some kind came out from behind the curtain, hahaha, dirty old git. There really was no privacy in this area, and everyone knew what was wrong with the people close by.

My head was banging, and I had been given IV paracetamol and co-codamol, none of which were working. I was told by the nurse who initially gave me the IV paracetamol that it's supposed to be as good as morphine as it hits your bloodstream straight away. I did not concur, and I had never had morphine before. My headache didn't pass, I was so tired and sore, and the waiting was slowly killing me. My mum thought the headache was probably from the fever of a Crohn's flare, and nothing was going to help it. About 8 hours after arriving, the surgeons came around, and it was after midnight at this point. I was called into a room as I needed to be examined, which I knew meant the inevitable finger up the bum test. I was in pain still from the surgery, so I was dreading it more than usual. As it was a male surgeon, he needed to call in a female, so the nurse who had given me my pain relief came in. I dealt with loads of nurses that day between how busy it was and shift changes, and they were all really great.

Dr Tan and the surgeon about to examine me, and the other surgeons with him, were all Chinese. They really are the superior race, I thought. The nurse was really lovely and understood it was an uncomfortable situation as the surgeons went to have a snoop. She asked me about my Crohns, and we discussed. When talking about ulcers, I said yeah, I had them, but it's weird when they pass, they look like when you boke your stomach lining. She asked me if it was like jelly, but my mind was distracted as the surgeons felt around for the abscess and I had already been internally pissing myself at the "cool jelly", aka lube in coming. I apologised and asked her to repeat herself, then agreed when I realised what she said. My brain was jelly at this point.

The surgeon confirmed the abscess had been drained and not returned, and I was unwell due to a flare-up. They needed to decide what to do, and should I be admitted under the medics or surgeons. However, they weren't happy with me going to the medics as they tend to use their own treatment plan instead of my consultants. I had spoken to a doctor in the medic's team earlier who was soo lovely and had said about IV steroids, so I guessed this was what they were talking about. This doctor was really informative too, as people had been making weird comments about my weight. As I was getting sicker, I was looking heavier from the steroids, and a few people had said to me that the people they know with Crohn's were skeletons. Thanks for basically calling me fat was usually my thoughts after hearing this. I asked her about my weight, and she said what people were saying to me was extremely ignorant, and it entirely depends on where in your GI track your Crohns is for it to affect weight drastically. Good to know. I was also happy going to the medics as the sexy junior doctor from earlier was in that team, so all I was thinking was, get me to the meDICKS, please! The surgeon wondered, though, because it was a flare whether I should be there or go home.

At this point, my mum, who had come back in the room after being asked to leave for the examination, piped up and said I wasn't going anywhere, I was extremely sick and needed treatment. The surgeon left and when he came back said, he was speaking to "CJ" (what took me a week to realise was my surgeon, Dr Tan's first name. Only when my gastro doctor on the ward said "Hi CJ" to him did I click), who was a good friend, and they were admitting me under the surgeons. They said as they needed to get me on infliximab ASAP, they were starting to fill out the paperwork so I could get it, but it would take a few days.

It turns out that special funding has to be applied for outside of the NHS due to the cost of the drug. WTF, how much did this bad boy cost. It was also only secured for a year of funding at a time. Mental. Thankfully it is renewed if needed and it's your treatment plan, but to only put an initial period of a year on it due to cost is insane. Nobody wakes up and goes, I know I'll have an incurable lifelong illness that takes low-grade chemo for the rest of my life to attempt to treat it.

It was really late, like after 1 am, and my mum had work in the morning, and I felt really bad, so I had been telling her for hours to head on home and sleep, I'd be fine by myself. But although I was a 24-year-old adult, I was still her baby. We waited a while longer until a porter came, who then took me to my room. My mum waited until I was in my room, and a nurse brought me toast to eat. It was really late, and the ward was silent and dark due to the time. It was a bit eerie, and I was also a bit scared and nervous to be by myself overnight in hospital. I was exhausted, and fatigue was in full swing, but I didn't think I could sleep due to nerves. It also really wasn't a priority, but any time I was regularly in hospital for appointments or admitted, the skin on my hands would go mental from all the handwashing. I had asked my friend Conal (the doctor), and he said it's from all the cheap soap irritating my skin. I'm very clearly delicate and wondered what my skin would be like by the end of my stay. It was always just very dry and red every time. I got ready for bed and put my laptop on quietly so I could fall asleep watching TV. I slept a bit, not well, but exhaustion must have taken over, as I remember being surprised that I actually got any sleep.

The hospital was in full swing by 7 am, being woken up to the daily "Breakfast?" question and receiving tea and toast. It was always cold and half stale/hard from sitting, as it had obviously been made in the hundreds/thousands to be sent around the wards. Obs and bloods were next, then later the surgeons and gastro team came around as I had been admitted under both, it turns out. Most of this was all done by 10 am; the mornings were so busy. The nurse looking after me that morning was a similar age to me and super lovely; we got on really well. Time passed quickly as I had been on the phone to one's calling to see how I was, so I didn't feel so alone. I'm also very content in my own company, so having my laptop there to watch Netflix or something on was grand, and the nurses were in regular. I also got to experience great joy when my surgeon and his team came in. I recognised that hair anywhere....it was only bloody Steve Harrington!!! I recalled his arrogant prick demeanour and oversized hair, which I imagined reflected the size of his ego and the fact he was probably trying to compensate for something. Dr Tan introduced me and announced to his team of juniors, "This is Sarah, a 24-year-old who has been recently diagnosed with Crohn's disease and had emergency surgery on Monday to drain an abscess." Steve obviously recognised me and looked sheepish as fuck. He could barely look up from his notes. Dr Tan said they were going to try to get me on infliximab ASAP as they didn't want to deviate from my consultant's current treatment plan. They needed to check things with him as I had also just had the chickenpox injection and needed to know how long it would take to kick in, as infliximab would wipe it. They said they'd be back tomorrow for a further update as also prior to infliximab, I would need to be tested for every infection going, including TB and need CT scans etc.

They left, and shortly after, my lovely nurse friend came back in, and I went to tell her about the junior doctor. Hilariously before I was finished with the story, she asked, was it him with the hair? Hahaha. We both burst out laughing, and she agreed saying, she thought something had gone on in here because before they came in and were looking for my notes, he was a prick to her and had talked down and shouted, "where are the notes?!" in a horrible tone. She said he then came out nice as pie and was very polite, asking her to do stuff. I said they had asked me if

I had been given anything else medication wise, and due to the story, I had told her about him sending me off with buscopan, she said how funny would it be if I had said, "yeah, buscopan, but it didn't work" and then stared at him. We pissed ourselves laughing, and I wished I had thought of that. She also said that if he had thought something wasn't right back in November, especially due to my high blood inflammation levels, he should have admitted me and figured it out, not said I'm not a consultant. She was totally right, and I think him seeing me and what had happened probably (well, hopefully) gave him the boot up his hole he needed.

I wanted on infliximab ASAP, and I wanted off the steroids right that second as the weight gain and hair was really fucking with my vanity and body image/mental health. I've actually never felt the same about myself since being on steroids. The uncontrollable changes to your body whilst not getting better is a bit soul-destroying. I still constantly look at my face and check if I look fat or how defined my jawline and cheekbones are, just in case others might see what I see, even months after the moon face is gone. I would call it to the point of paranoia, but it's a mental block I think I'll be slightly stuck with forever. I was constantly embarrassed about how I looked and needed to explain or tell people as I thought everyone could see it and were internally judging me. Those closest to me were definitely fed up hearing me go on about the roid weight, especially when explaining myself to others. But I felt like a fat ugly mess and needed to blame it on something/let people know it was out of my control.

Later on that day, I moved hospital room to another part of the ward, and my immediate worry was would my family know where to find me. Now with hindsight, I realise my mum would've probably been so tired she wouldn't have remembered where my room was anyway. I think I had been in 5A and was now in 5B. Before this, I had a Pilipino lady come around and ask me to fill out my meal requests for the next few days. It was all so lovely I could hardly choose... I learned the hard way mass produced scrambled eggs are not the one. Think cold flavourless rubber. How can something so simple go so wrong? Also not meaning to brag, but I make some pretty sweet scrambled eggs myself, so I wouldn't want to offend my taste buds in such a way. I was now glad I had been moved wards as hopefully, they'd lose my meal requests, and I had no appetite. The wee lady was like a mini Hilter, when she came in and announced in broken English I had to move rooms and start packing. I said no problem and proceeded to do so, then waited to be moved. She somehow thought as I lay back down on my bed that I mustn't have done anything and repeatedly kept coming in and announcing the same thing and walking out again. After about her third or fourth time doing this, I told her I was packed and waiting and where was I to carry my stuff to? I then got told I wasn't to carry anything, it would be placed on my bed, and I was to be wheeled there. Thank fuck I was thinking, as I was weak and tired and no way could carry all the things I had. A nurse or porter came, and I got wheeled down the corridor to my new room. I had liked the slightly different aesthetic of my old room a bit better as it was brighter, and this new room faced the inside of the hospital. I mean, I didn't have much choice in the matter, but on the plus side the en-suite was actually a bit closer. It's the little things.

My first day was fine; I just stayed on my laptop and continued watching Friends. Each hospital stay seems to have a TV show I was watching, and this time it was Friends. My parents and Conor came up later and brought anything else I might need from my family house and flat. Thankfully because I was in a side room, Conor came up early straight after work and stayed later as there was no one to tell him otherwise. I was looking forward to seeing him, and I missed our life, flat and normality. I was also used to sleeping beside him too, and no longer had that comfort. It was always sad when I said he needed to leave, as he tried staying really late but had work in the morning. I assured him I was fine and was just going to be watching Netflix's.

I couldn't usually sleep until closer to 12 am as the last set of obs and medicines came round at that time. I was on a mixture of steroids, cholestagel, antibiotics, and was usually getting my last antibiotic for the day at this time.

You never sleep properly in hospital, so I had a restless night's sleep, being woken at about 6 am for obs and bloods, so they could be sent to the labs before the doctors came around at 9ish. After that, I was awake as breakfast came at 7. A lot of the tablets I was taking all had to be taken at certain times, some with food and some on an empty stomach. Due to the first round of medicines coming about an hour or 2 after breakfast, this was not happening. Prior to being admitted, I had written a meticulous tablet plan, all organised in my shitty falling apart £1 Poundland dosette box. I didn't really care as I was hopefully coming off most of them soon and knew the steroids weren't making me any better. They had to be taken at least 30 minutes before breakfast. I also believed the antibiotics were making this flare-up worse as well. Cholestagel, I didn't even care about it, so fuck it. I was on so many tablets it was insane; I literally lost count. I was also on regular pain relief as I was still sore from just having surgery. It wasn't beyond excruciating pain, but I was continually sore and aching for over a week, especially needing the toilet so much in a just operated on area. I remember there were times it was really painful especially mixed with the continuous stomach pain that week. I definitely forget the pain to an extent, though, as at various points, my mum came into the bathroom and was practically holding me as I wiggled about on the toilet with the pain. Not something any 24-year-old thinks they'll be having their parent do for them, but here I was.

I did dread the morning medicines the most, though, as it was "hospital policy" for everyone to have a daily blood-thinning injection to prevent blood clots due to all the lying down. I saw the nurse come with the injection and thought it wouldn't be bad; injections don't bother me. Oh, how wrong could I be! I didn't realise these injections were really painful. It wasn't even the needle, but when the fluid got injected in, it burned. The burn also lasted a good 15-20 minutes. I was so shocked the first day this happened and didn't know what was going on. A nurse later explained they are very painful injections and the worst one's pain wise. You don't say. A bit sadistic of the hospital really, I'd rather risk the blood clot. I also don't think they realised that all this lying down was really child's play with the amount I had been sleeping recently. Give me a real challenge, pfft. Every day I dreaded that injection and, without a doubt, was the worst part. I didn't even mind the repeated poking with needles to try and get blood out of my shitty veins.

The doctors and surgeons then did their rounds, and gastro felt my stomach, with the words "very tender" being heard every day for the next week. I asked was it the antibiotics causing this level of flare-up, and the doctors confirmed it wasn't, they don't help but certainly don't affect you to the level I was on. Dr Tan had said they were organising the CT's, chest x-rays and whatever else was needed prior to infliximab. They were still waiting to hear back how long the chickenpox's injection took to kick in. After they left, I mustered up the energy to get showered. The hospital rooms were really warm, and I was very sweaty come the morning. The permanent low-grade fever and my resting heart rate in the 100's probably weren't helping either.

Shortly after getting showered and snoozing whilst watching my laptop, Dr Tan came back. He was by himself and sat down beside my bed and explained how the chickenpox injection took 6 weeks to kick in, and due to how unwell I was, I couldn't wait 6 weeks on this injection. He said on top of the Crohns being severely active (going a nice 30 times on average a day now), my heart rate, dehydration, and currently losing too much weight (I lost about a stone in a week but was still a puffy fucker on the roids fs), this was all not good. The following sentence gave me the shock of my life. He continued with, as he was my surgeon he was here to explain the surgical options and what would happen if this was to continue. He had looked at my colonoscopy and the biopsy results from it, and proceeded to draw a picture. He drew a rough image of where the small intestines are, then the large and coloured in the three areas I had the disease.

"You have perianal disease where we drained the abscess, but your terminal ileum (last part of the small intestine) and the start of your large intestine are badly inflamed. I know you have been told this could be removed with key-hole surgery, but you are so unwell your body needs a break. What we would have to do is cut open your belly down the middle and remove both the diseased and a percentage of healthy tissue on each side to try and knit it back together again. But because of how unwell you are, there is no guarantee it would knit, and the disease is too active, so it would only come back again in healthy tissue. This means you would need a bag put in, and it would be an ileostomy." If I could've fallen out of my bed I fucking would have. I couldn't believe what I was hearing, I thought only extremely ill people got bags and how the hell was I one of them?! No way was I on that level; I still to this day don't think I'll ever accept I was that level of ill. I mean, I now know I was, but this was insane. I wanted to burst out crying, I felt like my world was crumbling around me. I had never thought I would ever need a bag. That just wasn't supposed to happen to me. I think after years of misdiagnoses, I never have believed when even at my worst, this could happen to me. Surely, if a doctor can't diagnose me, it can't be that bad, can it?

Dr Tan proceeded to say, that if this were to happen, they would in time try to reverse it, but a lot of people end up really loving their bag and don't want to have it reversed. I actually understood and empathised with that. But if I was to have it reversed, there is no guarantee the tissue would knit together again, or if it did, the disease could come back aggressively, and I would have to have it redone, and this time, it would be permanent. I think I was in shock. I was holding back tears so badly, and I was worried about what my voice would sound like. But I done what I always do, and I smiled and laughed through the pain and told him it's fine, I understand. He said he was going to check with the gastro team as they want to try all medicine possible first. Also, he wasn't in the business of giving 24-year-olds bags, and it was definitely the last option even for him, but as my surgeon had to let me know it was on the cards. I appreciated this but was massively in shock. I had been barely diagnosed a month; WTF!

As he left, I was grabbing my phone, telling myself, wait until you're in the bathroom to cry, don't let any of the staff find out, I don't want to make a scene or look scared and pathetic. I tried phoning Conor, but he didn't answer at first as he was at work. Unfortunately, I was already hysterical and had only got to about the bathroom door before the tears started. Everyone I phoned didn't answer at first as they were at work, but then I got through to my mum and told her what was happening, and I might be getting a bag. She said she needed to leave work and come to the hospital, and I told her I was fine, just shocked. She told me, of course, to shut up, there was no way I should be by myself and in no state to be. I felt bad she was leaving work, but she was probably right. Conor then phoned back, and I explained the same to him, and he also said he was leaving work to be with me. I must've sounded in a bad way. I was so embarrassed then as I heard my name being called, and it was Dr Tan returning. Oh fuck I thought, I'm hysterical, and I don't want him to see me or feel bad; he was literally doing his job. I tried to brush away tears with some tissues and compose myself. It was very obvious I had been crying, and the look on his face said it all. He told me, don't worry, the gastro team are saying no surgery, they're going to try infliximab first and then proceed. I said no worries, thanks as he left again, then went back to trying to calm myself down. I felt so bad, he was so lovely and just doing his job, and I knew I needed to know this, but I was extremely shocked. Stay strong Saz, stay strong.

My mum and Conor arrived up, and I composed myself. My mum had phoned my dad, and he was coming up after work. It was a lot of news to hear, especially so unexpectedly. There ended up being a lot of people around that day. My mum had also told Anna-Marie, who was really against the idea of surgery as she thought an ileostomy would leave me very dehydrated and sicker. I think it's because its output is very watery in comparison to a colostomy, as the large intestine absorbs the water out of stool and would need to be drinking more water. Something they were aware I wasn't great at; if only it had a flavour, then I'd be sweet. I literally only drink it at work because there's nothing else. That day was emotional, but it wouldn't be my last. I felt bad as my mum then booked off work so she could come up every day. I hadn't realised and wasn't told until after I was let out, but the gastro doctor, when talking to my mum privately had told her, "You have a very sick daughter". Probably why she booked off to be there so much.

That week thinking back is a bit of a blur now. I remember it felt really long, and as tired as I was, sleep wasn't great. I wasn't getting to bed each night until about 12 and woken up between 5-7 for bloods and obs. A wake up call with a needle was not the one. My veins were gone at this point, between dehydration and overuse. They were resorting to taking blood from the veins in my hands and wrists. The bruises were ever-growing.

I was monitored so closely that the doctors requested every time I go to the toilet, I went in one of those grey cardboard carton things. The same poor nurse, Heather, I think her name was, was on with me for 2 days as well; that was not a pleasant job. They then had to fill out a stool sheet based on what they saw. I can now confirm I know the "bristol stool chart" very well. I was producing type 7, 30 times a day. The build of cartons awaiting the nurses was not pretty, I apologised every time, and they kept telling me not to worry, it wasn't the worst bit of their job. I remembered the nurse Heather telling me someone having their stomach emptied was her least favourite part of the job, and it nearly made her sick every time. She asked if I ever had it done, and I said thankfully not. Quite literally boke city. So horrendous, I couldn't be at that for a living. Every time the poor nurse came to check the cartons, I unfortunately was also already in the bathroom, so she had to keep coming back. After about 2 days, I was trusted to fill the sheet in myself, and of course, had to keep asking for more pages along with the cartons.

They sent off another stool sample to test for c diff, which is a bad bowel infection that people tend to get post-surgery. One of the auxiliary staff regularly looking after me that week was a lovely Pilipino man, and he was so funny, kind and caring. I really liked him, and we chatted away whenever he was in looking after me. He normally took my weight every day in one of those sitting chair scales, which I didn't know existed until told to sit in one, and then each day informed me I was lighter than the day before. He had told me that if I had c diff, I'd probably know about it, as it was a really nasty infection, and the smell would let you know alone. Unfortunately, I was producing black cement/water at this point, and due to my lack of eating, it was mostly body fluid and didn't overly smell.

I had my chest x-ray and remember in the short time I was away panicking in case I needed the toilet when waiting for the porter. I was thankfully fine. However, I was so paranoid I thought I saw a trace of shit on the string part of my nightgown and was super embarrassed. I said to my mum when I was back, and she laughed when I tried showing her. She asked how did I even see anything, and whatever it was she would clean anyway for my peace of mind. Her and Sharon, who was there visiting at the time, thought it looked like a faint pen mark, and upon reflection, it was most likely that, but I was so paranoid I didn't care. The chest x-ray was different from the type I normally had, I had always been lying down, but I had to stand and put my hands behind my back for this one. I remember being exhausted, and it took it out of me even those few minutes of standing.

The cannula that had been put in my arm when I was admitted, was starting not to work anymore, and a really lovely junior doctor came around to put a new one in my other arm. I asked why they were putting a new cannula in, and he explained that after a few days, the vein starts to shut down, and it'll not allow anything else in. I apologised in advance for my shit veins, and he said, don't worry, he lets medical students practice on him. I couldn't believe it, no way would I let some uni students practice on me. Fair fucks to him. He said it's because they're given fake plastic arms to practice on, but they're really rubbish, so a person is better. He put his money where his mouth is with all this practice talk, and effortlessly in one go, got the cannula into my vein. I was so relieved. He asked how I was and what they were doing with me next, and I said I had Crohn's and waiting to get on infliximab. He told me his friend was on infliximab and was doing really well, and after an infusion, came and met him and their other friends for golf. I was feeling optimistic about infliximab, I had heard so many good things, and it had got a lot of people into remission, and after everything, I hoped to be one of them. Especially as it was meant to be so good at curing fistulas, so hopefully no more operations. I know now that was wishful thinking.

I can't remember if it was the day I got the new cannula or the next day, but I was to go for a CT scan. As I had MRI's previously and knew how long they were, I was sceptical in case I needed a toilet during it. Sharon, who was there, told me they're over really quickly, and you just feel like you're wetting yourself due to the sensation from the contrast/dye. The nurse told me they were waiting for the drink to come up to the ward (I think that was the contrast) as I needed to take it 45 minutes before the CT. As I waited with my mum and Sharon, Heather, the super lovely nurse who was still looking after me, came in apologising and was raging as the contrast had been brought up, but no one was told, it was just left at their reception area. I only had 20 minutes now to drink what was approximately a litre. Tough going, but I got it down. Mostly because my mum practically shoved it down my throat. In typical Laura Donnelly, a.k.a. Lazza D fashion, "no fucking about and get that down ya." I was worried because of the effects of the MRI contrast and said to the nurse, who said not to worry, it wasn't half as strong and had way less of the stuff the MRI contrast would have in it. This settled me a bit, but the sheer volume of liquid was making me need to pee anyway.

The porter came, and I was brought down for my CT scan. I was left in a corridor outside the CT room and was really worried because there was no toilet. I thankfully saw one to the left of me and, of course, used it in the time I was waiting. When I went in for the CT, it was pretty underwhelming in comparison to an MRI. I remember the staff were lovely and said it was over in less than 5 minutes. They weren't wrong. When injected with the dye, I got told it would give a sensation of wetting myself due to the warmth and might even feel it go up to my chest. I got in the CT machine that is basically a big open circle, not claustrophobic at all compared to the big enclosing MRI. The scan basically was getting moved on a bed through this big open circle. I think you went in and out of the circle a few times, I can't remember now. When they injected the dye to give the warm sensation, I knew what they meant. I remember it being really warm to the point if I pissed myself and it was that hot, I'd know I need to see a doctor because something would not be right. The feeling also did spread up to my chest. After that, it was done, and I waited on a porter to take me back to my room. When I was back in my room, that was me done with tests for another few days. Once the doctors were happy I had no other health issues or infections I could get on infliximab, also once the funding was approved.

Another test they performed was an ECG. My resting heart rate had been so high, normally between 100-120, so they checked for any irregularities. There was one morning it was 140 and something, but that was more to do with the fact I had been woken at 5 am for obs, and the nurse had scared the shit out of me. Even she looked alarmed at its speed as she jotted down all my ob results on my chart. The nurse doing the ECG was funny and said this is something she did know how to do due to it being a cardiac ward. The poor nurses had been thrown in the deep end; they openly admitted to having no idea about Crohn's as they were cardiac trained, and I was on a cardiac ward. They were all soo good and soo eager to learn, help and find out answers though, it was really impressive and greatly appreciated by both myself and my family.

The ECG was a really simple test; they stuck sticky things to different points on my body, like on my chest and feet, then hooked them up to a machine as I lay very still. It told them straight away there was nothing irregular. My mum had asked the doctor what was causing the raised heart rate, as there are heart problems on both sides of the family. Her dad had died of a massive heart attack aged 35 and just dropped dead one day. My uncle, her brother, had also had heart problems since his 30s and a few years ago had a double heart bypass operation. My cousin on my dad's side had an attack of the heart aged 25 when his heart just stopped, and he technically died on the spot. He was extremely lucky, and doctors who were also out for dinner saw him and kept his heart going until the ambulance arrived, and something like ten electric shocks later, it finally started again. He was in intensive care for weeks and hospital for months, now having a defibrillator in to keep his heart going as it still sometimes stops. The doctor said any of the above was unlikely because it tended to be male traits and no irregularities found on the ECG, but inflammation and dehydration cause the heart rate to rise. Also, the main reason was due to how sick I was, and my body was basically working double-time to try and fight the Crohn's. Unfortunately, Crohn's was currently winning.

It was really busy whilst I was admitted, some evenings my parents would leave as there were too many people there. Michael, my housemate, kept bringing me up my favourite food. God love him. My flare up was so bad that I had literally no appetite and couldn't eat anything, so I had to send it home with my mum and dad. I think he noticed my lack of eating, as I hadn't touched my beloved pepperami's every time he visited. It was probably the tell-tale sign something was very wrong. My mum had also been bringing up nice food to try and get me to eat, instead of the rubbish hospital food, but saw that there was no appetite and how quickly the little I was force-fed passed through me. It was always good craic when I had visitors. One evening it was me, Conor, Michael, Ryan, Caitriona, and Aisha all squished into my room. Michael took it upon himself to start playing with my bed settings and put me up to the roof. Everyone was so lovely. Caitriona had brought me lovely stuff from Lush, Aisha had got me lovely flowers and a card, and one of my friends in Vietnam, Odhran, got Michael to send me flowers and a card. Michael, of course, signed it on Odhran's behalf, and I was informed of his new life choice of becoming a ladyboy now Vietnam had him. I messaged Odie to thank him and congratulate him on the new life choice.

When my cousins Danielle and Shannon visited, they brought lovely pyjamas, lip balm and body sprays. It was all so nice, and there was no need for any of it. I felt so bad when my cousins visited; my auntie Paula (their mum) had to sit outside and look after Danielle's daughter, Bella, who was then one, and really sick with an ear infection and tonsillitis not long out of hospital herself. I would've loved a baby Bella hug, but she wasn't even allowed in the room as my immune system was so suppressed and her being so sick. Also, if I caught anything, I wouldn't be able to get this much-needed infusion. I had to blow kisses out the window to her. She even tried pulling the door handle to get in, but we had to stop her heartbreakingly.

I kept being told how well I looked for how sick I was, but it was definitely lies. I was bloated, ghostly pale with red cheeks from my low-grade fever, and felt disgusting and weak. Some nurses openly told me they couldn't believe what was wrong or how unwell I was due to how well I looked. Conor thought I just looked run down like I had a cold, but didn't look unwell enough for everything that was going on. My loving mother, on the other hand, was the only one brutally honest. She thought I looked like shit and repeatedly told people I looked like crap. I appreciated the honesty though, I did. She also proceeded to poke my arm one day as I lay in my hospital bed, commenting on the bloating due to water retention/weight gain from the roids. Thanks, Laz. I told her she actually looked sicker than me, as she had been at the dermatologist to have a bit of pre skin cancer burned off her head, and was rocking a big plaster with a stitch underneath. My friend Bebhinn who was a nurse in the Royal, also came and visited on her breaks. All these visits were great and really lifted my spirits. I got to pretend like I was semi-normal for a while and kind of forgot about what was going on for a minute. Even when all my lovely nurses, doctors and auxiliary staff for that week were in, I pretended like I was normal, telling them about my travelling plans and what I did with myself when they asked. They really tried in all aspects of looking after me.

On Saturday, when I was in, it was sad as I would normally be on a night out, but instead, Conor came up with a Chinese for us to eat. I ate what I could as I tried to pretend that any part of this was normal. We sat and watched Netflix's on my laptop, and he spooned me in my hospital bed. A night-time staff member who brought around food and was a bit of a slabber, came into my room unannounced, saying how we needed to cut it out in case a doctor walked in and cracked up, but as he was so sound, he had no problem. He kept trying to show off in front of Conor, and I felt like he was making one too many "woman" jokes. Neither of us found it overly amusing, especially when trying to chill out and spend time together. Also, if we were at anything, I'd like to think I'd at least have locked the door or pulled the curtains first;

I wasn't here to be thrown out or arrested.

I was also so weak at this point I needed help walking out to get water literally less than a couple of metres away. I was actually out of breath and even dizzier than before. I had constantly been dizzy for about a week now, especially when I stood up or down. I was starting to need help even getting to and from the toilet due to weakness. I embarrassingly also needed help when getting washed, especially washing my hair. In the morning, when I got up, I was now waiting for my mum to arrive so she could help me into the en suite. I sat in the chair while she hosed me down, and she washed my hair, and I washed my body. 24 and washing like a 90-year-old, it was degrading, but I was so out of it at this point I didn't care. I needed to lie down after washing as that little took that much energy. Looking back now, I realise how sick I was. At the time however, I kept saying for how sick I kept being told I was, I didn't feel THAT bad. My auntie Sharon, who was told she has terminal cancer but has outlived her diagnosis for years now, agreed and said she felt the same when being told she was dying, she didn't feel like that. It was strange, and this becoming my new normal probably wasn't helping. I had been getting progressively worse for years now, I just didn't know what feeling "normal" or "healthy" was anymore. I kept thinking, should I even be in hospital and concerned I was wasting a bed, but looking back, yes, I definitely should have.

These social interactions greatly helped in keeping me distracted and speeding up the time. I was fine on my own too, and sometimes liked the quiet because I was so wrecked, but socialising was definitely good for me. Hospitals and illnesses are lonely places. My only really embarrassing interaction was realised after my friends had visited one evening (I can't remember which one as the days began to blur) that from being instructed to shit in a carton every time I went, there had been an overspill. I was usually in the en suite for obvious reasons when people visited, and as friends arrived, my parents let them know

I was in the toilet. I could hear the standard "haha of course" jokes start and, "oh, her favourite place". Yeah I've Crohn's, we get it. Anyway, whilst I was doing my business into the carton for my really impressive sheets, some must have overspilt as I was carrying it due to my weakness. After my friends left, when I was talking to Conor, who normally stayed later apart from when he was playing football, I unfolded my legs that I had been kneeling on. It was then I saw the shit on my fucking slippers. I was literally mortified. How the fuck did that get there?!? I then realised it had transferred to the back of my pyjamas when I was kneeling. I said to Conor, actually soo embarrassed, and he was a proper champ. It didn't faze him at all and helped me look in case it got anywhere else. It had also transferred to the bed of course, as I had been sitting on it, and he lifted all the sheets off immediately and called a nurse to come to change the bed.

He helped me change into my spare PJs, and we discovered it was definitely overspill, as of course, I also started thinking, have I accidentally shit myself and somehow not noticed. Conor took my shitty slipper and PJs and actually started scrubbing them with soap in the sink in the bathroom. Wow, he must really love me I thought, then put them in a plastic bag to take home to put in the washing machine. It wasn't much hence why it wasn't noticed straight away, but I was still mortified. The nurse who had been looking after me for a couple of nights was so nice and was like, seriously Sarah, don't worry at all, this is the least of our concern. She actually could barely see it and even asked where it was when changing my sheets. To be fair, it wasn't much across all three items; you would have had to actively search to find it, but I was obviously mortified nonetheless. On her last shift with me, I remember she actually wished me luck with all my travel plans, which was really nice. After this incident, I messaged my mum to ensure she brought up more spare pyjamas the next day and spare slippers, as I was now without. I had fluffy socks, though, that done the trick in the meantime, and it wasn't like I was travelling far distances.

On Sunday, I was told they were still waiting on the C diff results as they took the longest (a few days) to process but as soon as they were back, the infliximab infusion was sitting, waiting, ready to go. As it was the weekend, it was only skeleton staff, and I had been warned that if I take a reaction to this, I will go down like a ton of bricks, and my life would be in danger. It was not filling me with hope. As sick as I was, I was happy to wait until Monday, but the doctors said I needed it ASAP. The IBD nurse had left a handover note on how to administer it, and I had been prescribed IV paracetamol and antihistamines prior to it in case of a reaction.

I had friends and family that were coming to visit and had been told due to how low my immune system would be, I'd be in quarantine after. I was actually really scared about getting it, purely because of all the reaction stuff I had been told by the nurses and doctors. I didn't want to experience anaphylactic shock, thanks. The different nurses that had been looking after me all week had repeatedly told me they weren't confident administering it either, as they had never done it before and what would happen if anything went wrong. It was Sunday afternoon at this point, and I didn't think it was going to happen. Then one of the doctors that had been looking after me came in and announced my C Diff results were back, and it was all clear. I was free of TB and all infections, it was definitely a bad Crohns flare I had, and they were going to do the infusion now. I had to message my granny and friend Ashleigh who were coming to visit, telling them not to come because this was due to start. The poor nurse looking after me was dreading it, God love her, and prepared the IV paracetamol first. This was set up to be administered over 20 minutes, but my mum and I noticed it wasn't going in, the bottle was still mostly full, and the nurse didn't come back until closer to an hour later. Straight away she said it's because the vein was shutting down as it had been in a few days now, and a doctor would need to come around and put in a new one.

We waited until a junior doctor came and I was concerned because it was getting late. This infusion was 3 hours long, and the later it got, it was going to be time for staff to swap over. What happened next I think still scars me. We began chatting to the doctor, and he said he was from South Africa. During the previous summer, a group of friends and I went Greek island hopping and met South Africans we became friendly with. I had said to the doctor we didn't know where they were from originally as they went between English and Afrikaans, and we had never heard the language before. He took immediate offence and began to say he did not speak Afrikaans; oops, I did not mean it like that. Maybe he thought I was a racist due to the connotations of speaking Afrikaans, but I did not mean it like that. I was just making conversation about a foreign language I had never heard of prior to meeting them, in my already scared and sick state. The cannula was in my left arm, so he tried my right arm, and I was hoping because I had previously had a cannula in there a matter of days before, the vein would be healed enough to take it. I got the standard "sharp scratch", and as I looked at the needle go in, my arm literally blew up in size. Why the fuck am I swollen?? I heard my mum go, "you blew it", and the doctor goes, "oh no, I've never seen a vein blow that quickly". "What does that mean?" I asked, and he explained it was an inflammatory response to my body not liking the needle and rejected it. I, of course, google what it really meant; he basically shredded through the vein with the needle, and the immediate swelling was all the blood exploding out of it and rising to the surface. It was actually really sore, and I had a huge black bruise the size of half my forearm for closer to a month.

He then tried another vein in the same arm. Nothing, he continually pulled the needle in and out for minutes trying to get the vein, and it was again getting really painful. The same thing happened when he tried the other arm. That was the 3rd attempt, and now out of cannulas, so he had to get more. WTF! Me, my mum, Sharon and Conor were all saying. I was so nervous and drained at this point I was fighting back the tears. I know I had shit veins and was dehydrated, both really not helping, but wtf was this! I said to them he was really hurting me, as he was continually for at least a minute at a time going in and out of my arm hitting tissue and veins but not getting it in properly. I think he was getting progressively more nervous too, especially as at this point my mum was making comments. I couldn't blame her; it was really shocking what was going on. It was like he had no training at all. I was also worried about what if he damages all my veins and no cannula can go in, and I can't get my infusion. When he returned, I told him they had been starting to take blood from my wrists and hands, so there might be veins there. My mum definitely scared him, she had left the room for a few minutes to answer a call, and when he arrived back before his 4th attempt, he sheepishly asked did I want her in the room. I said, Nah, don't worry, and to fire on. I was hoping he would get better if she wasn't there, maybe less performance anxiety.

He tried putting the next cannula in the side of my wrist, which really hurt. Getting blood from there is nippy too, the skin is so thin. I could actually feel him scraping my bone, so at this, I actually started saying "ouch" aloud to try to make it stop. I couldn't hold it back anymore and I hadn't said anything the other times it was sore, but feeling the needle scrape my bone was too much. Attempt number 5 was in my hand, and of course, it didn't work either. I fucking hate hand cannulas too. They're so much sorer as the skin is so thin and pulled against with the weight of the cannula. At this point it was a joke, and he had wasted about half an hour. It was about 4 pm, and he said he needed to get a superior as he was aware of the time and how it needed to start soon due to the swap over of staff. I was fucking raging. As soon as he left the room, I burst out crying. My mum tried calming me down, and Sharon was saying she didn't know how I could watch him going in and out with the needle, especially so many times, I was very brave. Conor sat and held my hand.

We waited another while, and eventually, a more senior doctor came. They were so short-staffed as it was a Sunday, and I was aware that if something goes wrong at the weekend, the likelihood of you dying is extremely high compared to during the week. One of the nurses during the week had agreed with my mum when she said this and also confirmed weekends mean skeleton staff. The doctor came in and had a look at my arms. He said, "Ah yes, all the normal entry points have been used." FFS, this was a joke; where the fuck was he going to go. He apologised and said he needed to go in my hand as it was the only one left. NOOOOOOOOOOO! Fucking hate stupid hand cannulas so much and knowing that was me for at least another few days. He thankfully got it in one go, and it meant they could prepare my infusion now. I was relieved I could get it, and hopefully the agro was all over, as I was still really distressed from that previous situation and full of nerves ahead of the infusion. But of course, things aren't that easy for me. As the nurse said she was preparing the infusion, we eagerly awaited her return. Ages later, she came back and said bad news, the infliximab infusion has to be administered with a special filter, and there was none. She said they had phoned different departments and the City hospital and no one had any, but they were continuing to try and get one.

It was after 5 pm at this point, and it was not looking optimistic. I was really stressed, and because we thought the infusion was starting, my mum had sent Sharon home, and it was just me, her and Conor. I was past caring about holding back tears, massively out of the norm for me, and instead just sat sobbing, feeling ridiculously sorry for myself and frustrated. I was massively fucked off that my veins had been destroyed and I had a hand cannula for nothing. Also, I had turned away visitors as I thought I was getting this infusion for definite today. I waited until after 6 pm, and it was confirmed that it definitely wasn't happening, as no one had the correct filter. I asked what would happen if I had it without the filter and was told that my veins couldn't handle it and it would destroy my arm due to the strength of the medication. Better not risk that then. I had two cannulas in at this point, and as they are uncomfortable and you can feel them in your arm, I struggle to sleep with them in and always worry about pulling them out by accident. I asked could I have the old cannula in my left arm taken out, and the nurse said no as my veins were so bad. She explained they were worried if something happened when I was getting my infusion, although that one wasn't working great, it could still get something in to try to treat me immediately. I was gutted as I hated them so much, and the one in my hand was hurting as it was pulling against the thin skin. I was upset and frustrated and wanted home now. I had had enough at this point and even thought about discharging myself. I remember thinking if I were strong enough, I'd love to throw a chair against the window and jump out of it. I had already looked at the drop days previously and noticed it's probably why the windows only open a matter of centimetres. I thought about finding the roof of the hospital and jumping from there, but I could barely walk a matter of metres, never mind devise a master plan to find the roof of the hospital, which would probably be blocked off, and try to jump from it. I'd probably need a few toilet stops on the way too.

I was really upset that evening but was told one of the IBD nurses would be around in the morning to set up the infusion and get it started. My mum promised she'd be up first thing and should be there before 9 am as it would probably start around then. My lovely Pilipino auxiliary friend saw my hand and commented on how uncomfortable it was. He suggested bandaging me up to hold it in place and help me not knock it off things. It was a really good idea, and it did help as it held the cannula in place better, so it wouldn't pull as much on my skin. The running joke with him and the nurses then was to call me Rocky as I looked like a boxer ready for a fight. Well, my right hand did, not the rest of me. The rest of me felt like I'd been through 10 rounds with Rocky.

Later after everyone left, I couldn't sleep that night. I lay there angrily, wanting to find the cannula drawer (which I was told was probably locked up) and repeatedly stab the doctor who did this to me. I was so irrationally angry at this hand cannula, but now with hindsight, it was a combination of everything manifesting into one specific point of anger. I lay there, the anger growing and growing, knowing there was nothing I could do about it. As my mum said, it wasn't his intention to fuck up so badly. But my counterargument was that if I fucked up that badly at my job, I'd probably lose it or be disciplined. How could someone dealing with a living, breathing human be let off so lightly? I was so angry I literally wanted to discipline him myself and see how he'd like a couple of veins shredded. I was also really nervous about the next day. I hoped my mum made it up on time as again was nervous about taking a reaction.

The morning came, and I had my standard approx 6 am bloods wake up call before breakfast at 7 am. I hadn't slept, so the wake-up call didn't really bother me. It mustn't have been long after 8 am and one of the IBD nurses, Noreen, called to my room. She had been up visiting me during the week, getting stuff sorted for the infusion and providing me with information when I first met her. I knew there was a couple of specialist nurses from phoning the IBD helpline previously, and they're all really lovely. I was shocked at how early the infusion started, and my mum wasn't here yet. I explained what had happened the day before with the filter, and she explained that the infusion can never be given without the filter and is therefore already attached to the tube it's administered through. So the filter had been there the whole time, pre-attached in the pack. I was actually raging. Part of me thought was it because the nurses were too scared to administer it yesterday they lied and didn't do it, or was it a genuine accident. Apparently, this had all been left on the handover note, and all I had heard all week was how none of the nurses on the ward felt comfortable administering it. I didn't blame them, but I also didn't want messed around.

I messaged my mum to say it was starting soon, and the IBD nurse was just making it up. Infliximab gets made up by your weight, so you get 5mg for every kilo you weigh. I hoped my mum would get here on time because I was again by myself and still extremely nervous about this, especially if I took a reaction and no one was here. Any time I had buzzed for a nurse that week, it took them approximately 20 minutes to come. Usually, someone from the ward would come within 5 minutes to see what was happening, then turn off the buzzer and say a nurse will be with you shortly. The day before this happened and a girl younger than myself, who I actually think was a physio (she wasn't a nurse anyway), had come in. My mum had asked for the nurse, as she was concerned about me being left unsupervised as I was unwell and due the infusion soon, still thinking I was getting it at this point. The girl very cheekily rolled her eyes and said, don't worry, she will be fine, nothing will happen. I thought my mum was going to rip her head off, especially as she was not a medical professional and had no idea what was actually going on, but telling one of my parents not to worry, all is good.

When the IBD nurse came back, she brought one of those poles that has a machine that sets the speed of the IV medicine with her as well. She said the one currently in my room wasn't able to do more than a certain time, and I needed one that could do 2 hours. Infliximab was going to be administered over 2 hours, then a 1-hour flush with saline after. I realised the lack of correct machinery in my room was another hiccup that would have occurred if they tried administering it the day before; it just really wasn't meant to be that Sunday.

The infusion was set up and in it went to my hand. Noreen told me that because she knew how busy the wards were, I was better buzzing every 15 minutes or so for a nurse because I need my obs done every half an hour. She knew the score. Also, the machine was detachable, so if I needed the toilet, which I more than likely would during it, I could unplug it from the wall and drag the pole with me, and it would keep administering. After that, I sat and waited for my mum to arrive and the next 3 hours to be over. I was worried about a reaction, and no IV paracetamol or antihistamines were given, but I sat and waited and hoped all would be ok. I had remembered Noreen telling me the other day that in America, as they're notoriously mental, some hospitals knock you out for the infusion, but that is not the norm in the UK. If anything, it sounded dangerous when you needed to be monitored so closely. In my boredom when waiting for my mum, I wrote an Instagram/Facebook status, as I had been receiving a lot of messages asking how I was. It was mostly pisstake as per usual, and I referred to getting a bag if this infusion didn't work, that wasn't a 10p Tesco one, and all I wanted to do was to go home and eat kebabs. Therefore, 1 prayer = 1 kebab and, of course, hashtagging kebabs. The picture was of my IV'ed hand getting the infusion; the world wasn't ready for my moon face and moustache. Within minutes of it being posted, I was inundated with messages, even from people I hadn't spoken to in years. I was really overwhelmed. Lots of thinking of you, and you are in my prayers, all really touching, and I couldn't believe it. I had been bored and was posting for a laugh, and it was returned with so much love. It was really greatly appreciated. You often feel forgotten about when lying in hospital or sick, especially as the world keeps going. But this was a nice reminder that I wasn't.

Shortly after, my mum arrived; I think the infusion had been on for nearly an hour but had gone by really quickly as I was so busy on my phone responding to all the messages. She apologised for not being here while it started, but I said it was fine; it seemed to be going well so far. The nurse was in every 30 minutes checking on me, and everything seemed fine, but my heart rate high as normal. I was starting to get this like surge of energy from it, something I hadn't felt in a long time. I yet again got emotional, so of course, I started crying like a fool asking my mum,

"Is this how a normal person feels?!" I think I irrationally burst out crying three times during it. I was so emotional but couldn't even tell you why, probably a mixture of everything over the last few weeks or even months, or dare I say years. For someone who never cries, I had done a lot of it that week.

When the 2 hours were up, I was relieved of no reactions, and it went onto the flush. I, of course, had needed the toilet a good few times during it, and manoeuvring the heavy pole, especially when fatigued and weak, in and out of a tight space proved difficult. I was glad when my mum arrived to help me move it in and out. Once the flush was over and I was unhooked, I asked for the unused arm cannula to be taken out, and it was. Thank fuck. I lay down for a few hours trying to sleep but couldn't as exhausted as I was. I just lay there with my eyes closed, resting and thinking as my mind was going 100 miles an hour. My mum actually did sleep on the chair next to me, and she said she was wrecked too. I probably should have given her my bed. Later she told me more people had been asking how I was. I told her I keep being told people will say a prayer for me, and although I'm not religious, I really appreciate it because people genuinely believe in it. However, my good Irish Catholic Mother informed me, of course people are praying for me. I just found the concept strange, appreciated, but strange. I think it's because it seems like such a caring, intimate thing to do for another person. To pray to your God for another's wellbeing when I struggle with the concept of a God and perhaps of even being worthy of their prayer. I realise now I was struggling to love myself with everything going on, so the thought of some higher entity caring for me was really alien. Now I believe there is a God or something higher; I don't know what but something. I still find the word "God" intimidating and weird, though, so I'll stick with "something".

Later that evening, Conor arrived, and I was glad to see him. I told him I was already feeling a lot better and couldn't wait to get home. I even felt up for walking down to the hospital shop, so

I put on my trainers for the first time in a week and nightgown and down we went. I definitely pushed myself too far though, I had not moved that much in probably closer to 2 weeks. I was exhausted and out of breath when I had to make the journey back to my room. I was cringing at how unfit/unhealthy I currently was, but Conor just laughed, appreciating I wasn't ready for that much movement yet. I should have realised how unwell I still was but was expecting miracles as I had noticed I wasn't going to the toilet quite as much, and had maybe gone down to about 15-20 times that day. Yeooo score! Lol, imagine thinking that was impressive, not going to the toilet 30 times a day but instead around 20; that is what my life had become. When he left that night, I was a lot more content than I was the night before, also absolutely exhausted and slept a bit better.

The next day the doctors and surgeons confirmed I could go home and didn't need to take any more antibiotics as infliximab would do the same job. Very unfortunately, I had to be weaned off the steroids. The one's I was on, normally you can just stop, but as I had been on them such a long time, I needed to be weaned. As I took 9mg daily, which were three 3mg tablets, I reduced one tablet weekly. Damn fucking steroids. I was delighted to be going home though, and threw my clothes on immediately. I had really appreciated all the lovely staff, nurses and doctors I had that week (minus a few), and my overall experience was good. I was going to say great, but that's far too strong an adjective to describe any hospital stay.

The last thing to come out before I went was my hand cannula. I was ecstatic to have that fucker removed and be needle-free. The nurse looking after me was concerned about my heart though, and said if anything felt wrong or even in a few days, go to my GP for an ECG to make sure the heart rate is coming down. Ruth, I think her name was, and she looked after me for the last 2 days. She was super lovely, really funny and had a big cheeky, sarcastic personality, right up my street. I said I would, and she gave me a big hug before I left. I got my mum to bring up a card for me to fill out and get sweets and chocolates as a thank you. I left them with Ruth and told her they were a thank you to everyone on my ward for how well they had looked after me that week. Shortly after my mum carried my bag and off we went, home at last. I looked back at the Royal as we drove past, thinking the immortal words of Mr Chow, "tooodaloo muthafuckaaaaa".

Not again

When I got home, I slept for ages. I was so wrecked, and you don't sleep properly in a hospital. I also was now in quarantine with my lack of immune system whilst I recovered. My mum took time off work as well to look after me, and I think I was off between 4-6 weeks, both my GP and hospital signing me off. I think it was because the consultant who I saw every day in the hospital, said if I was to get even a cold, it would likely turn into a chest infection, which I couldn't fight and would be on a breathing machine in intensive care. No thank you. When I did have visitors, my mum had them wash their hands or hand sanitise before coming near me. I also didn't really want anyone seeing me, and I was really embarrassed about how I looked still. I was hoping that the moon face and facial hair would be on their way out by the time I returned to work. I had posted on a Crohn's forum too, asking about when it would go and if it would go. Part of me was still sceptical even when doctors told me it would go. Those who replied said the hair would all fall out and become so weak I would be able to pull it out without barely touching it. That's exactly what happened, but it took weeks and, for some hair, months. Apparently, hair grows in 3-month cycles, so by the end of 3-months, it was gone; I literally shed a layer of peach fuzz.

One day, Conor rubbed my shoulder, and a layer fell out; he kept doing it as the 2 of us pissed ourselves laughing as I shed like a dog. He found it strange as he said he couldn't see it or notice it as it was fine blonde hair but now it was coming out it looked like loads. On the other hand, I could see it up close and was very aware it was there, and it had not been prior to steroids. I think the moon face took closer to 2 months to fully go as well. The only plus was the hair on my head had grown amazingly long and thick, which looking back, I did not appreciate enough. I got so impatient with waiting on the steroid side effects to reverse, one day, a few weeks later, when I was taking the dog for a walk, I called into the chemist opposite my house to ask when I would lose it all. The pharmacist asked when did I finish my steroids, and I responded 5 days ago. He laughed and said I'd definitely not have lost anything yet but was really helpful and looked up when they should be out of my system. Unfortunately, there was no information listed for the steroids I was on, but he said to give it time and it would reverse. Patients really is a virtue.

The day after I was let out of hospital, I had a PIP interview. As soon as I had been diagnosed, the number of people who told me to apply for it was crazy, and I had never even heard of it before. It's basically a small benefit for those unwell, to cover the costs of hospital appointments and when you're sick and unable to work. I had heard bad things about the interview and how Tories had changed the scheme, meaning it was ridiculously hard to get. But being naïve as I was, I thought there's no way I wouldn't get something, especially being signed off work, just out of hospital/after surgery and all my medical evidence. Of course, that didn't happen. The woman came in and pretended to be very nice and asked me a load of questions about my health, loads of sympathetic aww's and that's awful, sorry you're just out of the hospital, etc etc etc. Even needed the toilet during it for dramatic effect. I had the standard response of, I just write a report, and someone else decides (that's a lie) and off she went. It then took probably 2 months later to respond, saying there was nothing wrong with me, and I didn't get it—disgusting bastards. I've since read newspaper articles where they have even turned down cancer patients. Just not sure how they live with themselves.

I had my second infusion 2 weeks later in the ambulatory care centre at the Royal. The second dose is given 2 weeks after the first, the third then 4 weeks later, and after that, every 8 weeks, but can be dropped to 6 if you need it. My mum came with me and sat for the 3 hours reading, and Conor lent me his tablet so I could watch Netflix's. There was already a huge improvement in me; I was feeling a lot better, and was going to the toilet about 5 or less times per day, it was also starting to form normally again. What a time to be alive. I thought this was a miracle drug and couldn't understand why everyone wasn't put on it. From my first day in the ambulatory care centre, I learned that if your infusion was 3 hours, you could be there anywhere between 3.5-5 hours. It's busy with loads of other patients, and it's a whole process. Your weight is taken, they then only make the infusion once you arrive due to the cost of it, and only if you pass the criteria of not being sick and your obs are fine with the nurses. Someone then needs to put the cannula in, sort your next appointment, regular obs, the infusion being made and dissolving time; there's basically a lot going on. Also, very dependent on how many patients are in, how many staff are in, who's free at the time, it's a lot of waiting your turn at the different stages.

This infusion went fine, and when I think back again, I also naively thought after this second dose, I would get into remission after the first one had been so successful. I thought this miracle drug would fix me in weeks. I wanted normal life back and to get back to work. My work colleagues had sent me beautiful flowers as well when I was off, and they were greatly appreciated. Of course, I wasn't entirely better and needed the toilet during this infusion, embarrassed as I unplugged my machine and dragged the pole out. There was a paramedic waiting outside the 2 patients toilets, and I hadn't noticed an old man sitting on a bed behind her in his nightgown. Both cubicles were in use, and I waited growing impatient as I needed the toilet now. A second later, someone came out of one, and before I could run in, the paramedic stopped me and said, excuse me, he was here, about the old man behind her. I understand she was doing her job and probably thought I was rude, also didn't realise what was wrong with me from how I looked, but I wish now I had said something. I just looked shocked when I saw him as I had completely not noticed him in my one-track mind for a toilet, and she helped him potter up from his bed. Thankfully within those few seconds, the other paramedic who was in the other bathroom came out, so I ran in after him whilst trying to maneuverer those poles with my infusion on it. It's the wheels they're on at the bottom that makes them difficult to manoeuvre in small spaces, and they're heavy enough; they're not made for dragging in a hurry.

The 4-6 weeks I had off felt long and short at the same time. I also wasn't earning, and unfortunately as most know, statutory sick pay wasn't cutting it to pay my bills and rent etc, and I wasn't awarded PIPs, so I really had no money. Shove your £95.85 per week up your fucking hole, Tory cunts. The only silver lining was I didn't want anyone to see me and was embarrassed when friends called to visit and could definitely see my moon face and pre-pubescent boy moustache. All of which I was told wasn't bad but was definitely lies to spare my feelings. As I began feeling better, I felt sorry for myself and how I was missing out on life but also didn't want to be seen by any member of the public as I didn't look like myself.

One day, a few weeks after I was out of hospital, my mum dragged me to Forestside and Connswater with her. Baker boy hat in tow, I tried hiding my face, and anyone we bumped into told me I looked brilliant, but I really didn't think so. The trip out actually exhausted me, I hadn't done so much walking in weeks and passed out when home. When in Forestside, I also learned about the radar scheme; I had heard of it but had never really looked into it. When I inevitably needed the toilet, I saw the "radar scheme" on the disabled toilets and needed a special key to access it. I didn't have the time to go looking for this key and later realised I could buy one due to my hidden disability.

Instead, I went to the women's toilets and sat in an end cubicle until my mum started texting, wondering where I was. I still wasn't really up for outings and was totally embarrassed with my appearance and the fact I still could need the toilet at any point, just like what was currently happening. I wasn't as well as I thought and still recovering. On the car journey on the way home, as I looked in the passenger seat vanity mirror, the light shone in brightly. It really highlighted the facial hair, and I noticed a little tuft on the lower left-hand side of my face. It was soul-destroying. The only consolation was when it started coming out, and as I was told, it would be so weak it would literally fall out when I touch it. I was overjoyed the day that happened, and it felt like an incredibly long time coming. Valentine's Day hit me hard for some reason. I was never one to particularly do anything or even bother with presents; what a stupid consumer waste of time, man. But that day, when I went on Instagram and saw a million stupid stories with people and their red roses and presents, I got really jealous. I realised my boyfriend of nearly 4 years hadn't bought me a single present when unwell or for Valentine's Day, in fact, I don't even think I saw him that day because he was playing football and I was still temporarily living at home. I wouldn't normally expect anything, but I felt really down and had even been getting gifts from my friends. He was dropping the ball. When I said to him, he said that I had been unwell, and we couldn't do anything even if I wanted to and would another time.

So, a few weeks later, we went mini-golfing and for dinner as a date day. I also told him what presents and flowers I wanted and made the whole thing very easy for him. He was never particularly romantic, which I didn't mind at all, neither was I, but it would have been nice for once. I did really appreciate the beautiful Swarovski bracelet and roses, though, and he left them on our bed as a surprise for me when I got out of the shower. I had done a full face of makeup and dressed up nice, but I felt disgusting and thought, what was the point; everyone will just see my fat face and facial hair. I almost didn't want to go so I could avoid the public and people seeing me. Also, with my immune system being so low and so scared of getting sick again, I was genuinely scared of germs for a few months. It was a fun enough day, but my heart definitely wasn't in it. I think all the recent isolation and worries had been affecting me more than I realised. Everything I was feeling was because I was missing out on trivial normal events. If I hadn't been sick, I wouldn't have cared and probably wanted nothing, but now I was craving normality back as I watched the rest of the world get on with their lives.

I returned to work, went back to my flat and thought I was getting into remission. But that would've been too easy. About 6 weeks after my operation, the pain started coming back. It wasn't as bad as before, but it was there. Of course, I tried to ignore it, thinking it would go away, but instead, it got worse. I didn't want another surgery; I just wanted this abscess/fistula to fuck off. I was just getting my life back; I was back on nights out, and telling people who asked how well I was doing. I even managed 2 days of heavy drinking over St Paddy's Day. St Paddy's Day was an eye-opener in relation to the radar scheme. I had got myself a key and was thankfully fine, but as the queues for the toilets were so long, when drinking in the Crown bar, I kept using their disabled toilets and letting my friends borrow the key. When I was peeing on one occasion, my friend Sile was waiting outside when a security man tried opening the door with the bar's key. She stopped him before he unlocked it and said I was in there.

Of course, he questioned her telling her it was impossible as he had the key, and she explained I had a medical condition, meaning I also had a key. He walked away apparently very confused looking and probably went to ask another staff member. Probably best workplaces educate their staff on the schemes in place to avoid future situations like that. I don't think that would be good publicity for any establishment, "Staff member opens disabled toilet whilst a disabled person is using it, as they are unaware of their works radar scheme". Not good. I had also been wanting to plan holidays and had my cousins wedding (I was a bridesmaid for), on the 1st June, and the Hen do a couple of weeks before. I really didn't have time for this and was not in the shape I wanted to be for the wedding as it was. It was now March, and as I had really enjoyed the Galgorm but was sick when I first went, my parents had got me vouchers for my Christmas present. So, I had finally got booking it and was also heading to that in a few weeks. I was not ready for Crohn's to steal more of my life. However, I was kidding myself as I noticed my Crohn's was generally getting worse and the tiredness and pain were all creeping up again.

I got to the Galgorm and again loved it, but I was not feeling great and back to being in quite a bit of pain again. Easter was the following week, but I had been really looking forward to it as it was 2 friends' birthdays and excited for their nights out. On Saturday (Easter Sunday was the next day), my mum insisted I go to the hospital. I was not amused. I was supposed to be out that night and brought my makeup bag to the hospital with me to do my makeup at the hospital while waiting. Nah, they shouldn't admit me; all those times I was really unwell, and they had done fuck all and got sent home with buscopan, I'll be on this night out, no sweat. It was late enough on a Saturday afternoon, and I'd say even after 4 pm, and A&E didn't seem overly busy. There was still the hour's long wait, waiting on blood results; I, of course, had a cannula put in, waiting to see the doctors etc. The whole process was painfully familiar.

The junior doctor I had was lovely, and he was concerned the abscess was back and, of course, needed to do the standard finger up the hole trick to check. Oh, how I had missed this... I wondered because he was young like I did about all the other junior (straight male) doctors if seeing a young woman's bum was a perk of the job. I mean, they probably weren't loving what they had to do, but with what their job entailed on a daily basis, you've got to take the silver linings. He said he couldn't feel an abscess but also said he wasn't trained in finding a fistula, and the abscess could have drained itself, therefore someone more senior would need to see me. They were still waiting for blood results, so I had to go back to the waiting area. My mum and I waited a while longer, and the doctor came out to us. He said my bloods were back, and inflammation looked alright for someone with Crohn's (I heard that a lot), but my white blood cells, which show infection, were raised, and due to the abscess probably being back and the massive immune suppressor I was on, he had spoken to a superior who wanted me admitted. You got to be fucking killing me. I'm supposed to be in Revolution de Cuba in an hour for cocktails FFS. This young doctor had also previously said about not admitting me because I was in good spirits and laughing and joking with him... THE FAÇADE WAS WORK-ING! Stupid more superior doctor taking charge. I was brought through and made wait for a bed. I don't think I had to wait that long, it was the day before Easter and it wasn't as busy.

I was put on the emergency surgery ward, and it was only me, a young girl who I think said she was 19, and an old lady who I remember being noisy, with her loud breathing and snoring. Shortly after I was at my bed, the superior doctor came around and said he needed to feel for the abscess again. I told him the junior doctor had already but couldn't feel it. He then explained he wouldn't have been trained, and he is trained in feeling for a fistula and was sorry this had to happen again. Two fingers in one day, I think this was a new record. What an excellent substitute for cocktails at happy hour, FFS. Then on my side I lay, the standard knees to chest, that paper towel thing wrapped over me to "protect" my modesty (it covered fuck all), some gloves, cool jelly and off he went. I heard him say fistula at 3 o clock, and my immediate thoughts were, where the fuck in medical school do you learn that?! Christ, that's someone's job. Imagine wanting to train in that?! Is he a smart specialist getting paid loads or a fucking pervert?! Who knew asses could be so complicated?! So many questions, not one seeming appropriate to ask. Once he removed his finger and I pulled my kacks back up, he said he could feel the fistula still and it hadn't closed yet, meaning I was right; the abscess would still be there filling, and I would need another pelvic MRI to confirm. However, it was Easter, and they didn't know when that would be. Let me go then, I thought.

I hadn't eaten all day, so my mum left and brought me up a Chinese with knives and forks from home as well as anything else I might need. This was my second time eating one of my favourite foods in a hospital, and it just wasn't the same. I got my mum to pull the curtain and when I was done eating, got changed into my PJ's. I hated changing clothes when I had a cannula in my arm, it always got caught. She left soon after, and I sat miserable, unable to sleep. The old woman was up most of the night; there could have been a touch of dementia or confusion as well. I put my headphones in my laptop so I could try to fall asleep watching TV, but I couldn't sleep. I was also worried my Crohns wasn't in remission still and I was on a shared ward; I did not want to be waiting for the toilet in the morning, especially if it was bad and I couldn't hold it. I think the anxiety of the situation kept me up as well, and my bed being at the wall beside the main door, so it was extra noisy.

I was also getting drunken messages from Conor, which was depressing as fuck as he was out having a good time as per usual, and I was stuck here, a weekend I had been really looking forward to. At closer to 2 am when I was actually nearly asleep, Conor's friend phoned me looking to know where he was when drunk. He had used to live with Matthew, and I was also very friendly with him, meaning my response was short and sharp, "I'm in hospital, Matthew". I was also aware it was 2 am, and I didn't want to wake the other two on my ward. Then the OMG, I'm so sorry, I love you etc., started. I knew it wasn't intentional, but I was not in a good mood. I couldn't sleep after that. The FOMO was real.

The next morning, I was wrecked, but glad it came as I couldn't sleep. Thinking back, I had been a bit scared being by myself again and frustrated at missing out again with friends. I remember the distinct feeling of fear, but I didn't know why; it could also have been adrenaline. I think the stress of being on a ward with others, meaning sharing a bathroom, set me off too and kept needing the toilet. Thinking back, I wish I had said something as I would've got a sideward. Of course, embarrassed as well, as I was thinking they'll definitely notice how many times I've been to the bathroom in the space of 30-60 minutes. I was talking to the young girl opposite me, and they thought she had appendicitis, so was waiting for a scan. She was lovely, and before she went for her scan I wished her luck. The ward was really filling up now and every bed was full. I gathered a few had been moved here from different hospitals as well. This had happened to a nice girl, similar age to me, who was moved to a bed beside me, and we had been chatting.

The doctors came around, and they wanted to look at the area, aka my hole. No examination today, thank fuck, they just wanted to check for inflammation. You're welcome Doctor, you're welcome. The pyjamas my mum brought me I could barely get pulled up, they were embarrassingly too small, and I made a joke like, "sorry, put on some weight". The doctor laughed and said, that's a good thing with Crohn's. He then decided it was fine if I wanted to go home for the day as I would definitely need an MRI before any more surgery and said the place wasn't a prison. I mentally begged to differ but took that as bittersweet news as I only got to go home for the day. I also missed last night for no reason. The thought of coming back in a matter of hours was killing me, but I was delighted to leave for now.

I phoned my mum to let her and my dad know and then phoned

Conor who then came and got me. I was really excited to see him, although it had been less than 24 hours since I last did. Perhaps that's how dogs feel when their owners return, that familiar comfort after being abandoned. They took the cannula out of my arm as you can't leave hospital with it in, in case you administer drugs yourself. It was probably safer to remove it as I probably would've tried heroin at this point, to be fair. I got changed, packed up and took my valuables with me; the rest I would return to later. My mum laughed because I had recently treated myself to a £70 Charlotte Tilbury face cream, and that was not being left behind; it was up there with my laptop value-wise.

I was so glad to be home and soo exhausted. My grandparents were coming for dinner, but they're farmers, so their dinner was lunchtime. Conor stayed and had dinner with us, and then we went and slept for 3 hours, he was hungover, and I was sleep-deprived. I showered and packed more things for my stay and really put off going back; I couldn't face it. We watched TV on my laptop, and I kept telling him, "Please don't make me go back, I want to stay with you and go back home to our flat." I probably sounded whiny and pathetic, but I didn't care; that simple normality and comfort was all I wanted. It must've been between 7-8 pm before my mum said I really needed to go back they would be changing staff soon. I also wasn't feeling well, I had the shivers but was apparently feeling warm, so again potential sepsis was the first thought, and I knew I needed to go as much as I didn't want to. I said my goodbyes, and Conor and I took off, of course making him stop at the shop first so I could get snacks.

I arrived back at my ward to find an ancient old man with a breathing machine giving him oxygen in my bed. WTF. Did I have the right place? I asked a nurse who said I had been moved further down the ward into another area. Oh please let it be a side room. Nah, not that lucky; it was just another wardroom. I saw my name above a bed that was on the left-hand side in the middle of the room. The ward was full of women of all ages, and I was quite nervous yet again to be sharing with a full ward. They were also all settled, and I felt like the new kid in town. It was a bit intimidating, and the feeling of fear came over me again. I now realise that feeling I continually repressed and ignored as I got on with it. Conor helped me set up my stuff, and I pulled the curtain around my cubicle so I could get changed, but I asked him to leave it like that so I could try and sleep. Shortly after, he left, and I wanted to cry. It was going to be another long night, in what I hadn't yet realised was hell.

Welcome to purgatory

I didn't really sleep again that night. A lady across the way had been up vomiting, and it had woken me up, not that that was hard. There was also a bad smell which I had assumed was the vomit. I and the others on the ward also noticed and discussed that week that at night time, for some reason, nurses don't use quiet voices but the same volume all day round, even with a ward trying to sleep at 3 am. In fact, it seemed the quieter the ward, the louder they were or, the more they shouted rather than spoke. I didn't know what was wrong with the lady opposite, but I heard her say, "It's the smell that's making me sick, I can't get past the smell". To which the nurses replied loudly, "you just need to try and get over it, then you'll stop being sick", and repeatedly told her this. I learned the next day the very lovely but very ill Marilyn had started vomiting a lot of blood on Saturday night. When she came to hospital, it turned out that her bowel had died, and if she hadn't had emergency surgery to remove it right then, she would have died. She said she woke up with a bag for life, which had quite literally saved her life. She had the bag changed a few times when we were on the ward together, and I understood why she felt sick. She hadn't been allowed to eat, so the output was pure body fluid, and the smell was terrible. I now think back to how unprofessional whomever the nurses were speaking to her, telling her to "get over the smell" literally a matter of hours after she was out of intensive care and trying to adjust to a massive life change. The smell was also putrid, I concurred. If myself and others were also nearly sick at the smell of something across a room, then an incredibly sick woman who is having the contents of her bowel emptied right beside her was understandably going to be sick.

When the morning came, it was the standard 7 am wake-up call, and the lights in the ward came on. The nurses liked to pull your curtain back, which I didn't overly appreciate. They did this at all times when you had it pulled shut, during the day, during the night and in the morning. You could never have it pulled completely shut for that long; not sure why. It was always done loudly/forcefully, so it would wake you up if you were sleeping. I wasn't allowed my breakfast for a while as they didn't know if I was fasting or not. I also felt shy surrounded by a ward of people who all knew each other already. Some seemed really sick too, and as per the name of the ward "emergency surgery", some of them were heavily drugged up, having just had that. Someone came round and took our bloods, and then the doctors made their way around. Each patient had a different doctor due to the different surgeries, so it was a guessing game who got seen to first. When my doctors were finally around, they said Dr Tan, my surgeon, would be back on Wednesday but again was waiting on an MRI before they could do the surgery, which wasn't looking likely due to the Easter holidays. The hospital wouldn't be properly running again until Wednesday. Fucking great, I thought; why am I waiting here wasting a bed. I was then allowed to eat, which I was thankful for as I was absolutely starving at this point.

There was so little staff in the hospital that the nurse looking after our room was actually agency staff and in a different uniform. She was nice when you got talking to her but came across as very old school, stern, harsh and, to be honest, a bit scary to start with. I think it was the tone of her voice and how she said things, but she actually was dead on when you got chatting to her properly. I was also very aware that I had no cannula put back in and really did not want one. They made everything more difficult, especially to sleep, and I also thought it was pointless if I wasn't getting IV drugs. So, I kept trying to hide my arms in a bid to hide the lack of cannula. However, thankfully got told that they don't give it on that ward unless you need one, so I didn't need one the rest of the week. Phew.

That day was slow, probably due to the lack of staff and the emptiness of the hospital. It was good though, as I got to know the ladies around me. There was Jean, who was to my right, waiting to get her gallbladder removed. I just wanted to adopt her as my granny and thought of her as my ward granny. She was just so lovely and sweet and chatty; we got on so well and chatted most of the time. There was Elizabeth to my left, also a lovely lady, who was quite posh and a feminist, what I absolutely loved. She had been there something mental like 6-8 weeks as she had an operation (done by a very good female surgeon, and she wanted to see more of them, YASSS QUEEN), but had fainted and hit her head off the bathroom sink a few weeks before. Her face was still black and the blue, God love her; it must have been a very nasty bang. She also couldn't leave until an occupational therapist package was put in place to help her when she got out. Deborah, who was a similar age to me, was opposite me to the left and had sepsis after a kidney infection. She was super lovely too, and we would go over to each other's beds and chat. I had noticed her boyfriend stay later the night I had arrived and left closer to 12, which she said hadn't been a problem and give me hope Conor could stay late too.

We also discussed the pros of the strong co-codamol the hospital prescribed, none of the shit over the counter stuff. They give you a fuzzy head, made you feel stoned and sleepy. I was in pain, so taking them regular enough, but when it came to nighttime, and I wanted to sleep, I made sure I took them. There was Ursula, who was opposite me, and she became like my hospital mummy, I loved her. I loved them all but especially her, that mummy bond yano. She said she had just stopped going to the toilet for about 2 weeks and was taking laxatives, and nothing was working. Then she got what felt like a leg cramp except all over her stomach.

She said the pain was beyond excruciating, and Jean had said she was climbing the walls when she arrived on the ward. I wasn't surprised to hear that; when I think of how sore and intense a single leg cramp can be, never mind that pain all over your stomach and it not stopping. It turned out her bowel had stopped working and had twisted itself, so she had emergency surgery to untwist it and remove the waste. I can't imagine the agony. There was then Marilyn on the opposite side to the right.

That day the nurse who was in charge and was coming across quite stern had a run-in with Marilyn. She was obviously in agony, having just had her stomach opened and a major organ removed. Her doctor had told her the medicine she was allowed and how often, but because that ward was a shit show, it hadn't been relayed to the nurses correctly. Or there was some sort of misunderstanding about medicine, as when Marilyn asked for her pain relief, the nurse told her no. Marilyn, obviously in agony argued back, and told the nurse exactly what she had been getting and what her doctor had told her she needed to be getting, and asked why she couldn't receive it. The nurse argued back harshly, it wasn't on her notes, and she wasn't getting it, but was basically shouting at her. This continued for a while until the nurse shouted she would get a doctor to explain, as poor Marilyn was visibly upset and angry at this point. When the nurse left, we all spoke up and said WTF was that about and how she was spoken to was completely not on. I said I felt extremely uncomfortable witnessing the whole thing, and Marilyn said she was going to report her as she had clear instructions from her doctor about what she needed and had been receiving it regularly. We completed supported her in this. When a doctor returned a while later with the nurse, they said there had been a mix-up, and Marilyn was given her medicine. Later, when her husband and family arrived, they were also upset at how she had been treated, especially when so unwell and a complaint was made. I saw the nurse cry, and I also felt bad for her as she was just trying to do her job, but the situation wasn't handled well. Tensions were running high, and it just escalated badly.

The ward was weird, and at 1 pm, they had "rest time", what as a 24-year-old I was not happy about, as it was essentially forced nap time, and even the lights were turned down. I was not tired at this point and did not want to sleep. I mean I love napping and would love a daily rest time normally, but on my own time, not dictated to. We were usually "ssshhed" as well to encourage rest. The food had been absolutely rotten as per, so my mum came up early as she had been in town shopping and brought a chopsticks Chinese with her. I seemed only to eat Chinese takeaway when in hospital, not that I was complaining. I was so glad of something that actually had a flavour.

Hospital mash is diabolical, and no amount of salt and pepper can add flavour to it; it just lessens the cardboard taste. When Jean woke from her nap, she smelt it and ask "ohhh, what's that smell". I completely empathised with Poor Marilyn, as she asked maybe it was her, as she was paranoid of her bag smelling, but it didn't at all. When I asked is it me, as my mum and I had Chinese, Jean replied, yes it smells lovely. I offered some to all the ladies, but nobody had any. I was kind of glad, it was pure great. We assured Marilyn we couldn't smell anything from her as she was worried. I totally got it, fuck I had been there with shit myself, thinking it had somehow got on things it hadn't, my moon face and facial hair. When it's on your mind, you can't help but be paranoid.

This ward was really strict on visitors as I heard auxiliary staff comment on my mum being here before 2 pm, visiting time. It was 1.45. I wasn't sure if he was joking or not, or on a power trip, as he and his friend were referred to regularly as "dumb and dumber" by the other staff, which they seemed to enjoy. They came into the ward trying to make jokes and a scene all the time, and speaking very loudly throughout "quiet time", making as much noise as possible whilst telling us all to sssh and sleep. Ironic. They were funny to start with, kind of like ward clowns, but they grew very tiresome and annoying very quickly, depending on the patients' mood. A few of the ladies threw comments at them, as their behaviour wasn't always work place appropriate in our opinions, as they announced they played practical jokes on new staff members, asking them to find feathers for the pillows etc. I'm all for having a laugh at work, God knows you need it, but this was incessant showing off. This also included when you were tired/trying to sleep and, in fact, waking you up so they could talk/show off, especially to the older and post-op ladies. It just wasn't appropriate and really very annoying. It's a hospital full of sick people, and they were completely desensitised. I did like them, but when not feeling well or in a bad mood, it really fucked me off.

Visiting time was busy, probably as many people were off for Easter Monday, which helped the day go a bit quicker. That evening my friend Gareth was coming up to visit, and Michael and Conor too. I had been in pain, so I was taking the strong co-codamol and was off my tits by the time they arrived. Gareth arrived first but couldn't see me as I had been chatting with Deborah on her bed. When he saw me, I was up full of energy, and the first thing he asked was why was I so happy and giggly. Pain meds, mate, was my response. We laughed, and Conor and Michael arrived shortly after. It was actually really good craic as I was on top form being essentially stoned out, and the four of us laughed. They left when the bell rang at 8 pm, and I was then left sad and alone. I knew Michael and Conor were going on a night out that I was missing, but Gareth was flying back to Leeds where he worked. That put a dampener on my evening, and I tried to go to sleep but, of course, couldn't sleep properly. I had friends messaging saying they wished I was there, and I wished I was there too. More life being stolen at 24 and I hated it.

Later that evening, Deborah's boyfriend had stayed on, and she had done what I had planned for Conor and me when he stayed. Pulled the curtain, and sat and watched TV on a laptop with the headphones in to make no noise. She had told me the nurses had no issue with this, and some had told her previously it was fine. At about 9 pm, although no one was sleeping and no noise was coming from her and her boyfriend (you couldn't even see them), a woman who I think was auxiliary night staff (as she was just asking if anyone wanted tea before bed), pulled back her curtain and began shouting at her whilst telling her boy-friend to leave. She was really unnecessarily rude, and Deborah had said the nurses allowed him to stay what was the issue. She proceeded to tell him he had to go and would only be al-lowed to stay if Deborah was incredibly sick. I sat there not believing what I was hearing as she told a girl with SEPSIS, THE LIFE-THREATENING BLOOD POISONING ILLNESS WITH A VERY HIGH MORTALITY RATE, she wasn't incredibly sick. She wasn't even a nurse and had no idea what was wrong with her. He left shortly after, and I went over to see if she was alright and said, WTF was that all about. She agreed and said nothing had been said before and had been told by nurses there was no issue. Even some of the other ladies agreed as they weren't disturbing anyone. If anything, they were making the least commotion. I also said I couldn't believe what she had said about her not being incredibly sick. Deborah told me that she had actually swollen up and turned orange when she was first admitted due to the sepsis, but she was now looking normal again due to all the IV antibiotics. This made sense as I had heard a doctor say to her, he didn't recognise her now, she was looking much better as she was soo ill when she arrived.

Shortly after, it was nighttime medicine; I was only on regular pain relief, as I was solely on infliximab for the Crohn's. I had forgotten about the bastarding blood thinning injections too, so when they were doing their rounds, it was pain relief and blood thinners. I couldn't have had the pain relief an hour or so be-fore the injection. They were worse this time around as I don't think the nurses on the ward knew how to give injections. I'm not being cheeky or funny, but it was genuinely worrying. The last time I was in, it was injected into your stomach, and I was only left with little bloody pinprick marks, bar one small black bruise about the size of my thumbnail. This time I was given the choice of my arm or stomach. I said to try my arm as I had only had it in my stomach before, and the fucker was, if not equally, more nippier. I also was left with a black bruise about the size of my fist. I had my cousin's Home Hen that Saturday too and was concerned (if I got out which I intended on), I was going to be black and blue. That's exactly what happened, as both arms had huge black bruises from different nights. I actually watched one nurse wipe up the remainder of the fluid as it ran down my arm post-injection. I didn't think that was supposed to happen, and when I spoke to Conor's auntie, who is a nurse, she confirmed it wasn't, and those injections should never be administered into your arm. She also said the ward I was on had a terrible repu-tation throughout the hospital, as she also worked in the Royal, and it was referred to as limbo. I personally preferred the term purgatory as I felt like I was paying for all of my fucking sins. When she saw my bruises, she couldn't believe it and said they were never administered correctly. When I told the nurses to move onto my stomach as I could hide those bruises, one even-ing, deep into my muscle was definitely hit with the needle and that injection area hurt for months after, it must have minorly damaged it. I somehow hated those injections even more by the end of the week.

Another practice in that ward that baffled me was, as it was a surgical ward, we were expected to wear surgical stockings at all times, even if we weren't having surgery. They are not for long term use; they're really tight and cut off circulation, marking up your leg from the tightness. It was actually the auxiliary staff that was weird about it, and Jean and I had been shouted at when seen not wearing them. Needless to say though, we pretended to put them on, we gave each other a look, and never wore them. They were also really hard to get on and off and took forever as they were so tight. They came in small, medium and large, so I was always given a small. Wonder if the medium would've been more comfortable. They were somewhat stupid looking, white knee-length socks with the toes cut out, so they were flashing. It's not a lewk. I again thought it was a stupid "compulsory" practice considering it wasn't necessary to have a cannula in your arm. Yet everyone here is sick, and there's a stronger possibility of them needing IV medicine urgently than preventing blood clots by wearing ridiculous socks.

It was the same story the next day, still waiting on the MRI, but it was Easter and nothing running. I was optimistic after sitting here idle for days I'd have it tomorrow. Jean was also waiting on her operation and, likewise, needed a scan before it could be done. The 2 of us were growing impatient, as she too had been in almost a week waiting. The only plus so far was how well my Crohns was actually behaving for once. It turned out sticking to the hospital's low residue food from the menu, regular pain relief (co-codamol constipates a normal person), and all the rest from barely moving was working wonders. I was only going to the toilet once or twice a day max, and it was all normal. I couldn't believe it! I was still passing stuff from the abscess, though, and it was getting more painful, so I knew I needed this MRI. When I got asked how I knew I was passing stuff from the abscess, I did my standard and gave the brutally honest truth. It feels like I need the toilet, so I go, and instead of shit coming out, yellow goo and sometimes blood comes out instead, and it relieves some pain. Noiceee. Crohns really is beautiful...

That day I had a good few visitors, my mum, Conor, and Conor's mum called up at the 2-4 pm visiting hours. Conor's mum told me how you wouldn't think there is anything wrong because I looked so well, which I always get told. I, however, felt like an ugly pale troll who was now heavier than normal due to lingering steroid weight. Especially as when my mum had arrived, I really didn't feel well and went to be sick, but a nurse brought me anti-sickness tablets and pain relief what helped. My mum kept saying I was flushed looking, but it probably gave a somewhat healthy ruddy glow. It was most likely from the infection, but I was used to the redness when my Crohns was severely active.

After they left, I didn't have long to wait until the evening when my parents came back up, and so did Conor. In the meantime, it was fine too; all of us on the ward sat and chatted. It was then I realised how soon out of surgery Marilyn was, as I asked her about her bag. We were all talking about why we were here (think Hospital Block Tango, not Cell Block Tango). I said I hope she didn't mind me asking, but as I had Crohn's and what I had been told about getting an ileostomy myself (retelling her and the others what my surgeon had told me), how was she managing it? She said she only had it a matter of days and told me what had happened and why she needed it. It was a real shock to her, as she had never had any bowel problems her whole life, and then her bowel died out of nowhere, and they had to perform the emergency operation to save her. It was mad what had happened to her, same with Ursula, how their bowels just decided not to cooperate one day and needed massive lifesaving surgery. Ursula had said her mum had died of something bowel related as well, and before she died, she was producing "black cement". As I thought back to my first hospital stay, I couldn't believe it when I was being told about getting a stoma bag, and that was literally what I was producing. Fuck, my bowel must have actually been dying. I said this to her, and she agreed; it kind of put into context how unwell I was and didn't realise. I could empathise massively with these stories with obviously having Crohn's and the joys of it.

Marilyn told me I was so brave and so young at 24 to be faced with all this. It was very kind of her, but I had taken the last 2 months to fully come to terms with having an ileostomy and the pros of it. I had thought about the stigma so strangely surrounding it. If someone's heart stops working, they perform heart surgery or a transplant to fix it and save their life. Someone's bowel stops working, and the only way to save them is to remove it and put a stoma in place; no one wants to know about the stoma, or it's taboo. Fucking mental and ignorant. I think those with that opinion need to realise that they themselves do, in fact, also shit. It may be something they struggle to come to terms with but believe it or not, all living things need to shit. Yes, maybe not a particularly nice topic, but how is it any different to someone saying they vomited? It just comes out the other end. Your bowels are major organs with major functions, and guess what? You need them or you die. There needs to be serious change or re-education when it comes to this. Most people don't realise the importance of their bowels, as this is where most of your food is absorbed; you don't actually need a stomach. I completely empathised with Marilyn though, she had no bowels problems her whole life, and she must have been in her 50s, got sick very suddenly and woke up with a bag for life. Something she didn't have time to come to terms with or probably never thought of her whole life. On the other hand, I had a lifelong chronic illness with a big chance of a bag and a big forewarning, so I had come to terms with it and done my research in the meantime.

Due to it being Easter and fucking everybody being off, something I fundamentally do not agree with (it's a fucking hospital providing a necessary lifesaving service, not an office that can happily close for a few days), she had been left with no stoma nurses. Meaning there was no one there to teach her how to use her and change her bag until Wednesday. Like everything, fucking Wednesday. I had also heard her ask about bags that were scented, as she had worked in a pharmacy and knew you could buy ones that were scented on the inside and smelled really nice. Also, therefore, helping her as she was still struggling with the smell. Of course the answer was no, we don't have them, this is the NHS, it's basic shit, or something along those lines.

When my mum was visiting, the bag was being emptied, and she was nearly sick, but my mum voms at anything. That's also when I realised when I had heard the vomiting on my first night and smelled something, it was actually the bag being emptied. It was a very fresh, distinct smell and smelled like a mixture of shit and body fluid, which is exactly what it was. I think it was also mostly just body fluid as she hadn't been allowed to eat for a good while, which is never a good smell. When my mum was so openly gagging, I told her to shut the fuck up or leave; I wasn't having poor Marilyn more conscious or paranoid at a stranger vomiting from the smell. I mean, I got it. We all wanted to be sick; the smell is that distinctive, and you only understand when you've smelled it yourself. It was now actually the main concern for getting a bag myself; could I too hack the smell. But my only concern right now was the poor struggling woman across the way and how she felt. My mum did actually leave temporarily and proceeded to breathe through tissues she had sprayed perfume on when she returned. I also felt bad for Marilyn as she was told she had to stick to a low residue diet and couldn't eat all the things she loved like tomatoes etc. I told her I was also on it, and it is hard to stick to as you don't realise what has high fibre and what doesn't, but it's not too bad. Another massive lifestyle change overnight. I know she thought I was brave, but I think she was also incredibly brave and just hadn't realised it yet. She probably felt like I felt so often, a scared isolated little girl struggling to understand why this happened, but she just hadn't realised her strength yet so soon after this major ordeal.

That night I really wanted Conor to stay later but was worried about the same woman who had shouted at Deborah and her boyfriend. Conor, being Conor, didn't really give a fuck about her and said he was staying a bit later anyway. He was back to work the next day, so he couldn't stay that late anyway. We pulled the curtain, and I put my headphones in the laptop so we could listen to the laptop that way and not disturb anyone. Deborah and her boyfriend were doing the same and chancing their arm, but of course, the woman was still on and asked both boyfriends to leave. She was a lot nicer with me for some reason, and when

Conor asked can he please stay another wee bit, he's leaving soon anyway, she just said because she said to the others, she had to say the same to us. He left a while after, but there's something really heart-breaking when your loved ones are asked to leave in hospital. Hospital stays are long lonely days where you see almost the full 24 hours of it. You're only allowed to be visited between 2-4 pm and 6-8 pm. That's 4 out of 24 hours max. You only see your nurses and doctors for 5 minutes at absolute most at any time sporadically throughout the day, so the social inter-action side is minimal. I was actually glad to be on a ward this time so the rest of us could all chat; we were all longing to go home as well.

The next day was a real down day; it was affecting everyone on the ward. Elizabeth was still waiting for her OT package, and Deborah wanted to go home and it was dependent on the in-fection level in her blood. Both Marilyn and Ursula had noticed something was wrong and were both waiting on scans and sur-geons to come around to check their healing progress. And poor Jean was in the same boat as me; she had been in a week and still no scan so they could perform the surgery. Dr Tan was back in, and as he understood loads about Crohn's and infliximab, he said we definitely needed the MRI ASAP as infliximab closes off fistulas, but if there is an abscess there and the fistula gets closed off, it's very dangerous and much harder surgery. Especially with my lack of immune system and having essentially a pocket of trapped infection. They better hurry the fuck up then I thought. I was then told they were pretty sure pelvic MRI's are done by a specialist and are only done on a Thursday, but they would let me know as mine was urgent. Great, I'd probably be waiting an-other day, but I was hoping they'd just do it or squeeze me in.

Deborah got to go home as her infection levels were down enough and was sent home with a load of tablet antibiotics to keep taking. We all said our goodbyes and were very jealous she got to go, but also happy for her and sad to see her leave.

Marilyn and Ursula got their scans. Ursula had a positive outcome and did not need further surgery, but poor Marilyn needed her operation redone. Not sure what actually happened, but she needed more surgery. Myself, Jean and Elizabeth waited but with no success as it approached late afternoon. I surprised myself as there were no lunchtime visitors today; I actually napped as the visiting room was full. Later I was visited by one of the hospital Chaplains, though. He was a really nice Reverent and we chatted away. I was initially shocked as to why he was there, and he asked if I wanted a Priest or anyone to come to visit, he would arrange that. I thanked him and declined; I didn't think I needed the last rights just yet. A lady named Margaret had also replaced Deborah; there was no wasting time here with the beds. She had come in during the night though, and again the noise of doctors and nurses bringing a sick person into a ward didn't help with sleep. When I woke up from my nap, I thought I saw Jean crying, and God love her she was. Before I could ask her what was wrong, a nurse saw and came over to ask. She said about her scan and the op and how she wanted to go home. We all completed empathised and tried to console her. The nurse then phoned, and later on she got her scan thankfully.

As I sat there, I was getting progressively downer myself. I was off work and therefore not earning, something I was very aware of and felt like I was wasting a hospital bed. I was extremely fed up and frustrated having had nothing done yet, but just sitting here for closer to a week and still no clue what was happening. The staff were mostly horrendous with no bedside manner and obviously didn't want to be here. Something I found when you work with sick people and it's a vocation, isn't really the right attitude. When Jean was away for her scan, I went out to the desk outside our room, where there were a few auxiliary staff and one nurse. I asked them if they could phone and ask when I was getting my MRI. One of the dumb and dumber members thought he was really funny and picked up the phone and went something along the lines of, "hello MRI, nope, Sarah's not getting her scan, not now, not ever and has to stay here". The others laughed hysterically, and I said, this isn't funny. I'm not getting paid as I'm off work and I've been here nearly a week. The loud-mouthed cunt then went on like he was big balls, and started going on about how I needed to be like him and get off the agency and into a proper contract as that had just happened for him last week. Fuck off you annoying twat with your delusions of grandeur. The young nurse, whose bedside manner I already hadn't rated (she was always painfully awkward), gave a semi sympathetic "aww", as she didn't know what to do. Without sounding rude, she didn't seem to have much of a personality, so I wasn't sure if that was all she genuinely could muster up.

Another one of the auxiliary staff was an old man that Jean had told me about. She said she had run in's with him, as he was a psycho and moved your belonging when cleaning if they were sitting out, and said the lady who was previously in my bed kept fighting with him. He had joined in the hysterical laughs with the other twats, and I just walked away humiliated and fighting angry tears. I wish I had reported them now as their behaviour was severely unprofessional, and it wasn't the first time they had fucked me off. I didn't care how they thought they were funny and could have a laugh with me; it was unprofessional, and I wasn't their mate, I was a patient in their care. I walked back in, and the tears were rolling down my face already. I had my head down and didn't want anyone to see, I was just going to go to the toilet and cry.

Ursula saw me though, and called me over. She was so lovely and consoled me, and I was so embarrassed to be crying, but she told me not to be worrying. She said she had heard them and how they were getting on before I had even gone out, and they were all loud-mouthed fucking wankers. Especially the dumb and dumber one and said everything that came out of his mouth was a pile of shite, and was constantly looking attention on the ward when he needs to fuck off and let us rest. She wasn't wrong. She said how they're all useless and only pretend they care, then they go home and forget about us, they don't really give a shit. Everything she said couldn't have been truer. The staff were so desensitised and hardened, this is just a job, and when they go home, like most, they switch off. My previous experience had been soo different, but I think due to the high level of very sick patients around the staff here, they were completely desensitised. We talked for ages, and I thanked her for looking after me. We got on so well, and she said I reminded her of her daughter. We had that mutual mummy daughter bond on the ward, and I was so thankful for her. I was mortified as I was sobbing and snotting everywhere, but she didn't care. My mum thanked her that evening too for looking after me; they also got on well. When I went back to my bed, I was still a bit teary and kept wiping my eyes. The nice nurse who had seen Jean crying then saw me and asked what was wrong. I said about my MRI and waiting, and she said she'd also phone as she had phoned for Jean. I wasn't as lucky, though, and there was no scan for me.

My mum and dad called up later, and my mum was extremely fucked off. Well, they both were, but Laura is the one who likes to vocalise it. She wanted to know why an MRI hadn't happened if my case was so urgent. When she was speaking to a doctor, he blamed it on the politicians up the hill and lack of funding, which, although a massive factor, was a bit of a cop-out. I had seen first-hand the lack of organisation and lack of wanting to take responsibility for anything going on in this ward, and it was actually a shit show. I don't think they could organise a piss up in a brewery. Unfortunately, this is just not the area for that kind of neglect and incompetence. I was seeing a different side to the NHS now, and every single stupid Facebook or social media post about all the great they do by people who have no experience was fucking me off. I was aware it seemed just to be this ward as my experience last time had been so drastically different. But I was in a bad place now and really unhappy. That night the stricter woman wasn't on, and Conor stayed later. When getting my daily blood thinner, a nurse did comment about the time and visiting hours, but we both ignored her. I actually told him at about 10 pm he probably needed to go, but he didn't want to. I didn't want him to go either but knew he needed to.

Thursday came, and Marilyn went off for her surgery. I shouted, good luck and see you after with a smile on her way out. I hadn't realised that would be the last time I saw her as she was going to intensive care after. Elizabeth also got her OT package finally, and got to go home after what I considered a record-breaking hospital stay in what could be considered hell. She's some pup. Jean finally got to go home too, after they again massively fucked up. She had come in with a chest infection and been using a diffusor breathing thing every night for it (I can't remember the name of it). Her chest had sounded really bad all week. I think it let medicine or steam into your lungs and helped clear your chest. I had originally been worried with my lack of immune system and catching it but was thankfully fine. Her surgeon had been around and told her the two options for her surgery, and she could decide what one. Poor Jean was in the same mindset as me, as I sat there and eavesdropped; she didn't know. After all, he was the surgeon and should be deciding the best option. He told her he didn't think she wanted the surgery as she wasn't really responding, and she said no, of course, I do. He then commented on her chest and her chest infection and wasn't sure about surgery with it. But of course, they got her ready for surgery, and she was sitting waiting in her surgical gown and socks to be brought down before the surgeon came back up and told her that her chest was too bad to do the op. So it was arranged she would go home with antibiotics to clear the infection, and they would do it at Musgrave in a few weeks. She said this suited her better as her house was closer to Musgrave, and she was delighted to be going home. I was delighted for her but was going to miss her terribly.

The thing that took the longest when someone was leaving was waiting on the medicine from the pharmacy; for some reason, it took hours. Jean said what I had been thinking about myself, and felt like she had wasted a hospital bed, but she did not at all. She, like myself, needed the surgery; it was the hospital that wasted the bed themselves by not being organised. She could have been on IV antibiotics the amount of time she was waiting, and had her chest infection cleared, and the surgery could have gone ahead. It was the evening when she was leaving, as pharmacy took so long, and I said to Conor to offer her a lift home, but she was so polite and refused. We kept asking if she was sure as it was no bother, but she insisted on getting a taxi. I had said to her one day as well that if she wanted to bring up something to watch TV on, I could help set it up for her, as she saw me watching Netflix's on my laptop, and said she was missing her shows. Again, she had said not to worry, she was just the loveliest chattiest little lady. When she left, I was so sad; I was losing another mate/ward granny but also delighted for her she was getting out. Every time someone left, it was bittersweet. Bitter for us left behind missing them, but sweet for them. I think of all the wonderful women I met during my time there, and I am so grateful for having met them. I still think about them and how they are and what they're up to, hoping it's all only the best and they made full recoveries.

The beds weren't long being filled. An old lady named Rose was placed in Jean's old bed, and a girl similar in age to me was placed in Elizabeth's, but I didn't see her until the morning as she came in late, and my curtains were closed. They cleaned the beds with those alcohol baby wipes, and I had the familiar thought of, seriously, how the fuck do those baby wipes clean anything. During visiting, a lady had also joined the ward and was placed where Marilyn originally was. My mum had made a pass remarkable comment about watching out for her as she seemed like the type to cause a scene. Me trying to be nice said, you don't know, and you can't say that. She said, just you wait and see. Why is it mothers are 99.9% of the time, right? (Do not tell them that).

That night was the worst night me and the rest of the ward could have ever had. The lights were out, and I was chilling, getting ready to sleep, and the ward was silent. Sleep hadn't been great all week, but daily naps were helping. I kept amazing myself by sleeping through the daytime visiting hours. Sometimes when I woke, I had caught the other patient's family members staring, looking away quickly as I opened my eyes. They were probably wondering WTF was wrong with me as I was decades younger than most there, or I looked that horrendous they couldn't help but stare.

Poor Rose had been really unwell, so they had put one of those tubes down her nose that basically brought the stuff up from her stomach and did the vomiting for her. Margaret had been coming around after her surgery and hadn't long had hers taken out. I can't remember exactly what happened to both of them, but Margaret had just had emergency surgery on her stomach. She was really ill and would have died if not treated. She said the pain was the worst she had ever felt in her life, and she had 5 or 7 children (can't remember) and would take childbirth any day. That was a common theme with the ladies; they all agreed the pain they had been in when ill before surgery was the worst they had felt in their life, and childbirth was so easy in comparison. I thankfully couldn't comment on that topic. Rose had said she was waiting for scans but was really sick, and the stuff coming up her tube was green. Not healthy.

I think we were all nearly sleeping, and the old ladies were already asleep, then this noise started. I have never heard anything quite like it in my life. The snoring was so loud it sounded as if it was in my ear. I was used to snoring; Conor's a massive snorer, and regularly got kicked, or his nose pinched. I actually thought I need to call a nurse as it must be poor Rose next to me, and she must be really unwell, as she definitely wasn't making any noise when sleeping earlier. I also voice noted the sound and sent it to Conor to be like, WTF is that, and how is it so loud. I put my headphones in and turned my laptop up full volume, and that wasn't even blocking it out! Conor couldn't believe what he could hear as I said I was just holding my phone in my hand, and that's what still was being picked up. Shortly after, I could hear Ursula on the phone with her partner, and she was not happy. I got up and walked over and mouthed at her WTF is that, as she was on the phone. She saw me and said, "OMG, I know I'm going to explode", and was very angry.

Understandably so, as the noise was actually coming from the new person beside her and was extremely unbearable up close. I wish everybody could experience what we heard as there are no words. Poor Rose was awake now and looked distressed, and Margaret had also been woken and was getting progressively sicker. She was so sick during the night, the next day they had to put the vomiting tube back down her again. I heard the doctors apologise as apparently it's extremely uncomfortable and even painful going down when awake, as they normally do it when under anaesthetic. It sounded it; imagine a tube being shoved up your nose and then down your throat to take your vomit up. I'd be boking if they even tried doing that to me. Fucking heroes, those ladies. When Ursula was off the phone, she called me over. I was sure the new girl beside me was also awake now too. I told her when I went to the toilet, which was located at the opposite side of the ward to the snoring, and the toilet was located at the back of the room and behind a heavy thick door, I could still hear it as if she was in the room with me. Ursula wasn't surprised and said she was fucking Peppa pig, hahaha. She really fucking was. We talked and complained about her for an hour, hoping it would stop, and when nurses came in, we said to them. They kept panning us off, saying it was snoring and not much they could do but would try turning her on her side as she was lying on her back, making it worse. Please anything we begged, the whole ward was awake because of this one pig, and no one was sleeping with this noise.

This actually helped, and we tried sleeping again, but it was too good to be true, and soon, she was back to full volume. Poor Ursula was nearly in tears at this point, and I wasn't far behind. I got up and said I'd go out and ask a nurse to move her again, as when I crept into her cubicle to assess the situation, she was back to lying like a roasting hog on her back. Fucking swine. Don't even feel bad for that comparison after what we endured. I also thought of moving her myself but knew it probably wasn't the best idea, as I was also contemplating strangling her. Ursula said yes please, and said she would move her herself if she weren't attached to the bed. She hadn't been able to move in a week as she had a catheter in, so she was hooked to the bed.

I went out and saw some staff at the desk outside our room and politely asked if one of them could please help as the whole ward was awake. Also, earlier, a nurse helped us move her as no one can sleep due to her snoring being so loud (it was also easily after 1 am at this point). Some cheeky fucking bitch of a nurse who was walking past and overheard, interrupted and shouted at me! "What do you expect us to do about someone snoring?!" she scowled as she pushed past me. WTF. I followed her in, horrified at how I had just been spoken to so rudely at 1 am when asking a question not directed to her on behalf of a distressed ward. She came in and was all over the snoring lady, "Oooh pet, I'm so sorry", as she moved her onto her side, then ran out again. The fat hog wasn't even waking when they were moving her; why were they so concerned?! I told Ursula what just happened whilst in shock at how I was spoken to, and she was raging. She shouted, she's fucking lucky I'm attached to this because if she had spoken to me like that, she would've got an earful, and that's not on! I agreed, and as we slabbered about the nurse, I was encouraged to report her. That is exactly what I did in the morning, I had had it with this fucking ward.

My Fitbit, which was originally purchased to monitor my heart rate after my first hospital stay, said I slept for 1 hour that night.

Most annoyingly, when I did fall asleep, I was fucking woken up at 5 am for obs. The auxiliary staff doing the obs was a young guy who nearly gave me a heart attack. After finally dosing off, I was in such a deep sleep, he had come right into my face saying my name to wake me. It was a little alarming. I jumped and then burst out laughing when I realised what was happening. I couldn't get back to sleep after that due to the ongoing noise. Also, at 6 am, the fucking hog woke up and phoned her daughter, proceeding to make loads of noise, hysterically laughing and waking everyone else up. She then proceeded to put her radio on full blast for us all to listen to, again my earphones and full volume not even drowning it out. Ursula's face said it all, and we both were going to kill her. Ursula even commented about its noise and to turn it off, but the rude bitch never paid attention. We were all sleep-deprived, exhausted, and found out that the woman had been moved from another ward. Ursula and I discussed and believed she had obviously caused issues on the other ward, and that's why we got landed with her. I said about my mum having prejudged her, and I hated to admit it, but she was very right. Ursula said my mum was 100% right and was like her; they had a good judge of character. She thought she was going to kill Peppa pig, purposely phoning her daughter at 6 am and making loads of noise, also constantly trying to get attention off the nurses. I agreed and said her cackles had ensured I was awake at 6 am.

I was hoping today I would get my MRI, but I also wanted out. I was supposed to be at a Hen party the next day, and this was massively fucking everything up. I waited, and the doctors told me the same thing; they were hoping for the MRI today. Later, when talking to the nurse that was on, I became confused as she said about drinking a contrast, so I asked her if I was getting a small bowel MRI and a pelvic MRI? To which she very abruptly and rudely told me, "I'm not your doctor, how would I know that? If you want to know, ask your doctor". WTF, you're the nurse in charge today; you should probably know what's happening. I had thought she was a bitch when she was first coming around the ward, and everyone was visibly annoyed at the noise from the radio. Instead of addressing this or telling her to turn it down/off, she instead called across to her, saying how she loved the song/channel or something stupid. I strongly disagreed; it was old shit I had never even heard before. Later on, I mentioned the noise to the nurse, and how no one slept last night and how rudely a nurse had spoken to me. Straight off the bat, the nurse very shockingly said, if I want to report it, I can, and she'll get the staff nurse in. I said yeah ok, not quite believing how quickly she was ready for me to report a colleague. Maybe she knew who it was and didn't like her. I reported her anyway, and the staff nurse basically agreed with the rude nurse, and said there isn't anything you can do about snoring but would report it. That fact I was very aware of, I'm not stupid, and aware people can't help it. It was how I was spoken to that was completely not on. I knew reporting it would do fuck all; they're all so protected in the NHS, but I was at the end of my tether and should never have been spoken to like that at 1 am when going out on behalf of a ward.

The loudmouth one of dumb and dumber, also had his 2 pence to put in as we sat there angry and sleep-deprived. We said about the noise the night before, and his response was, "Oh don't you worry, I know, we hear everything in here. What you need to do is get yourself a pair of earplugs." To which I responded, "No, I had my earphones in with the volume up full blast, and it still didn't block the noise out." He obviously didn't like I was right and tried interrupting me and kept repeating, "no, no, you need earplugs". I thought I was going to climb the big bastard and punch him. I had already been fucked off at comments about my profession. As a paralegal and someone who has a law degree, there's a strange assumption of a certain level of intelligence. Also, there are strange assumptions made from working in a legal job, which I gather people relate to snobbery and think they can make jokes at. He had tried making jokes about "those legal types", which wasn't going down well and was fucking me off these ignorant assumptions. I have gathered over time, however, a lot of boys (won't call them men as they aren't) do not like intelligent women; it threatens their fragile little egos. After the week I had had, I would have loved to tell the ward that if they had the work ethic of the majority of solicitors I knew, maybe the place wouldn't be a fucking shambles. They work outside of their 9-5 hours all the time for no extra pay to ensure everything is done for their client. There are solely and massively responsible for every matter they touch, and even one fuck up could lead to them being reported to the Law Society or struck off. Whereas doctors and nurses practically had to intentionally kill someone for anything to happen or be taken seriously. I don't often defend the profession I'm in; if anything, these boring responsibilities are why I put off qualifying. I'm also in a profession that's massively overworked, underpaid and stressed, yet everyone assumes it's big money. Not until you're a partner, mate. If a client phoned and they got told that we missed the deadline for something completing, because we forgot or didn't organise it then refused to take responsibility, it would be a very different matter. Basically, at this point, I thought the medical profession could go and shove its delusions of grandeur up its incompetent ass.

My mum had been phoning asking what was happening, and I told her I didn't know, still waiting. Shortly after, I heard the mouthy one of dumb and dumber say my name on the phone and how we can't give out details over the phone. I was thinking what the fuck is going on, and if this is my MRI and he's fucked it up, I really will lose my temper and go out there and fuck him up. I went out and asked what was happening, and all he said was, we can't give out any information over the phone. I didn't understand what was happening and was just left confused. But my mum phoned me a few minutes later to say she was waiting for my nurse to phone me back, as there had been no update on the MRI. I then realised that was her phoning the ward and was raging my next of kin wasn't told information about me. I said to Ursula, and she was also raging, WTF was that. She had just had her catheter removed and was really gearing up to leave. She said she couldn't stand this hellhole and needed out and would be ASAP. They had also fucked her off the day before at visiting time when her son and his wife and their kids came up to visit. They only allowed her son in and wouldn't allow her grandchildren to come in, again WTF. They had brought presents and pictures, and her son had to bring them in, and they were also upset they couldn't see her. I just didn't get this stupid fucking ward. Peppa pig's grandkids had been all over her when she arrived last night!! They had me with no immune system beside a lady with a chest infection for a week, yet your loved ones couldn't visit you. Seriously check your priorities. Ursula was visibly upset too.

My mum called me back again and was livid. She spoke to the nurse looking after us today, but I literally hadn't seen her since speaking to her that morning. Apparently, she came on the phone with an attitude, and told my mum she didn't know what was going on with me. If I wanted to know I was a 24-year-old adult and ask myself, why was my mum phoning for me... understandably, that didn't go down well with Mumma bear Laza D. She might be 5 foot, but she will literally cut a bitch. So obviously, with my mum being my mum, she ended up getting in contact with the head of something organisational in the hospital. I can't remember who, but the contact was high up anyway. Laura doesn't do half measures. She told the lady what had happened and what was said by the nurse, and apparently, the woman was horrified. The lady said she couldn't believe the nurse had said this, and they were going to report her. Also, how dare she, as although I'm 24, I'm still obviously my mum's baby. My mum agreed and said she had said to the nurse that although I'm 24, I'm not going to speak up, this is not a natural environment for a 24-year-old, nor should it be, and I was scared and sick. She wasn't wrong. There was one of those weekly meetings where cases are discussed, and the lady said this was definitely being brought up. Just in case all my doctor fans missed me yano x.

It turned out they only done the pelvic MRI's on a Thursday, and they had missed organising it for the day before. So they decided they were going to let me go, and I'd come back next week as if I was still an inpatient for the MRI. I needed to leave as well as I thought I was getting sick as my throat was sore and my glands were swollen. When my surgeon came around that morning, I asked him to check my glands. He did, and I was shocked at how official it all was as he got me to sit in the chair and stood behind me to check, agreeing they were swollen. Get me out of here. I was black and blue from injections and bloods, sleep-deprived and extremely fucked off. I was delighted I could go, and when they realised my MRI wasn't happening, I was allowed to finally eat my breakfast as they had me fasting. My surgeon asked me did I feel ok and in good health to go, to which I replied, "yes, definitely", so I could start packing my bags. I phoned my dad to come and get me as he was off.

Peppa pig was already away for her surgery, and I hoped she didn't bother the ward much more. Especially as Ursula was able to move now, and she might just strangle her. I had laughed internally, though, as Peppa was getting her pre-op questions, and the doctor had asked her how her health was. She exclaimed loudly she was perfectly healthy bar this operation (I think it was her gallbladder), to which the doctor replied, "You have type 2 diabetes, and you're very overweight" hahahahah. I think I bit my tongue to keep that one in. She was commended, however on trying to lose weight. She was definitely 4 foot something and probably between 12-14 stone; she was a wee warthog like. Terrible to say, but she evoked that level of anger in me. I spoke to a girl similar in age to me and she was just back from her surgery. It turned out she kept getting abscesses in the same area as me but didn't have Crohn's, so had to keep getting them drained. Rose, I chatted to loads that day; she was funny and in her late

80's closer to 90 and was telling me about her family. I think she had something like 10 kids, mental. She kept telling me how people were amazed at her brood, and it wasn't hard to have that many as she got pregnant so easily, but then realising what she said and shouting, "not in a dirty way!" Aye right ya wee cat, I know the score, secrets safe with me Rose hun. Margaret had been really ill and wasn't long after having the boking tube put back down and coming around. I spoke to her children and told them how awful the ward was, and they completely agreed. They told me about the nurse my mum had reported that morning. Something similar had happened to them and how they were treated, and how she treated Margaret. They wanted to report her but were worried that it would impact their mum's treatment if they did. I hated to agree, but it's true it probably would have, having witnessed the high levels of unprofessionalism that week. I played them the recording of the snoring and said it probably didn't help poor Margaret, as she had been woken because of that, then she started to get sick. I had also seen a nurse shout at one of her sons one day during visiting time. A nurse saw him picking up the notes that they keep at the foot of your bed and came running over, shouting that he wasn't allowed to look at them and took them off him, then left the room angrily. A bit weird; the last time I was in, I was allowed to look at my notes. In fact, I took pictures and sent them to my auntie in Australia. Maybe they didn't want family members to realise their incompetency. Who knows? Her children also told me that as their mother was suffering in silence, the doctors weren't going to do a CT scan, only her kids kicked up a fuss. It turns out if they hadn't, she would have died as that's what showed she needed the emergency lifesaving surgery.

I lastly said goodbye to my beloved Ursula. We gave each other a big hug, and she told me to get out there and live my life. Forget about this horrible shit show, and she wouldn't be long behind me as she refused to stay much longer and needed home. I really hoped she got out soon, and now she was on her feet, I think she would've been ready to fight back. Don't blame her, the place was a shit show. I actually loved her. One day when she would've only been a day or two post-op, I heard her shouting at a doctor or nurse saying there was a tablet she needed to take every day at a certain time and had been doing this for years, and since she had been in hospital, she hadn't been getting it. I spoke to her about this and said last time I was in and on loads of tablets, they were never administered correctly. I was going to really miss my hospital mum.

When my dad was on his way, I left the ward, not waiting for a porter to carry my stuff and just ran out to my freedom. My dad came, and I told him angrily about the shit show and what had happened the night before and that day. He agreed some nurses are shit and don't want to be there, making it awful for patients. He had kidney stones years before and had a procedure in the Royal to blast them, then had a catheter or something put in for a few days but was allowed home. The nurse then told him that he could remove the catheter himself after a certain amount of time, which he did and ended up rupturing his insides and vomiting with the pain. My mum then drove him straight to hospital, and it was uncovered that the nurse who told him to remove it himself was completely wrong, and he should've come back to the hospital for them to do it. He said the nurse who then took the rest out, spent her entire time moaning about how she didn't want to be there and basically hated her job, whilst he was lying there in agony. Seriously WTF. The whole experience had left me so down and disheartened that one evening, while I had been in hospital, Conor had felt really bad for me, and bought me the new Kim Kardashian eyeshadow palette. It was very nice of him, and I was very excited about its arrival. As they say, "boy done good". Cringe. But I was seriously delighted.

I was so glad to be out but was soo angry; that whole week had been a shit show of an experience I never wanted to relive again. I actually thought of other people who were going to experience something similar on that ward, and I actually got the fear for these potential unknown randomers. How is that even possible. How is a ward THAT bad? My cousin phoned me as it was her Home Hen the next day and she was really glad I could go. So was I but I was embarrassed as I was literally black and blue from injections, and there was no hiding them on my arms. I was soo tired, and a few friends had said they would visit, but Michael had told them already I wasn't up for visitors today. I needed to go to my flat and sleep. Conor picked me up from my family house after work, and I passed out early. I think I slept over 12 hours and was still wrecked the next day. At about 4 pm, I needed to muster up the energy to get ready for the Home Hen but couldn't believe how wrecked I still was. I thought I looked rotten in my dress too, as last time I had worn it, I had undiagnosed Crohn's disease and was also exercising, so I was tiny, I think closer to 7 stone. I was now about 9 stone, and it did not fit as well. Between being so inactive with illness, surgery and hospital stays, none of this helped. Also, the steroid weight was still shedding as my face was still not quite back to normal. I glammed up anyway and went. It was a really fun night, so glad I could make it. I think I slept the whole next day again and then went back to work on Monday, still wrecked. I needed to earn as I had missed a week's wage, and who knew what more I would be missing.

Brace yourself, more surgery is coming

My MRI came on Thursday, and I dreaded the thought of return-ing to THAT hospital. I literally couldn't be fucked. I remem-bered back to January to my last pelvic MRI and thought it only took about 10 minutes, so I was hoping not to be there for long. It was different from the Ulster Independent, very different. No fancy rooms but cubicles and lockers and a small waiting room. My mum came with me, and instead of a hospital gown, it was scrubs. WHAT I LOVED! Apart from what I assumed was blood-stains, but I seriously looked good in them. I could imagine my-self in Casualty or Holby or something as chief nurse. Not a real-life nurse, of course, but a fake one. I don't have time for real-life vomit and shit of another person to get on me. I got my mum to take a picture of me, but unfortunately, she was sitting as I was standing, and the double chin angle was not good. I needed a professional to capture this iconic hospital lewk, but of course, it still went on my Insta; I loved them that much. I did however feel a bit bare in them as they were baggy and loose-fitting, and I was only allowed my knickers on underneath. I always forgot to take piercings out prior to the appointment as well, due to the no metal rule. It was always a minor inconvenience as of course I struggled to get them out when I actually needed to, typical.

They put a cannula in, and I got ready to go in the MRI machine. Just before going into the machine though, I realised there was a metal heart on my pants. I said to the nice woman looking after me as I now realised I was at risk of having the machine rip off my knickers. Hilarious but not ideal. She said she knew what I meant, but those bits are usually plastic, but she would check. I refrained from saying, "I think it's metal, these are fancy pants" and proceeded to show her the metal heart. She agreed she thought it was metal, and I was given scissors to cut it off.

I wondered what would have happened if I hadn't realised I had this single little metal heart attached to me. I went into the MRI room and was placed in feet first lying on my back. It was more claustrophobic than last time, but it didn't bother me; if I rolled my eyes back, I could see out of the machine. This one lasted ages, like about 30 minutes. But MRI's don't bother me, and I just lay there very still in the noisy machine with the headphones on, listening to the poor quality recorded music. This one also had a recorded automated voice telling me what to do, like when to breathe and not to breathe etc. Previously it had been the imager telling me what to do over the mic. I remember being really tired and thinking if it wasn't for the breathing instructions, I could honestly probably zone out this noise and have a nap. I even closed my eyes a few times then made myself wake up. After it was over, the lady looking after me said how well I had done, I literally didn't move a muscle. I wasn't that surprised as I was both strangely tired and relaxed in the machine. I got the cannula out, changed and went home, now waiting for my results and a phone call from my doctors. I remember the abscess being really sore that day and was kind of glad as I knew that meant it should definitely show up on the MRI.

It must have been the following Friday I received a phone call from my surgeon. He said I had been coming up at their weekly case conferences. Absolutely cringe; I had literally been a Royal local celeb for months. He confirmed there was still an abscess there, and him and my Crohns doctor had to sit together and brainstorm what to do as it was a very complex MRI. Basically, as the abscess was a product of a fistula, a product of severe inflammation from Crohn's disease, it couldn't be treated like a normal abscess where they just cut into it, drain it, stitch it up and it's gone. Due to inflammation that would basically make it explode and not work. Draining it again would only be a temporary solution and would be too dangerous if it came back and the fistula closed. So the shocker I received next was, "Also, the fistula is in a very dangerous place, and it needs to be moved. If more inflammation occurs, there is a chance another fistula could develop and create a tunnel between your bowel and vagina, meaning you would be passing stool out your vagina, which is very dangerous and hard to fix." Again, WTF. "I don't think so", I responded. That really was the straw that broke the camel's back. If I started shitting out my vag, the whole NHS was getting sued. He continued that it had happened with previous patients, so they were ensuring it wasn't going to happen with me. It bloody better not, or I really would lose my shit (pardon the pun). My surgery was going to be the following Friday, and they were going to move the fistula to a safer place and hold it with a stitch while also re-draining the abscess. I was delighted I was finally getting the surgery, I had been going on and on about when the fuck they were gonna do it, as I felt like I was in limbo. I was also told I had to take the bastarding ciprofloxacin and metronidazole antibiotics again and was already dreading them.

I started the antibiotics that day, and you can't drink on metronidazole, which was majorly fucking me off, as it was really sunny and my last weekend of freedom. Apparently, it makes you violently sick if you drink on them, and I heard someone say they give it to alcoholics, so if they drink, they'll be really ill. Not sure how true that is, also a bit cruel, but maybe effective. My mates weren't even heading out, just drinking in our flat, but I was raging. I was quite irrationally down as well, I think it was the fact more of my life was being controlled and stolen by this. Something as normal as drinking with your mates on a Saturday. This time something strange happened though, I started taking a weird reaction.

Of course, the standard of annoying my bowels/Crohn's happened, as the main side effects of those antibiotics is stomach cramps and diarrhoea, so always a bad combo. But it also was making me really dopey, I felt massively stoned, and my brain literally wasn't working. I was dizzy and confused, and when putting food in the oven, I turned around 5 minutes later and asked Conor who was cooking. I had no memory. He was a bit worried at that point, and by Sunday, he and my mum told me to phone the out of hours doctors. As dopey as I was, I agreed. The only plus was because I felt so out of it; everything was kind of funny. But the lack of awareness permanently was also annoying. The out of hours doctor told me to stop taking metronidazole as it was probably causing it due to its strength, but as I had said I was seeing my consultant for a hospital appointment the next day, to definitely bring this all up. Don't worry, I was going to.

Within the 24 hours of stopping it and seeing my doctor, I was a lot better, and it must have been the metronidazole. He thought it had brought on some kind of neurological migraine, which was also a side effect. I had to keep taking ciprofloxacin though, and its side effects alone had me unwell the rest of the week. I didn't make it into work the few days prior to surgery, it triggered a bad Crohns flare, or the side effects were the exact same. I went back to my family house on Thursday evening, and my mum had bought Milton what is apparently for sterilising baby's bottles etc. She told me to have a bath with it and I smelled like bleach/chlorine. I had been over-optimistic yet again that this surgery recovery shouldn't take too long, and I'd be fine and at my cousin's Hen party the following week, no problems. This was sadly not the case.

The next morning came, and I had to be at the City hospital again for 7 am. It was the same as last time, when I waited in a room filled with others getting surgery and their families until the nurses told us where to go. The antibiotics were disagreeing with me really badly again; it was like a repeat of last time, and I kept needing the toilet. Embarrassingly I kept walking in and out to use the bathroom, again the others probably thinking

WTF is her problem. Déjà vu. Also, the horrendous journey over with the worry of me shitting myself being at the forefront of my mind. The anxiety and stress Crohns causes for the simplest of things, like going on a car journey, is so tiring. We were told where to go, and it was the same room as last time. I had the same lovely nurses as before, and they actually recognised me. They were also sad to see me back and asked what was wrong. I told them the abscess had come back again and needed more surgery.

The standard peeing in a cup to make sure you're not pregnant started for the whole ward. Again, a lady in her mid to late 50's laughed at this and said there wasn't much chance. The doctors then did the different rounds of questions. I remember them all being really nice and really liking them. I massively preferred the City, it was a nicer hospital and the staff I had encountered always seemed nicer. My judgement was definitely clouded from my last hospital stay experience, though. I was chatting away to the junior doctor for one of my question rounds; we were similar in age and got on well. She had asked about different tests I had received, and I told her how difficult it was to get my diagnosis, but was confused as I had Crohn's in my small bowel, but when I had the barium x-ray to check it, it came back clear. She said it was a really old, outdated test that wasn't very good and would need an MRI to see what was going on properly. I agreed as the MRI had shown up ulcers and everything. I really liked my anaesthetist as well. I had to do the cringe thing and say to her about smoking grass for pain relief as it's meant to affect doses, and she was really dead on, unlike the previous one. She was really chilled and cool; it had a real calming effect on me too. She said it's no problem at all, and thanks for letting her know, no lecture about how there is more effective pain relief out there and then not suggesting anything. Morphine, I can confirm, is the only pain relief I have felt adequately deals with Crohn's pain, and they don't hand that out like co-codamol.

When my surgeon came around, I joked and said I'm sure he was sick of seeing me, to which he laughed and agreed. He didn't like operating on young people. He must have just arrived at the hospital as he was in casual clothes and had a bag with him. It must be weird being a surgeon, just driving to work in your scruffs, getting ready for a big day of cutting people up. It was a quick encounter and I was awaiting the standard finger up the bum trick, but I was surprised when that didn't happen. I still had to be examined, and he asked where I felt the pain and lump on the outside, so I said on the left-hand side, and he confirmed when he found it. He said he'd know for definite when operating what surgery was needed and said I might have a stitch for life and apologised. I remember being confused and thinking, what is he sorry for because if it's a stitch on the inside, I won't even know it's there. After all the rounds of questions were done, I changed into my surgical gown and waited. I was leaving putting my surgical socks on until the last minute as they were uncomfortable. I found they actually cut off circulation because they were so tight, or dug into the backs of your legs under your knees and became itchy. I had also hated having to wear them unnecessarily so recently, so I wasn't putting them on before I needed to. The last time I had to wear them in hospital a few weeks previous, they were so tight I couldn't get them on by myself. I spent about half an hour at least trying to get them on. I vaguely remembered my mum laughing and asking what the fuck was I doing. The first surgery I had, the lovely nurses helped me put them on so there were no issues, and I was going to get their help again.

As I waited with the curtains pulled around me before being brought down, my medical files were sat in front of me. I remembered seeing pictures they took during my colonoscopy of the Crohn's and looked through my file to see if I could find them. I accidentally ripped a page when trying to be careful, very annoying, but I was just hoping they wouldn't notice. I had 3 big files; quite impressive really to build up such a medical history in such a short space of time some would say. I found the pictures, got my phone and took pictures of them. I was going to show Conor them later, really make his day I'm sure. Who wouldn't want to see bleeding intestines and ulcers?

Shortly after, the nurses pulled back my curtain and said they were ready for me. I remember because of the antibiotics, I felt soo sick and had the familiar thought, was it possible to shit yourself during an operation. I got paranoid and panicky as I felt so sick and had it in my head, as soon as I was knocked out and everything relaxed, I was going to shit myself, and although be unconscious, be absolutely mortified. The anxiety of all this was probably making me feel worse too. One of my nurses, who I got on super well with (she was German, and I think her name was Catianna) and a porter began wheeling me in the bed down to surgery. As I was going out the door, one of them asked, have you got your socks on? Oh fuck, I had forgotten; I guess my subconscious really didn't want me to wear them. They were whipped on by me and a nurse (mostly the nurse) as I was being wheeled out the door, of course not very gracefully, and I was also trying to protect my modesty as nude under my gown.

I was talking to my nurse on the way down; we got on so well and had chatted loads, pre and post-surgery. I was saying I hoped I didn't have to stay after the surgery and got home, mostly because I didn't want the blood-thinning injections. She agreed and said before a long flight she took one of the injections and said they were the most painful going, and could definitely cope with being a diabetic if you can cope with them. I had also told her I hoped they could find a vein ok, as I had been fasting and my veins are now awful from overuse. I said about the junior doctor who had butchered 5 veins, and she was horrified. She said she was trained in putting in cannulas, and there was no excuse for that. It was bad technique and he should have stopped after 3 attempts to call someone more superior.

My auntie Annie had previously said in Australia it's policy to stop and get someone else after 3 failed attempts. I was glad when I heard this but also annoyed yet again at what I had been unnecessarily subjected to. My nurse and the porter left me outside the surgical unit, wished me luck, and said she'd see me afterwards. I had forgotten before they bring you into the operating room, you wait outside it in a bright medicine sort of room, and get asked questions about what medication you are on and if you are allergic to anything. Last time it was very quick, but this time it was longer. I had to tell them about the antibiotics I was currently on and taking the reaction to one of them. I was really nervous and really felt like I needed the toilet, but I couldn't tell if it was that or nerves. I said to the doctors, "This is so cringe but am I allowed to go to the toilet?" and they said they would check for me. I explained why and said the antibiotics were making my Crohn's really bad, and keep feeling like I needed to go, but I would probably be fine. They were really lovely and checked and asked when returning, did I still need to go just because I would have to be brought out and escorted back. I didn't want any unnecessary fuss or annoyance and told them it's fine, it kind of subsided, and I thought it might be nerves mixed with the Crohn's. They were really nice and empathetic, and said the antibiotics definitely upset people Crohn's or no Crohn's, so weren't surprised and to let them know if I wasn't ok.

I was then wheeled into the surgery room, and the anaesthetist came in to put the cannula into my hand. I apologised in advance. I remember her repeatedly flicking my hand to get the veins up, and after a while of this, she got it in in one go. She laughed and told me not to worry, my veins weren't the worst she had seen. I then had the pre-anaesthetic dose of diazepam etc., which didn't make me as woozy or relaxed as the first time. I think I was still so on edge over my bowels. The mask thing went on first, and I breathed in when instructed, then the anaesthetic went in and like before, then there was nothing.

This time I was woken by hearing my name being shouted; I then realised I was being shaken. As I opened my eyes, the anaesthetist was grabbing my gown with both hands, shaking me, and shouting "Sarah" repeatedly. I must've been asleep longer than planned as the nurses looked concerned, but the anaesthetist didn't. I wondered if she gave me an extra dose because I said about smoking grass or I generally slept on, as I was so tired and barely slept the night before. I don't think anyone really sleeps well the night before surgery. But these fleeting thoughts didn't last long as the pain kicked in straight away. Fuck, I remember thinking, this is worse than last time. The burn was insane, and it felt like someone had shoved a hot rode up my bum after dipping it in lava. That familiar post-surgery burn, but it was even worse now, but I also wondered did I just forget how bad it was.

A Lithuanian nurse came over and asked me to turn over so she could check my bandages. I gathered I was all wrapped up and could feel it. I wanted to know if I had a stitch or not but was in a lot of pain. I turned over, and she looked at the bandages and then told me I had a stitch in. I said I thought I might as I can feel it, it's painful. She rudely told me I couldn't feel it, it was the bandages, before walking away mid-conversation, as a woman who had just had her tonsils taken out had been wheeled up to the ward and was also from Lithuanian. She was far more interested in her due to the connection and walked away without saying anything more and was up the other woman's hole. Rude cunt, I thought. There was another lovely male nurse on, though, and he heard I was in pain. When he asked, I said, yeah, I feel like a hot rode has been shoved up me. He was really empathetic, and said no way am I allowed to leave here in pain and shouldn't be in pain, so he was going to get me more pain relief. They had IV pain relief going already, but I think it was just IV paracetamol; it had to be it was so shite (I don't care what medical professionals say, it is NOT, and I repeat, NOT as effective as morphine). He got me some morphine, and I was excited to try it. It was administered in small amounts each time to make sure I didn't take a re-action. It was given over 3 doses, and when the first one went in, I got a woozy feeling. Then he checked my heart rate, and then the next dose went in, again feeling woozy. This was repeated a third time and again felt woozy, but the pain was going. This was great. I was a big fan of morphine after this, it was such effect-ive pain relief. I was totally fine, like chatting away and aware of what was going on but pain-free. I remembered the last time I was in, and Ursula and Marilyn had morphine on tap and just pressed a button for it; that's what I wanted.

I chatted loads to the nurse, he was so nice, and I told him I preferred the City to the Royal. He agreed and said it was a much nicer hospital, as he used to work in the Royal. When the Trusts branched together, he told me all the staff got moved, and he much preferred working here. Although he did miss the riff-raff of the Royal sometimes, the City was much nicer to work in. I agreed from a patient front as well. I had found the staff I en-countered much nicer and professional, and in general, a nicer hospital. I had to stay in recovery a bit longer because of the mor-phine and, of course, needed to pee from all the fluids, but when I heard I was going back to the ward soon, I was glad. I didn't feel prepared to give those bedpans another go.

I was wheeled back to the ward by the porter and was told I had to stay in this other recovery a bit longer as well due to the morphine. I didn't mind; I was comfortable. The nurses laughed upon my return and asked why I seemed so bright-eyed, and bushy-tailed post-surgery. I laughed and said morphine. I was pain-free and really tired, but I stayed awake as I didn't want to doze off and then be woken up to go home. A few others were now being wheeled off for surgery, and a new woman and I presumed her boyfriend arrived as I was walking to use the ward bathroom. I was walking funny as I was a bit woozy post-surgery, but this guy walking past did not care and nearly took me out. I was bleeding so much the blood had seeped through my bandages, gown, the pad things the nurses put on the bed to protect against bleeding, the sheet, and finally through to the leather/PVC (more likely PVC) hospital bed. I remember thinking, wish I could fling some of my blood at him for his rudeness. I actually think I heard a nurse making a comment to him as I went into the cubicle. When I went to pee, I didn't know what to expect, and I had to pull the bloody bandages off that were taped on. I noticed a load of gauze or paper or whatever medical stuffed they used, and it was packed into the wound. I couldn't understand what they had done or what was packed, and I was still pain-free, so of course, I tried feeling what was going on, but couldn't understand. I also forgot they put iodine all down your legs and had thought the blood had spread really far down. It thankfully hadn't spread that far. I peed and embarrassedly came out to ask for new bed stuff as I had bled so much. The nurses told me not to worry at all and thinking back; I don't know why I was embarrassed. I think you always feel it more in the moment, and I didn't appreciate I had just been cut open. I also asked did they know if I had a stitch or was my wound packed out. One of the nurses got me to lie down, and she had a look and confirmed it was packed out. I was surprised at how much more painful this surgery had been, but I hadn't realised the extent of what was done. I was told I had a seton stitch but didn't have a fucking clue what that was and was too dopey to even look it up.

After a few hours, I was allowed to go, and my mum came and collected me. She helped me get changed as I was a bit off balance but overall felt fine. Before changing, however, I went to the bathroom to pee and realised as my mother laughed and shouted after me, forgetting about the open back hospital gowns. Full moon in the afternoon, you're welcome ward. The nurses said to me as much as they loved me, they hoped never to see me again and hoped I got on my cousins Hen do, which was now the following Friday. I was very optimistic about my current lack of pain. I would be in Magaluf sipping some sweet Rushkinoff vodka/paint stripper that day next week. I left feeling optimistic and had assumed not much had happened with the surgery as I wasn't given any post-surgery advice or pain relief. I had told the nurses I would keep taking the co-codamol I had at home, as I had also been given that previously in hospital. All I was given was another 2 weeks' worth of the shitty antibiotics to keep taking.

I was fine but growing more uncomfortable as the day went on. Anyone I spoke to, I told them I was fine, and pain relief was still working. I had been topping up regularly as well. All this came tumbling down at approximately 3 am going into the next day. I woke during the night, and that was me awake for the next 3 days. All the good hospital pain relief was wearing off, and co-codamol was not cutting it. I was now in agony, and nothing was helping. That day was a blur, and my mum didn't want me going to the flat that night. My wound was still packed too, but I thought it would be fine. Sometimes I wish I didn't think because I'm normally wrong. It was a Saturday, and I had barely seen Conor, so I wanted to just chill, get a Chinese, and watch TV with him. I also wanted to smoke some grass to help me sleep and relieve my pain. It had been the only thing that helped with the abscess/Crohn's pain in general, so I again hoped it would work. That evening and over the next few weeks, I learned that no amount of grass would help the pain I was in (well, whatever amount I was taking anyway). I was in so much pain I actually began to wonder how fucking sore it would be without pain relief in general as I felt it was doing nothing for it.

When I arrived at the flat, I sat and talked to our housemates Michael and Ryan, and Ryan's girlfriends who was also over from England visiting. I sat on the sofa with Conor in a funny position as I was in pain, and we all ordered food and talked. Of course, I was joking about the pain and asking if they wanted to see my bloody bandaged gooch for some Saturday night entertainment. The standard sarcastic, yeah, let's see, that's so sexy, get your gooch out, jokes were thrown back. I wasn't actually aware of what the wound area looked like, but I would have put money on it not being pretty. The wound was still packed, and I wondered when that would come out and I could see what was actually going on.

Our food came, and Conor and I went to our room to eat and watch TV. The smoke helped for a while, and I managed to doze for a bit. Unfortunately though, as the antibiotics triggered a flare-up, I wasn't resting for long before I needed the toilet, especially after treating myself to my fave of salt and chilli chicken. Another joy of Crohn's, it waits for no one. It was about 1 am, and I was just trying to sleep, and of course, I needed the toilet. I hadn't really been after surgery from all the pain relief that usually constipates a person, but that was now reversing. The pain that came next made me think I was dying.

The packing in my wound began coming out, and there was loads of it; it literally felt like I gave birth to the gauze. The blood had also unfortunately hardened in the packing, so as it was making its way down, it ripped its way out of the wound, fresh and old blood coming with it. As the flare-up continued, I shouted for Conor and woke him. I was sweating, shaking and crying whilst burning liquid shit was coming out of my wound where they had cut a hole as well as the proper hole. I didn't know this at the time as I had no idea what fucking surgery they had done. It was only when I requested a mirror to try to look and see WTF was going on did I realise a hole had been cut in me. I should've known, I just had fucking surgery. However, I was so confused, and in so much pain at the time, also nothing had actually been properly explained to me. The flare-up lasted hours, so it was hours of excruciating pain, and it was so bad undigested food was coming out. The wound was bleeding and raw, and wiping was agonising and not helping as anything the shit touched burned like acid. Conor said he had never seen a person in more pain, and I was so brave. He, however, shortly after, went

159

back to sleep and left me. I was starting to drift in and out of consciousness with the pain whilst screaming and yelping on the toilet. I was also concerned about waking my housemates, but I couldn't help it as I had never felt pain like it before.

I since learned from a doctor that the surgery they performed entailed cutting a hole in my gooch to move the fistula. They then put a seton stitch through it to hold it in place and allow anything from the abscess to come out. As this fistula was inter-sphincteric, meaning my inside and outside tissue was connecting, which includes the muscle, my body hadn't figured out yet that this new wound wasn't for passing shit, and it shouldn't have been coming out there. Very unfortunately, it didn't really stand a chance with the antibiotic flare-up when unable to form normal shit. Instead, I delightfully had uncontrollable burning liquid making its way through another part of my insides and out through a newly formed surgical wound. If you think that pain sounds unimaginable, I can safely confirm it was. This went on for hours, and I was really past it. Absolutely exhausted, the only thing I could think to do was crawl into the shower light-headed and try to hose myself down for some relief. It actually worked a bit, but our shower was so shit with the worst pressure, so it wasn't ideal. At this point, I was in a heap at the bottom of the shower, uncontrollably sobbing, whilst drifting in and out of consciousness with the pain, sweat pouring out of me and beyond horrified more undigested food was coming out. I remember this scared me so much I let out a scream, but it was definitely more a cry for help.

Conor slept through all of this, and I had been worried I might wake my housemates with the noise, but if he wasn't waking, they probably couldn't hear. They confirmed the next day; they couldn't. I kept texting my mum, but she was away in my granny's in Tyrone, and there is no signal there, and my dad would've been asleep at home. I didn't know what to do or if this was normal, and I was so exhausted. It had been over 24 hours since I last slept, and this episode had gone on for at least 2 hours. I was wrecked and weak. When my body decided there was no more acid and undigested food to shit out, I crawled back to bed. Exhausted, I tried to sleep, but every time I nearly dozed off, where the wound was sent a jolt up my body like an electric shock of pain, and I couldn't sleep. My body actually jumped as this happened every time. Desperate for sleep and in agony, I lay there waiting for an appropriate time to call my granny's.

I kept trying to wake up Conor, but it wasn't really happening. I felt like I had given birth and then had acid thrown on me. Was this normal post-surgery? Was I being a wimp? I didn't want to go back to the doctors or hospital in case it was just standard post-surgery pain, but I had never felt anything like it, and it was beyond excruciating. I must have been hitting a good 9-10 on the pain scale, and the duration of it was the worst; I didn't even think labour could be that bad. I don't think any amount of description could actually describe how bad this was or the pain; I literally wanted to die.

I phoned my mum in the morning and asked if she had got my texts. She hadn't and said I should have phoned my grandparents' house phone to wake her. I wasn't going to do that. I told her I would phone the out of hour's doctor to see if this was normal as I didn't want to go back to hospital. Of course, the out of hour's doctor told me I needed to go back to the hospital, and she said Conor was to take me, she was driving straight to the Royal to meet us there. I went up looking like the biggest tramp in the world. I managed to shower myself and put on a button-up loose sleeveless top as I knew I'd be getting another cannula and a pair of pyjama bottoms. My top was a red checked one, and my PJs were blue checked...talk about a style icon. I was actually mortified going up and being seen in public like that, but that probably should have been the least of my worries.

Conor and I went up, and my heart rate was high, showing the amount of pain I was in. I could barely walk from where they had done the surgery and the pain, and had been supported when walking. We actually bumped into one of my neighbours when waiting and told her what was wrong. She could see I was in agony from how I looked and how I was lying on my side. I couldn't sit normally or walk without help because of the pain. My mood was foul from being back in hospital, lack of sleep, and pain. I had a cannula put in, but of course, my veins weren't working, so it took 2 different vein attempts. The guy doing it I remember being soo lovely, I think he was Polish. He apologised for not getting one of the veins and had to go for a vein on my left arm, far enough down; it was pretty much at my wrist. It didn't bother me though, I actually preferred it here compared to being in the folds of my arm for sleeping and trying to get comfortable. Not that I slept for a while. He told me I needed to take the cotton wool and tape off my other arm after 10 minutes or it would leave a mark, what I had noticed from my 100's of other cannulas/bloods. I was in so much pain, and my Crohns was terrible.

My mum had arrived, and Conor and I were waiting in an A&E cubicle for the doctor to arrive. Of course, I needed the toilet and could barely walk. I was dreading the pain and there would be no shower to hose myself down if needed in the hospital toilets. The doctors let me out the back entrance to go to a toilet, and my mum supported me as I walked. We bumped into my friend Aisha's friend, who is a doctor, and I briefly told him what was happening. I couldn't talk too long needed the loo, and was in a lot of pain as I pottered on. My mum was helping me on and off the toilet, as any movement hurt, and of course, the inevitable pain happened, but it wasn't half as bad as before, thank fuck. I even wet tissues to ensure it was clean and minimise pain—the things you do.

When we got back, a junior doctor came around and said he needed to look at the surgical wound. Time to whip my hoop out again and get my knees to my chest. I think he was gay though what I weirdly found a bit more reassuring. Maybe I assumed he wouldn't be staring at that area too long; who knows. I can't imagine it would be particularly pleasant for a straight doctor either. It was so painful moving trying to get my PJ's even slightly up or down. He said it looked very clean and fine, but also very irritated and angry, to be expected after surgery. However, he wanted to admit me as a precaution as my surgeon was back the following day. FML, I thought, and really did not want to be put back on that emergency surgical ward. The gentleman who had put in my cannula walked past shortly after and stopped to ask how I was, and I told him I was being admitted again. He saw I had forgotten to take the tape and cotton wool off my arm and jokingly reminded me so I wouldn't mark myself. Of course, I had when I took it off then, but it was the least of my worries. When he left my mum said how he was lovely too. I heard my friends Doctor friend talking to an old man in the cubicle next to me, well shout. The old man had come up because he was apparently struggling to hear; it turned out his ears were full of ear wax. Imagine being so well and having so much free time that a slight inconvenience such as bad ear wax, you take yourself and your wife to hospital. This kind of incident is why the NHS is fucking slammed. So many irrelevant time wasters, he literally could have phoned his GP or, even simpler, went to a chemist. Needless to say, he was sent home the dirty old bastard, away home to clean his ears, I hoped.

A lady who sorted the wards came around, and I shortly after found out I'd be going back to that shit hole of a ward. I had also discovered their level of incompetency, as my friend at work had told me about how two agency staff on the ward took her dying mother in law on a syringe driver out of her bed to sit on the toilet unattended for over an hour. When this was realised, the main staff informed her family and apologised. Like seriously WTF! The lady hadn't realised I had Crohn's or the obvious diarrhoea that went with it, and when she found out, I was changed straight away from a ward to a side room. Thank fuck, I thought as I was so exhausted and in so much pain. I didn't want to talk or be seen by anyone; it was bad enough I was going to that ward in general. I waited for a porter and was brought up. I already recognised some of the staff and the loudmouthed one of dumb and dumber was there too. I could feel my blood starting to boil. I heard him shout when he heard my name, she's been here before. I had to keep my head down and began muttering to my mum and Conor if he started, I'd go fucking mental. I lay down on the bed straight away and, of course, couldn't sleep; I still had that electric shock feeling every time I relaxed even slightly. I was feeling delirious and frustrated from lack of sleep and pain.

Conor I think, was growing more and more concerned (or fed up with my mood) as when the nurse came to check on me, he had a million questions about pain relief and all sorts of medical stuff. He actually sounded like he knew what he was talking about, so when by ourselves, the nurse asked me was he a medical professional. I confirmed he certainly was not. I think he had just heard enough from other doctors and nurses in passing to know what to ask about. That nurse was really nice though, and shortly after, a young nurse, who I recognised as the awkward one I had dealt with previously when admitted, came into my room with IV paracetamol. I knew it was going to do fuck all but, of course, got the standard spiel of how "great" it was. How about you have your gooch operated on, have shit seep into areas of your body it shouldn't having just been cut open, and tell me how "great" the 16p over the counter pain relief in liquid form is. It's annoying how doctors and nurses have no actual real-life experience with these illnesses or pain and because they've been told "it is good and effective" (in a robot voice), they believe it and not the patient. They can study all the books they want, but they really have no idea until they actually experience something first-hand. The young nurse was nice, but she was so awkward; I could feel it radiating out of her as she set up my IV drip. Maybe because we were similar in age, or she could have been younger than me, I don't know. Quite a few of them lacked bedside manner, something I've since spoken about with my friends Caitriona and Dearbhla, as their mum, who is a nurse, has said the exact same thing. It's lost these days, and as long as you have a degree, you get the job. You get that with most professions now, but it is necessary for a carer to have some level of bedside manner.

Conor and my mum both left to get me my stuff, and my mum was also going to Newcastle in England the following day to visit her auntie. She had already cancelled and rearranged a few times due to my unpredictable health, and she asked if she was ok to go this time, if not, she would cancel again. I told her no, it was fine, and I was hoping I'd get out once my surgeon saw me the following day. I lay trying to sleep whilst I was by myself for a few hours, but of course, I couldn't with the pain and constant electric shocks. I was also moved rooms to a different part of the ward. When doing my obs, the auxiliary staff asked me if I was in pain, and I replied "Yes" very firmly. They didn't care, they were there to do their job, and I was bluntly asked, "Yeah, but how much on a scale of 1-10" so that they could write it down on their chart. I think I said either 6 or 8, it's a very difficult question to answer especially as pain is so relative. I was in agony but compared to someone who had had 10 bones crushed and their skin tore open in a horrendous accident, my pain was probably nothing. I was given morphine tablets, codeine, paracetamol, all regular, yet nothing stopped the pain or the electric shocks. The only plus of it was, it was stopping me from needing the toilet, good ol' constipating pain relief. I couldn't wait to see my surgeon the next day. It was lovely and sunny, and a bank holiday Monday the following day. I had noticed that my A&E wait wasn't as long or as busy, and the ward was empty compared to before. It's amazing how people aren't sick or have nothing urgently wrong when it's sunny and a bank holiday...

That night I asked for more pain relief to try and sleep, but the nurse told me I was maxed out. Fucking unbelievable, where is the IV morphine on tap when you need it. I didn't sleep all night, and when the standard busy ward routine started at 7 am, I was glad of it. I had the standard slice of toast and cup of tea, and it wasn't too much longer until my surgeon came around. He took a look and said straight away the stitch was in too tight, which was causing the pain and the problems. The wound had also become infected and needed IV antibiotics, and was extremely inflamed and angry. You're telling me, CJ, I thought. I could literally feel the swelling. Unfortunately, I had eaten that stupid rotten toast too like an hour before, so I had to wait 6 hours for surgery. I honestly couldn't wait to be knocked out and asleep, it was now 3 days, and I was massively sleep deprived.

After they left, I phoned my mum, and she had just landed in Newcastle. I told her what Dr Tan had said, and she felt terrible that she left, and asked did she want me to come back. Obviously, I said no, it's fine; she was back in a few days and wasn't going to be able to do anything here anyway. She told me to phone my auntie Annie to let her know. She had had similar sort of surgeries for a non-Crohns related abscess in a similar area years before, and had said the repeated surgeries were excruciating too. I think they thought I just couldn't hack the pain post-op and that was the problem, not my stitch being too tight and pulling the wound along with causing other issues. I phoned Conor to let him know and that he would probably need to bring me more stuff up; he was thankfully off work. I phoned Anna-Marie then and let her know. She said she thought it was just how painful the surgery was, as after hers, she used to lie on the sofa crying with the pain and knew first-hand how painful it was. She is allergic to most pain relief as well, so was just braving it out. Hero. I'm not a fan of crying, I don't like showing my emotions so openly, even when in agony. These last few months however I had no choice between the physical pain and emotional turmoil I had been in.

Soon after, the pre-op questions started, with different rounds of nurses and doctors coming in. Most of it was a blur apart from one junior doctor I distinctly remember. Thinking back, she was funny and dramatic, but at the time in my sleep-deprived state, she was like a whirlwind. When going through the different questions, I asked why I had to wait 6 hours after eating before surgery? She extravagantly explained if they give you anaes-thetic with anything in your stomach, you can vomit and die. Noice. Apparently, food stays in your stomach for 6 hours, but I had been internally questioning if I had just made myself vomit, would they do the surgery quicker. Like it was literally a slice of toast, and I was actually so hungry again already, my stom-ach had started rumbling. Also, I wondered with active Crohn's disease does food sit that long in my stomach. During flare-ups, I have witnessed undigested food making its way out approxi-mately 2-4 hours later maximum. I never got into it because it's not like they would miraculously speed up my surgery if I said all this. She reminded me of the coach from mean girls, as I distinctly remembered his quote, "Don't have sex because you will get pregnant and die!" Like pretty much every question she asked ended up ending with, "because if you have this/done this, YOU WILL DIE!" It was all very theatrical and amusing. I actually really liked her, and it certainly lifted my mood a bit. You keep taking your job seriously my little F1 hun.

Conor came up and sat with me until the surgery, it was a waiting game. My gown and surgical socks had been delivered, and I was going to get showered before changing into them. My cousins Danielle and Shannon had surprised me with a visit, which was lovely, and we sat and chatted before I got ready. Felt bad they came all the way from Tyrone for a quick visit, it was really lovely. The chatting also distracted me a bit from the pain, and they very nicely told me what was becoming my standard, you look so well for how sick you are—all very nice lies. We laughed and chatted, and after they left, I got a quick shower and changed into my surgical gown and socks. I thought it was better to have the socks on early this time, so there wasn't a repeat of the other day and a last-minute struggle before surgery. Also, Conor was there to help. The cannula in my wrist/lower hand area had 2 of the wee lead things attached, like thin tubes and then 2 bulky connector bits at the bottom. They had been knocking off everything, and I began questioning the sanitation of them, as they had definitely hit off the toilet seat along with pretty much anything else in its path as they dangled down. I wondered where the anaesthetic would go in before surgery as there were 2 connectors, or would they flip the lid of the capped bit and put it in through a syringe. I didn't have long to wait. I think Conor and I just sat and watched Netflix's on my laptop and talked in the meantime.

One of the nice auxiliary staff, who I remembered from before and he remembered me, came in to do my obs. My resting heart rate was in the 100's, and he worryingly asked if I was in pain. I must've come across as an absolute psycho as I had been smiling, laughing and joking with him. I explained to him I was actually in agony as my stitches were in too tight, and I hadn't actually slept in days, again all said with a Cheshire Cat grin. Smile through the pain. He looked concerned, but I was getting surgery soon anyway. I was so genuinely excited to be knocked out so I could sleep.

Shortly after, at 2 pm on the dot, a nurse came in to get me. I told Conor, "cya on the flip side mothaa fuckaaa" (out of earshot of the nurse, I'm not that bad), and I was wheeled out in my hospital bed. I always cringed when being brought around in the beds or wheelchairs as passers-by stared at you. Especially visitors as they usually had the most curious looks, and when you look like a literal tramp, in PJ's and no makeup on, it's very easy to become paranoid. On my first hospital stay, I vividly remember being taken to a test with a porter, and visitors were in the lift with us just staring at me in my chair. It's very uncomfortable, especially when feeling/looking like shit. I was wheeled down to theatre and it was dead quiet. I was the only one there, and for some reason, it reminded me of a morgue. Albeit I've never been in one, it was the clinical bright lights and emptiness except for cupboard/wardrobe things and metal units. It just looked like somewhere dead bodies would be stored. It was very different to my previous two times in the City; it wasn't as nice or as modern and seemed way more clinical. I waited in my bed outside the surgical room for the nurse to bring me in when everything was ready. I had felt bad Conor was sitting upstairs, probably bored, but I would most likely be back in a few hours, and he had my laptop and his phone. I was hoping for all the morphine afterwards as well, it was sweet. As it made you a bit dopey, though, I remembered back to the people who messaged me after surgery previously, and I said I'd let them know how I was recovering. However, I had completely forgotten being that drugged up post-surgery, so here's hoping nothing was taken personally. Also, it wouldn't have been a great update. Very shortly after, barely any waiting, I was wheeled in. My anaesthetist was a man this time, previously it had been two women. He was really nice, and I told him I couldn't wait to sleep. As my cannula hadn't been used since the day before, I, of course, worried what if the vein had shut down like previously. But thankfully, it hadn't, and just like that, I was out.

The familiar feeling of waking up not knowing the time, date, where I was, happened again and I was in a ward by myself. It was much bigger than the City's and again different, more run-down looking. It kind of reminded me of an empty milking parlour, all the machinery lying about and no beds making the area look bigger but very quiet. A nurse was straight over to me, and I remember really liking her and thinking she was lovely. She asked me how I was and as I began responding, my teeth began chattering and I could barely get a word out. She asked me if I was feeling cold because I had also begun shivering during the surgery, so they had put a blanket on me, as she also got me a blanket for now. I responded, saying I didn't feel cold and wasn't sure why my teeth were chattering, and she said it could be my body coming around after the surgery. I was asked was I in pain, and I again had that oh so familiar hot rode burn going on, so it was a firm yes from me. The morphine was whopped out and administered, but I didn't get the woozy feeling like before. It done its job, though, and the pain subsided. As I lay there in recovery for the next hour, only two more patients were wheeled in, and they began the waking up process like I had done shortly before.

I had a repeat of my first surgery, and from all the fluids being pumped around me, I needed to pee so badly, but again it was only the bedpan. I was getting desperate and couldn't see a clock, so I didn't know how much longer I would be there. So, I took my chances and asked for the bedpan. What happened next was the biggest surprise of all though. I thought it would never work or be a real struggle like last time. This time however, I managed to pull myself up, push all the wires out of the way, use what strength I had to fully sit up, crouch, and pull bloody bandages away to actually pee. Whoo-hoo, what a relief. I believe what helped this time was the morphine and the dopiness. Forget dutch courage, I was all about morphine courage. I remember being amazed at how much I actually had to pee, and when I was done, I called the nurse, and she pulled back the curtain to collect the bedpan. I was so proud; I felt like one of those old people heroes who use them on the reg.

Shortly after, I was wheeled back to my ward and was looking forward to seeing Conor, although feeling sleepy again. I was wheeled back into my room, and Conor had a smirk on his face. I was glad he was there as when I was first wheeled in, I couldn't see him and was worried he was gone, but he was just behind the door. After the nurse left, he burst out laughing, and I worryingly asked what? He asked had I had morphine, to which I replied yes. He said he thought so because I looked whapped out and had a stupid smirk on my face. Also, how airily I said "Hi" and smiled when wheeled into the room. I confirmed, "Yes, mate, I'm in a good place currently" and he continued to laugh. They started the IV antibiotics shortly after, and I was told I'd be on a 24-hour course of them. I wondered because the tablet form affected my Crohns so badly, would the IV form do the same. It thankfully didn't, and from all the pain relief, I hadn't needed the toilet much in the last 24 hours, which was a God send. Even thinking about the pain made me want to scream and cry. My dad came up later to visit, and I phoned my mum to let her know how I got on. I could thankfully sleep that night as well, but as it was a hospital, it wasn't a great sleep. My obs were being taken more regularly post-surgery too, meaning I was being woken at 1 am and 5 am for checks. Also, when trying to sleep that night, I was due IV antibiotics between 11 pm – 1 am, and each dose took an hour. So with a noisy beeping machine beside you administering medicine, it's hard to sleep. It was also now concerning me, I was supposed to be in Magaluf in a matter of days. I would probably be wrecked, but I was hoping recovery would be fine, and the previous had just been a mishap.

The next day I was still bleeding heavily, and the nurses and auxiliary staff were giving me loads of maternity pads. I had been given some when leaving the hospital the other day but had a long run out. Maternity pads are literally big thick (probably a couple of inches) pads of cotton wool. They were from the hospital, so they came in plastic packaging that had to be pulled back to be opened, like a packet of ham or something. They weren't like normal sanitary pads that are sticky; these were literally a big wad of cotton wool that you would think would take ages to soak through, but this wound of mine wasn't stopping for nobody. The doctors made their rounds that morning, and my surgeon wasn't in; it was another one. They came in, and the first thing he said with a smile was, "Do you want to go home?"

I laughed and replied yes, and he said to speed things up, he would write me a prescription for a couple of weeks of the ciproflaxin antibiotics. I asked him do I need to take them as I react badly to them, and he said to double-check with my surgeon. Shortly after they left, the nurse looking after me that day came in, and I told her they were looking to send me home with antibiotics. She was literally horrified and said no way, as she lifted my notes to show me, I had been written up straight after surgery to have 24 hour IV antibiotics. I'm due another 3 doses today before I can go anywhere. Not confidence-inspiring to find out my notes hadn't been read by a surgeon, and they had tried to send me home pre-emptively. I was also glad she said this as I wasn't entirely happy going home just yet after everything that had happened. I wanted to ask my surgeon how to look after my wound and if I could go to Maga that Friday. Also, I especially did not want to be taking those tablets as I knew exactly what would happen.

That day the annoyinger one from the wards, dumb and dumber, who had previously annoyed me, was around, and I have to say I was so happy when my opinion changed of him. Previously I think, he had been showing off in a ward situation, but he was really lovely and caring when checking on me this time. He even checked to see if I was alright when not working on my part of the ward. He said when he saw my name the other day, he recognised me from before. Which I remembered him loudly stating, and me being in a serious amount of pain and sleep-deprived state, was wondering if he was going to start. Later, when he was working on my part of the ward, he was in and out getting me stuff, and I was telling him I was hoping to make it to Maga that Friday. He wasn't as optimistic as me and said I'd probably be on some strong pain meds too. I knew he was right but wasn't ready to admit it. Not until the fat lady sings, and in this case, it was Dr CJ Tan. He had been joking with Conor, saying that them two would go to Maga in my place, and I told them I'd kill them. When he was doing my obs, my blood pressure that is normally low at the best of times, was apparently extremely low, and he took it 3 times. He also said if it had been any lower or hadn't gone up to the borderline level, he would have called a doctor as it was dangerously low. He seemed really genuinely worried when taking it, but I wasn't worried as it's usually low, and probably just lack of sleep and all the medication running through my system wasn't helping.

On Tuesday, I was alone resting most of the day, reflecting on how every bank/public holiday this year I had missed because of illness or surgery. It was really sunny outside, and as a good few people had run the marathon the day before, as I was having my second emergency surgery in 2-3 days, I wondered if I would be recovered enough to run the marathon next year. Yeah, I'll totes do that, I thought, as I do every year then never do it. Conor came up after work, but it was an hour before visiting time, and I was just about to get my dinner. I had to walk to let him in at the entrance to the ward as it was locked from the outside. The older auxiliary man who had been working on my ward last time and was a real stickler for the rules, came into my room to tell Conor to leave. Needless to say, it didn't happen, and Conor talked back, and I asked could he not stay as it was an hour to visiting and I was just eating my dinner (oh, that scrumptious hospital cooked dinner...). After this, he was visibly annoyed but didn't say anything and left. A small victory I was taking, I had been alone all day and was glad of the company, especially from my boyfriend who I'm used to living with. Later on, my dad and Michael also came up to visit. It was strange as it was so bright outside, but it was always dark come visiting time any other time I had been in hospital. The seasons were changing and coming into the good summer months, yet my Crohn's was remaining and getting worse. Fuck you, Crohn's, yet again fuck you.

They had sped up how regularly I was getting my IV antibiotics to try and send me home quicker. But it was going to be after 9, nearly 10 p.m. by the time it was done, and I wasn't going anywhere. The nurse looking after me that night I remembered from before, and she was nice. I explained to her what had happened, and my worries about going home and I also wasn't sure if I had the wound packed again. This had to be sheer desperation, as it basically meant I was volunteering for the nightly blood thinning injection. They had been their least painful but still sore this hospital stay and for one reason only, morphine. She completely understood and said she would be the same and asked to check the wound. She had a look, and as Conor was still there, I remember thinking he was getting up to look too, but was actually just moving in his seat. I had, of course, pre-emptively called him out and asked WTF was he trying to look at.

He laughed and said he wasn't, but curiosity would have made me want to look if it had been the other way around. I'm not squeamish, and when he had surgery a few years before, I wanted to see his wound straight away. The nurse said she wasn't sure if it was packed out as I was quite bandaged up and said someone else was on the ward with a seton stitch, but they didn't have Crohn's. She said they're not talked about as much but quite common. I've since heard of a few people with them; an old school friend had one put in during a different operation that I think was on his stomach, but his grew out over time. My best friend Katie's sister in law has Crohn's, and she also had one, and hers fell out after a few years. My surgeon said when your body no longer needs it, this tends to happen, or the removal is a matter of cutting and pulling it. I'm not sure if you're conscious or not for this, but there have been many times where I have just wanted to cut it out myself.

I remember having some lovely nurses and auxiliary staff this day, which was really nice as I was worried it would be like last time. One of them doing the night rounds, when I was talking to her, said she was going to say to the nurse to not wake me up for more obs during the night, as I was so sleep deprived. I really appreciated it, especially as I hadn't asked; she just gathered from what I was telling her I needed sleep. I was concerned, though, as one of the nurses on that night, who also remembered me from my previous admission, and I thought could be a bit funny or rude sometimes, I didn't think it would wash with. Another auxiliary girl I also chatted to for ages. My laptop with whatever I was currently watching was usually a good point of conversation when a staff member came in. From all my admissions, they always asked what you're watching or comment on it. She saw I was watching Grim on Netflix, and was telling me she loved it and was excited for me to see the end and how I had it all ahead of me. My arm, where the cannula was, was starting to become painful, and the skin underneath was rock hard and lumpy; a rash was also starting to appear. I asked her because my IV meds were done could I get it out also, I was going home the next day, and the nurse told her yes. After she took it out, she turned around to me and in shock, said, "OMG, your poor skin is all red and out in a rash." I think it was probably leakage of medicine getting out of my vein and into the skin/tissue, and it had irritated it. It went away within a few weeks, but it shocked me how long it stayed hard and lumpy and a bit sore to touch. I must have started to pass out, but the nurse, who I thought could be a bit funny, woke me to drink 2 glasses of water as my blood pressure was seriously low again, and they needed to get it up. I think I drunk a glass then passed out. I was also woke during the night from her needing my IV machine as she was banging on it right at my head. I tried being pleasant and laughing when I first woke, confused and half asleep, but now I think she could have wheeled it out of my room and banged it, and I wouldn't have noticed. I don't even think it was used or taken in the end.

The next day I was gearing up to go home. I just needed to talk to my surgeon, so I got up, had breakfast, showered, and began packing. My medication to take away with me had been locked in the cabinet beside my bed from the day before, so there would be no waiting for pharmacy. When the doctors did their rounds, I asked to speak to my surgeon for advice before going, and they said they would get him. I was also down to my last maternity pad and went out looking for a staff member to give me more. I couldn't see anyone except for the sister nurse of the ward, easily recognised by her bright red uniform. I went up and asked her if

I could please have more, to which she was not pleasant or help-ful. "What do you mean you need these?! Who has been giving them to you? We don't give those out unless you've had a baby or un-expectantly got your period."

At this point, I didn't want or feel the need to tell her my period had just started, so I was now in extra need. I told her the nurses and auxiliary staff had been getting me them, so she said she would see what she could do. Really helpful. A while later, she arrived in my room with a good few of them, and I was shocked she actually gave me any at all. I thanked her and said I unfor-tunately had a wound in a really awkward place and was still bleeding loads, to try and defuse the awkward situation. She said nothing and literally rolled her eyes at me. WTF is her problem.

After that, Dr Tan came around with her, and I asked him my questions and if I could be in Maga in a few days. He said be-cause of my age, and how young I was, he didn't want to tell me no, but I couldn't go to the beach as no sand could get in the wound or get in the pool, it had to be kept very clean. It was basically a polite no, but I was still trying to play it by ear. I really did not want to be missing my cousins Hen do. Especially as I was a bridesmaid and was also thinking of the massive waste of money because I wasn't earning when off work, I wouldn't financially be able to take the recommended 6 weeks off to re-cover even if I needed it. I really like my workplace, but this was seriously annoying and adding stress when not well. After speaking to Dr Tan, I thanked him, and he always shook my hand and smiled; he's so nice. As he was leaving, the bitch sister actu-ally turned around whilst rolling her eyes at me AGAIN and said, "I'll let you go, we've wasted enough of your time," and giggled to Dr Tan. He said nothing to her and left, and she followed suit. Fucking cunt. I was really taken back, and I think so was he.

I then began finishing packing immediately. My dad and Conor were both working, so I phoned my auntie Sharon to come and get me, and she was on her way shortly. The cunty sister came back in and, to top it all off, said, "Sarah, A&E is awfully busy today, and we need your bed, so you need to leave." I was currently dressed and all my belongings were packed on top of the bed, so she was either blind, stupid, rude, or an unfortunate combination of them all. I'll go with the latter. I said to her, " Yes, I know I'm packed and waiting on a lift ", and she left. I put my coat on and asked one of the nurses to get a porter so they could bring my stuff downstairs; I also needed the antibiotics from the locked cabinet beside my bed. Dr Tan had said as a precaution to take the antibiotics as the other doctor had prescribed them. I was dreading it and already knew it would fuck shit up.

There was a lovely nurse who I remembered from before that was sorting this out, when the sister came back into my room and said surprised, "Oh, I didn't mean you had to go now, I meant you could sit in our waiting room". WTF, stupid bitch, like I'm going to wait in your stupid fucking waiting room when I can go home. I responded saying, no, it's fine, my lift is coming anyway, and I was only staying until I had spoken to Dr Tan. She then said the porters are all busy and will take a while, so the older man on the ward (who Conor had refused to leave for the previous day) would take my stuff down. The lovely nurse who was there was really caring, and I remembered this from before. She got the antibiotics out of the cabinet and saw how many a day I had to take, and said she'd get me sorted now and start the dose, proceeding to pour me water and get them out of the box. The sister took great umbrage at this and intervened, actually telling the nurse to "stop fussing over her she can do it herself" then stood staring at her. The poor nurse was visibly uncomfortable but ignored her. The sister eventually fucked off after a few seconds of lingering as the nurse began a conversation with me. WTF is this bitch's problem!!

I said to my mum on the phone later, and she said the sister obviously remembered me from before and the complaining my mum had done to her on the phone about the staff and decided to take it out on me. How professional of a fucking late 50s, probably in her 60's woman who is supposed to be running the ward. The bitch had a stupid fucking fringe and some of the worst blonde, blocky, chunky highlights on top of brown hair I had ever seen in my life. I don't even feel bad for thinking/ saying it because she was a massive cunt. It takes a real icon to pull off bangs, hun, and you certainly ain't one. Her hair also clashed massively with her uniform, it was not a lewk. Grow up bitch, and don't take your annoyance out on a 24-year-old who had been treated like shit by your staff and was in for her 3rd emergency surgery spaced over a few months. The ward was completely desensitised; they need to do training/practice renewal seminars or some kind of shit to sort that out. Their behaviour and attitudes stick with the patients for life, yet this is the equivalent of just another day in the office for them.

The lovely nurse however, made sure I got my tablets into me and began asking what happened and how I was. I told her and she said God love me and that the pain from the stitch/electric shock feeling would have been nerve damage. So, it was why all the pain relief wouldn't have worked and been very painful. She told me she had nerve damage on her thumb one time, and that was sore enough and nothing you can do about it. As we continued chatting, I was laughing about the maternity pads and how they looked, and said my period had just started as well, so they're extra handy at the moment. She was so nice and sympathetic and said I was probably feeling worse just post 2 surgeries, and that was going on too. But it was a really good sign that it came, as I had so much going on in my body between Crohn's/medication/surgeries, the fact my body was still going ahead and doing that showed in that aspect I was healthy and continuing to power on through. She helped me out of the room with my bag, and I thanked her and walked down with the older gentleman.

We were chatting, and he said I needed to take the whole 6 weeks off to recover, and I said I didn't think I could because I wasn't getting paid and needed the money. He was really nice and helpful and began telling me different things I could apply for, as he had to do the same when having an operation previously. I looked into it but couldn't apply for them in the end. I was attempting to apply for PIP's for a second time too, and knew again it would be unsuccessful.

He wished me luck, and I thanked him and waited at the chairs by the window for Sharon. He was a really nice man, he just loved the rules. When I saw her, the taxi's outside the hospital were parked the whole way up to the entrance, so I knew I'd be quicker walking a bit further down to her. My bag was soo heavy though, and I would barely carry it. I was also obviously in pain, but had no choice but to lug it quickly down. I don't think I should've been doing that post-surgery, but I wanted home and didn't really have an option. I also looked fine to passers-by, so nobody moved, and I was practically walked through when struggling down with my bag. If only people could see what was going on underneath or inside. I threw my bag in the back seat and jumped in the front. I couldn't wait to get home, but it was bittersweet as I wouldn't be getting back to my flat for God knows how long. Sitting was horrible, but the journey home wasn't too long, and I was glad to get home and be out of that hell hole.

I was still heavily pain meded up and was feeling ok, sore to walk and I couldn't sit like a normal person, but was generally alright. When we got in, Sharon made us lunch and very kindly went to the chemist across the road to get me more pain relief. She said she also ordered one of those rings you can sit on and I didn't know what she was talking about. When it arrived a few hours later, it was literally a white foam rubber ring looking thing for sitting on. I think it's for people who have just had babies, but I used it anyway. I unfortunately then noticed I was getting sorer when sitting on it, so I googled if I should be sitting on it, and it said no because it puts more pressure on the surgical wound. Annoying as that was, it was greatly appreciated, and I thought it initially helped. We had been talking, and I felt like I shouldn't complain as Sharon's surgery involved having her stomach cut open and 80% of it removed, including some lymph nodes. However, she said she'd rather have her op 10 times over than go through what I did. I now agree, turns out having an open wound where they cut a hole in your gooch, put a stitch through it and having body functions whilst trying to heal is not pleasant. I had no idea what was ahead of me, and I'm glad I didn't. If I did, I wouldn't have done it, and I'd have taken the sepsis and inevitable death.

Game of Crohn's

My mum arrived back from Newcastle later and was off for the following week. I was hoping I could still make it to Maga, which was now 2-3 days away, and when doped up on pain relief and feeling ok, it all seems achievable. Needless to say, a repeat of before happened, the hospital pain meds wore off, and codeine and paracetamol were no longer cutting it. The bastarding ciproflaxin antibiotics I was unnecessarily sent home with began their work of causing a flare-up in a matter of hours. Normally with Crohn's, I've always found first thing in the morning it's at its worst, but for some reason, these tablets made it worse at night. The next few weeks were the worst of my life and were insanely brutal. The flare-ups from the antibiotics meant that shit was still seeping out of this new surgical wound as my body still hadn't learned yet it wasn't supposed to be used. The pain was excruciating, and my mum thought I had sepsis as I was sweating, shaking, and nearly losing consciousness continually from the pain. I was still bleeding as I was post-op too, but it was starting to calm down.

Numerous times during the day but mostly anywhere between 11 pm to 1 am when me and my parents were trying to sleep, the worst happened. The regular pain relief meant I should have been constipated, but the antibiotics were doing the opposite. So, unfortunately, my body was trying to do the 2 things at once. You would think it would perfectly balance things out, but oh no, instead had the shits for a really long time, and shit was coming out of the wound at a ridiculously slow speed. The only relief was when the wound was clean, and this was never-ending, going on for hours every night. My mum stayed up with me, holding me whilst I sat squirming on the toilet while screaming. I repeatedly screamed, "this is fucking brutal", and "please kill me, I can't do this", whilst physically shaking and sweating. She kept running me Milton baths so I could clean myself and get relief, but it never lasted long because, of course, there was always more.

Whenever I needed the toilet, it again felt like I was giving birth, then someone was throwing acid over me. The dread I had every time I knew I needed the toilet and what was to come. I initially fought back the tears, knowing what I was shortly up against, but after a few days, I just broke down before. It never got any easier or less painful. Afterwards, exhausted, I would stand in the shower or be on all fours in the bath; the pain was so bad I needed the water to clean the wound to get any relief. I must have been having at least 10 Milton baths a day.

I figured out pretty soon that I wouldn't be making it to Maga, and I was so gutted. I felt so bad as I was a bridesmaid and missing the main Hen do. I tried getting my flight money back from EasyJet, and I got 12 quid back. Thanks, EasyJet, so compassionate even with my medical note from my GP saying I was in no way fit to fly after emergency surgery. Off work, earning no money, missing out on an important Hen do, in constant excruciating pain, I was not in a good way. By Friday, I should have been in Maga, but Conor came to stay at my house instead. I had barely seen him and also had barely slept.

I was in so much pain I couldn't lie down without it being sore, and because I was lying in funny positions all the time trying to get comfortable, I was now sore all over. I tried sleeping with a pillow under me, every position, nothing worked, everything was painful. On my side, on my back, on my front. You name it, I tried it, and I could not get any relief. I was desperate for sleep. Apparently, I was "hard work" and "grumpy" all the time from being in chronic pain. My best friend's sister is in chronic pain and really unwell from doctors misdiagnosing her, and she has permanent spinal damage as a result. I had been told her personality had completely changed since this, and she was really hard to be around. I totally got it. Apparently, King Henry VIII went psycho and killed his wives after a bad horse-riding injury, which led to his bone coming out of his leg, and it never healed. Again, I got it. I thought every other person around me was a fucking lucky cunt, living their lives pain-free whilst I couldn't sleep and in so much permanent pain. I was done.

I had been googling how much pain relief I needed to take to overdose but how to best make it look like an accident. It turns out you need a lot, and it isn't easy to make it look like an accident. I was in so much pain my opinion on suicide had also completely changed. People who had committed suicide had become my heroes; they were all out of pain and finally resting. I believed the problem is all the miserable, selfish cunts left behind. The dead have ended their misery, and it's the rest of us that have to go on and feel guilty that we didn't do enough, throwing around phrases like, "it's so terrible, they should have said something". Humans are disgusting. You didn't care about your loved ones enough when they were alive, and they made a lucky escape getting away from you whilst you wallow in your pity party of misunderstanding and guilt. This rant isn't about anyone in particular; I just viewed death and suicide very different at the time as I longed for an escape. For all we know, this is hell we are living in now, and those that are dead have escaped it. I certainly was living in hell and wanted it to end. I kept wondering if I was a bad person and what I had done to deserve it. Or maybe in a past life, I was a cunt and getting my karma. I lay in bed every night crying with the pain and frustration, longing to sleep. Conor also told me I was becoming like our mutual friend's sister and did I really want to be like that, almost as a warning. I got really angry at this as he saw me suffering immensely but could only think of "how difficult" I was being, but not taking into consideration why. He was being extremely fickle, and he wanted the good fun, funny, laid back Saz. Not the exhausted, recovering, in extreme agony one. I barely saw or spoke to him compared to normal over those few weeks, and he was obviously staying away.

My parents, who were very against me smoking grass, had begun actually asking Conor to give me some to try to help the pain in any way. I took it, but it wasn't working. On the Friday after a smoke, I was so exhausted and just wanted some normality as we tried to chill in my back room and watch something on Netflix's. I was trying to lie on the floor on my stomach with loads of blankets and pillows underneath me to watch TV, but nothing helped. It must have been hitting around 11 pm as my stomach started to go, and I knew what was going to come. Before I even made it to the toilet, whinging and crocodile tears had started as I knew the pain that was ahead of me. I literally despised every second of it and hated all my doctors and surgeons for doing this to me. Conor wanted to make sure I was alright and came up with me.

Then the agony mixed with yelling, shaking, and sweats began. My mum had bought a load of cotton wool pads and brought in a basin that was filled with water so I could try and keep dabbing the wound clean whilst on the toilet. The screams became so loud it soon woke up my mum, who came in to try to help. I was sweating so much that she shouted for Conor to get a thermometer to check my temperature in case it really was sepsis. She checked, and my temperature was fine; it was visibly obvious the pain I was in, and my body was not responding well. I was concerned this was considered "normal" after surgery and what the fuck was the doctors putting me through. I was winching and screaming; all dignity was gone. Crohn's is not a dignified disease, and I thought I'd lost my dignity to doctors when subjected to their tests/procedures. This, however, was next level. Never in a million years would I have asked or expected either of them to do this, but here we were. Both my mum and Conor watched me as I screamed on the toilet, helping me in and out of baths or to hose myself down. I had remembered watching Loose

Women and Kaye Adams saying when giving birth, the window was open, and she lay there not giving a fuck. I remember being shocked, thinking no way you'd definitely care, but this was now again something else I totally got. When you're in that much pain, you really don't give a fuck about anything but getting out of it.

As these episodes were worse throughout the night, another one happened an hour or so later. Never long intervals in between either; there was no winning. Probably at about 1 am, I was back in the bathroom, but it was getting worse. Conor and I had gone to bed to try and sleep, and this had started. I remember being in the bath in just a bra screaming for him to hose the wound down. The pain was too much, and it was all obviously too much for Conor to handle too. His uncle, years previously before we were going out, had killed himself, and he was extremely sensitive to the expression, "makes me want to kill myself". I had learned this the hard way as any time I had said the expression without thinking, and he'd scream at me and really go off on one then not talk to me. He was unsurprisingly triggered. Well, at this point, sleep-deprived, on all fours with liquid burning shit coming out a newly formed surgical wound for what felt like the millionth time, crying, shaking, sweating, and screaming, I shouted, "I can't fucking do this, somebody fucking kill me I want to die". He snapped at this, and on the back, he hit me. Yes, he hit me on the back and shouted, "don't say that, you know how much that pisses me off", and completely went off on one. At this point, I was soo fucking done. The hysterics grew louder; how fucking dare he make this about himself!!! He couldn't have put his stupid emotions aside for 2 fucking minutes without this being about him and a phrase he didn't like. I was shocked, upset, and outraged on top of all the other emotions I was already feeling. I literally felt like collapsing and began to sink further into a heap. Not long after, my mum came in, as she heard the screams growing and saw the red hand mark on my back. She asked what happened, and I didn't know what to say.

I was obviously going to tell her but didn't want a fight on top of everything else going on, so I was going to do it when he left. He was embarrassed too and didn't know what to say. She asked again, and he said he had done it but didn't mean to. Surprisingly, my mum didn't say much, just shortly after told him to go to bed as he must be wrecked. HE MUST BE WRECKED!!!! I told her what happened, and she said, "Sarah, you know he's not coping and hasn't been. He literally can't cope when you're sick. It's very obvious." She was right.

This continuing cycle happened throughout the night, and of course, Conor had passed out and no waking him any time I was up during the night. A bit like the first night when I done it all by myself. It was another reminder with this illness how alone I am, even when the one person in the world I'm supposed to be the closest to is there. My mum helped me during the night, she definitely wasn't sleeping, and I felt really bad. The coming morning as the saga repeated itself, whilst yet again on all fours in the bath; blood clots started coming out of the wound. At this point, I screamed, "GET ME TO FUCKING HOSPITAL NOW!!!!" I had never volunteered to go to the hospital in my life. I normally put up a fight and refuse to go before being dragged. There were no arguments, and my mum brought me straight up. She said to the person at the A&E gates I needed to be left up outside the A&E so we could park there instead of having to walk from the car park. I couldn't physically do it, I could barely walk up the stairs FFS.

We weren't long in A&E as anyone post-surgery will be seen quite quickly if it was within 6 weeks of the op. It was also a gloriously sunny (for NI) Saturday early afternoon, so yano why would people be sick. My heart rate was really high when doing the obs, showing how much pain I was in, and some junior surgeons saw me quite soon after. They examined the wound and apologised as they could see how visibly angry and sore it was as they poked about. I was pleasant and told them it was fine, although it was agony, and I did twitch at the pain. My mum said if it was anyone else, I'd have probably told them where to go. I agreed and said, "Aye, they'd be told to fuck off", and the doctor laughed. It was a really nice young male and female looking after me, and I recognised the guy from my first surgery as one of the junior doctors doing the pre-op questions. He didn't remember me thank fuck, as I recalled asking him questions about smoking grass and anaesthetic. He said as long as it wasn't in the last 48 hours, and I felt like saying try 24 but didn't. With hindsight, I realise what I did pre-op was probably quite stupid, but I was unwell and didn't care or think at the time. He had a look at my MRI and came back and said, "Wow, that was complex", looking shocked. I laughed and said, yeah, that's not the first time I had heard that, and he said the surgery I had was the best option. I said my surgeon and consultant had explained the same due to the different complications and where the abscess/fistula was. I told them about the antibiotics, and when I was asked how I was sent home, they were horrified. No guidance and wrong medication. They apologised and said what I had been through, I never should have, and never should have been in the pain I was in. They told me no more antibiotics, which should help, especially as my body was learning that the wound shouldn't be used for toileting purposes and when things solid up, it would get a lot better. I was told when to take my pain relief and what I should be taking. Also given anaesthetic gel for the wound, which I should have been given before leaving hospital. I felt a lot better after the lovely doctors explained everything, I was just unbelievably frustrated at how I was left. I could tell when they apologised, they meant it and felt really sorry for me from their tone and the looks on their faces. It was sad to be such a pity party; I really hated it but knew they understood from their profession. The funniest thing the guy doctor said to me though, was when he was explaining the current bowel movements. Due to active Crohn's and the medication I was currently on, they were not normal. It took everything in me not to go, "What?! This isn't normal?!" extremely sarcastically, but it probably wasn't the time for a joke.

I went home feeling a good bit better and big-time, realising I couldn't have been on the Hen do. I mean I realised that when I couldn't sit properly and would need to be seated on the aeroplane for a few hours, I probably shouldn't go, but I still considered it. The pain was horrendous, and although the gel and new guidance etc., all helped, every time I needed the toilet, it was still horrendous. My mum was going back to work on Monday, and I was really scared about being by myself in case something happened. She told me she had to go back, and I'd be fine, but of course, I was worried. The pain was so bad I physically couldn't move to make the Milton bath and had to scream for my mum to help, but I'd have no choice but to power through. I was used to it at this point and didn't like asking for help, I don't in general, but at that time, I really desperately needed it. To prepare, I stopped calling for my mum even when I needed her as I'd have no choice from Monday. My mood was so low the thought of killing myself in an empty house was screaming, "perfect opportunity". But I was so physically weak and inept it would have most likely failed, and from previous research, my pain meds wouldn't make it look like an accident.

Monday came, and I learned to cope. I still wasn't sleeping well from the pain and watched a serious amount of Ru Paul's Drag Race to get me through. The pain was still excruciating when I needed the toilet, but things were getting better as I was off the antibiotics, so less frequent toilet trips. I had started pre-running a bath as I knew I'd need it after the toilet, then would hobble or crawl my way across depending on pain levels when I was done. This was my routine for the following week, and at the weekend, my best friend Katie, my granny and Sharon all called. I was still in pain, but seeing people was a distraction. The isolation wasn't nice as I was unable to do anything except watch TV, and my mind was so bored. Conor and I hadn't been getting on either, he was completely withdrawing, and I hadn't seen him in a while. It was very upsetting, as he would love to go on about how he was my partner and always there for me, but when I needed him most, he was gone. Talk is cheap, and he was really proving that. There was always an excuse as to why he couldn't come to visit when our flat was 5 minutes away, and I knew his schedule/routine. I was so lonely and in so much emotional and physical pain. I was spending all day by myself in agony for weeks. There was nothing he could do, and I knew that, but all I wanted was for him to be there and keep me company/distracted. He literally just had to sit there and hug or talk to me, but it was obviously too much. I hadn't asked for anything else just to see my best friend.

It was really good seeing Katie, and she had brought her dog Lola, who is the cutest bundle of joy ever. My dog Codi is scared of her, so the interactions were also funny to watch. When asked how I was, I was getting sick of my mum interrupting and telling people I was fine and coming to a turning point. Yes, I wasn't as bad as what I was, but I was still in a lot of pain and walking like a dick. She had this stupid 10-day rule or something her granny used to tell her about people recovering from surgery, and as I was just over the 10 days, this made everything fine in her head as I essentially hadn't died. After Katie left, I had been messaging Conor and was frustrated as I hadn't seen him in over a week. He was also actively making plans to try and go out drinking instead of seeing me. He literally could have sat and drunk with me, but he didn't want to be anywhere near me. It was so selfish. When he was sick, I had cancelled plans to stay with him and make sure he was alright when his ailments were much less serious. I was also thinking about the times both pre and post diagnoses when I didn't feel well or didn't want to go out, and he had practically forced me to just to accommodate him, justifying it with, "but you're always alright when you're out". There was an unequal balance of give and take, and I was becoming more and more aware of it. I financially supported him way more than he supported me, as he always said he never had any money, and there was always a stupid excuse as to why. When in reality, it was the fact he would happily spend hundreds unnecessarily on a night out but refuse to even spend a pound on his lunch, which I regularly slabbered at him for.

I was showing my granny something on my phone when Conor's responses started coming through, and it was clear we were having a fight. My granny read it and took his side and said how he needed a break too and should consider how lucky I am as most men would have just left me, and he was better than most. My mother agreed, and I was now fighting back the tears at their stupid misogynistic opinions. These are both cultchy women who have their husband's dinners on the table when they want it, and my grandad doesn't even know how to make himself a cup of tea. I might have been depressed and in pain, but I'm so glad that I recognised my value even in those low moments. I am a wonderful fucking person who deserves to be loved unconditionally by my other half and be supported in my time of need!! That is literally the foundation of ANY relationship, whether romantic or platonic. Any so-called "man" who leaves their loved one because they cannot cope during sickness is not a man and obviously doesn't love them very much. Those people are worse than the shit my Crohny bowels produce, and I have no time for that in my life; in fact, no one should. I should have pitied them for their warped views more than being angry, as they obviously don't have very high self-worth, or they are genuinely that brainwashed by misogyny. Or maybe they actually love their husbands that much, and maybe I should be jealous of that. They realised this struck a chord as I was holding back tears and said no more. I'd have stormed away if I could, but a pathetic slow hobble didn't have the same kind of effect. I talked about this with my mum a while later, and she said she only said what she did because she didn't realise the full extent of what was really going on. I had been keeping my relationship problems to myself, hoping this would all blow over.

Later the fighting with Conor continued as he decided to go out. I was so angry and fed up, and I messaged him, saying I didn't want to go out with him anymore. He didn't deserve any more than a text as I sat in a heap crying my eyes out. He phoned me not long after to try to calm me down and said he wasn't giving our relationship up over something stupid after nearly 4 years together. I appreciated it and calmed down after initially putting up a fight, repeatedly telling him I'm done. The worst bit was he choose to go to his mate's house and just drink a few beers and play Xbox. I found that insulting as I would sit with him and the boys in the flat and do this. So if that's all he really wanted to do, I again would have accommodated him. He said he would come to see me the next day, which I was glad of, but it was all becoming too little too late. Things got a bit better, and when I did see him, I explained how lonely I was and was spending nearly 24 hours by myself every day in chronic pain. The days were so long and painful, especially as I could do minimal, and I was so bored/fed up. He got it but said he needed a break too. I got it, he was 25, and none of this was normal. I did not want him as my carer, he was my boyfriend, and we wanted our normal life back. But what he had been doing wasn't a break, it was a fucking holiday from the relationship, and so many alarm bells which I had been repressing or ignoring for years were starting to ring louder and louder.

The next few weeks consisted of recovering and getting my next dose of infliximab (which really helped to ease the flare), brides-maid fittings and wedding prep. My days were so basic I considered the following a real highlight. One day, I was sitting in my garden, the weather was actually really sunny for Northern Ireland, and my ginger mother had the audacity to keep banging on about how my Casper like skin needed some colour ahead of the wedding (it's called fake tan Laura). I needed to be careful though, as I had been told that my skin would react differently in sunlight now due to the immune suppressors I was on. This was true as I burned way quicker than I normally would. I was sitting on my laptop trying to catch a pathetic tan, when my dog started going mental and chasing what I assumed was a large cat that had walked beside the bench I was sitting on. It was only when I saw the bushy tail and red fur did I realise he was chasing a fox away from me. It was the middle of the day, and 20 something degrees; what the fuck was a fox doing out. I must've looked like the equivalent of a tasty kebab at the end of a night out, all sun creamed up and glistening/sweating in the sun. Well done, Codi, for protecting me. But that was a highlight, showing the lack of excitement in my life.

Katie visited one day to record me for her work as a patient for her hospital's trust for some project they were doing. I wasn't part of the Dundonald trust but wished I was as I had heard their hospital is meant to be amazing (for a hospital), and the Royal currently wasn't in my good books. I felt better putting on makeup and dressing respectfully, not sweats and a nightgown. It was funny as we had to keep retaking the videos as I read too fast from the script prompter thing. Katie kept joking, saying I looked so well they wouldn't believe I had surgery or was sick when she had to show the video. That's what usually happened, and when I met some of her work friends on nights out months later, they said the same and that I didn't look sick and would assume I'm really healthy. The perks of makeup and an invisible illness. Katie told me I'd make a good weather woman from my sunny disposition, I'm not sure I would, but I'd give it a go.

My friends Erin and Caitrionia also visited one day, and it really cheered me up. They very kindly brought presents from themselves and our other friends Ashleigh and Rhiannon. There was honestly no need but greatly appreciated, and I still wear the PJs and nightgown regularly. We sat and chatted for ages, and it was a great distraction, especially when in pain. I was aware I looked like a dick when walking them to and from the door and apologised for the slow limpy hobble. It was so nice having a bit of normality for a few hours before going back to the ever depressing, lonely recovery.

I had bridesmaid dress fittings and was sad I was not in the shape I wanted to be. Ill-health took that out of my hands. I had intended to start exercising in January to be ready for June, but that didn't happen. Thankfully, the dress fit, though, and only needed to be taken up lengthwise. Zoe had said she was glad in the end I couldn't make it to the Hen do as they all came back sick and on antibiotics. That sweet rushinoff cough got them, and she said I would never have made the wedding if I had gone. It was a good thing in hindsight, but I was still gutted I couldn't go. I was telling one of the other bridesmaids, her husband's sister, Simone, about what had happened, and she said what Zoe had previously said to me, I'm not going to blink at childbirth. The number of women with children who have said that to me after I've described what happened post-surgery. I think I will be sweet though, but I'd take an epidural; nobody likes a martyr when there are free drugs on the go. The dressmaker was so lovely as well and asked how I was as she knew I had been going in for surgery. At the previous fitting, she told me about her daughter, who has Crohn's and what she had been through. Our stories were similar, she had abscesses that wouldn't go, but she had five seton stitches in. FIVE!!! I said God love her, and I couldn't even imagine the pain. She then told me that they needed forceps when her daughter was giving birth and pulled a stitch out. I screamed internally but vocally let out a loud, "FUCK". I think I'd have sued, stupid cunts. She said it was the unhealing abscesses that lead to an ileostomy, and her whole back passage needed to be taken away. I've heard other Crohnies refer to it as a Barbie bum. But her daughter never looked back after it. I was glad to hear this as she had suffered for years.

She had also said the same as me, the Crohn's she could handle, but the pain from the abscesses and the surgeries were too much. I was glad it wasn't just me who thought that. My mum's

friend in works sister was likewise going through a similar process; she had had Crohn's for years but was unwell again and
in hospital from an abscess. She had her wound dressed and
repacked every day, and the thought of the pain killed me as I
recalled the packing of my wound coming out and how horrible
it was. Her and her husband wanted to have another baby too,
and they didn't know what was going to happen after all this.
It's so sad how chronic illnesses can take away what is so normal
for another person. I was starting to do normal things again.
Conor and I even made it out for dinner one evening as I could
sit like a normal person again without it hurting. I had even
made it on casual nights out to our local pubs with friends, and
I think everyone expected me to look like shit. I kept being told
how good I was looking, and it was definitely makeup and also
the fact I hadn't had surgery on my face. Everything about my
illness and surgery was invisible, so nobody would ever have a
clue unless told. The bit of normality was nice, though, and Zoe's
wedding was super close now. I had been worried if I was going
to make it up the aisle or not or if I'd need a Segway to do my
walking for me. It would have been quite the entrance. At the
wedding rehearsal, the nerves kicked in for me (I wondered how
the fuck the bride and groom were feeling), and I began wondering would I need the toilet during the service and, if so, what
would happen. I had made an escape route in my head to discretely leave if I had to.

We stayed over in the Stormont hotel the night before as the
whole wedding took place there. I was already paranoid about
the morning as my Crohns is always worse then and about
bathroom access. Thankfully on the day, it was all fine, and the
Crohns was really settling again, but of course, I had a precautionary imodem just in case. From the night before into the
whole next day, everything was just amazing and really lifted
my spirits. We had such fun, and I, Kathy (my Cousin Martin's
wife, who is Zoe's sister-in-law), and Simone were in a room
together and couldn't sleep. We stayed up to 3 or 4 am when

we had to be up at 7 am, laughing and talking shite. We could hear the others sleeping in the other room and wondered how we didn't wake them with the laughing and talking. When 7 am came, we were surprisingly awake and had the best morning getting ready. The whole day was amazing and so full of love; I wished we could do it all over again. I kept being told no one could believe I had just had surgery for how well I looked, the power of makeup and a nice dress, I guess.

I was starting to feel normal again, and the following week, I returned to work. I needed to start earning again, and when off, I had reapplied for PIPs. Of course, it was unsuccessful, but I tried. The worst bit was when I was finally interviewed; when explaining my surgeries and illness etc., I had said how it sounds gross, and the guy had the audacity to say, "don't worry, I understand these things because of my medical background." No, hun, you informed me you were an occupational therapist, not a specialist doctor, who has sold his soul to become a PIP's interviewer, aka a massive cunt. Fuck off with your pathetic delusions of grandeur. Also, as PIP's is notorious for the interviewer lying and making up stuff you had apparently said, when I received the big fat NO letter, I was beyond affronted at the comments. The incriminating bastard had said I "walked my dog" when I never said such things, he purely put this down because he saw Codi. How dare you use my baby against me! Every rejection letter was beyond insulting and always left me feeling upset and deflated, along with furious, bewildered, and ready to slit the interviewer's throat. That death would be too kind for them though, perhaps slow impalement instead. I can't even remember the rest of the lies and insults I read. They always made me shed a tear, and I was always so upset/angry that this stupid fucking process did this to me.

It's all coming up Saz... oh wait

I returned back to normal life and moved back into the flat full time after the wedding and was beyond glad. It was coming into summer, and the weather I was actually able to enjoy now, not stuck inside, unable to move. As I settled back into the flat and my health began to return, doubts that had been pushed to the back of my mind for a long time were starting to creep up. It was getting to the point where I couldn't ignore them and was scared of my emotions. I didn't want to be with Conor. It was strange as normally before I go into a relationship, I get the fear and think, WTF am I doing, my single life is so sweet. But now I had been with him for 4 years, and we were living together. I had assumed that was it and hadn't thought of a life outside of him. I know we were so young and only 24 and 25, but nothing had gone wrong. We still got on super well most of the time, but my feeling were out of my control and rapidly changing/being discovered. It was really shit. This was the point where we were supposed to go travelling because my health was coming back, but I was facing the realisation I no longer loved him romantically and didn't want to be with him. Also, due to the fact we had been to-gether so many years and living together, melters had been ask-ing the annoying question every long-term couple gets asked, "When are you two getting married?" how about never, hun. We had never discussed marriage, well, not properly. Whenever the subject was broached, we both responded with, "we'll talk about it when we're 30". It was certainly not a priority. The thought also utterly terrifies me, and I'm just not sure I have that level of commitment in me. My mum says the cliché of "I just haven't found the right person yet", but I don't think that'll ever happen.

Weddings are great fun, but my own, I just don't know about. I'd love a day of partying in a fancy dress, but all the rest I'd leave.

I kept this to myself and hoped the feelings would go away, but the more I ignored them, the stronger they got. It was early July 2018, and so much had changed so far this year. The repercussions of breaking up with Conor meant losing my best friend, moving out of the flat with the boys, and back home permanently. Also, most likely causing a divide in our friendship group, and I was facing the harrowing thought that no one else would ever want to go out with me again because of the Crohns baggage. It's strange as I'd be horrified if another person said this about themselves in relation to an illness they suffered from, but when it comes to yourself, you're 10 times harsher. It was also the loudest thought, who could ever love me.

After a few weeks of the drowning thoughts, I had started to confide my feelings in a few friends, and they were all amazingly supportive. They told me I needed to do what was right for me, and if it wasn't being with Conor, that was ok. My mum and dad said the same; they both loved him and thought he was a great guy, but I needed to end it and do not dare think about settling if I wasn't happy. I was also beginning to think Conor probably should have been guessing something was up, I was kind of avoiding him in the flat, and we were spending no time together. However, I realised though that was part of the problem. Between me being sick and us being so comfortable with each other, even previously, we barely spent time together in the evenings. We were both always doing our own thing or entertaining ourselves. We only ate dinner and watched TV together before bed, but this summer, I had been convinced by friends to start watching Love Island, and he was refusing to watch it with me. So, for that month to six weeks or whatever it was, I was always asleep by the time he came upstairs.

It was one day, about a month into these feelings, he started talking about a holiday. I froze with guilt and didn't know what to say. I kept avoiding the question and walked out of our room into our bathroom, shouting behind me, "I don't know", and shut the door. I had tried bracing up the courage a few times to talk to him, but there never seemed like a right time. WTF do I say to him, the one person in the world I don't want to hurt, and I knew this would kill him. I didn't think he was coming into the bathroom, and I had burst out crying. I'm really not a crier, but I didn't know what else to do. He walked in, and I tried pretending I was fine, and he hugged me and said, "Aww, I know you're worried about your Crohn's, and it flaring up, but don't worry, you're doing really well."

The guilt nearly killed me. I walked out again into the bedroom and literally couldn't speak. He followed me again and asked what was wrong. I kept trying to speak but muffled half words that made no sense is all that came out. I kept repeating then, "I just don't know, I just don't know", whilst pacing and crying in a tizzy. He definitely thought I was insane. When he asked what about, I managed to get out, "About us. I just don't know, I love you so much, and nothing's happened, but I just don't know about a future." I couldn't believe I said it. I knew once it was said there was no getting it back. He was confused and upset but was taking it better than I thought. He was probably in shock. I really didn't know what to say when he asked me to explain. How could I try to explain it to him when I couldn't even get my own head around it? He didn't understand that, and I get it; I wouldn't if it was the other way around.

The minefield that was currently my mind and emotions was not making sense, and articulating was extremely difficult. What could I say really to soften the blow? Thanks for four great year's babe, but I just woke up and didn't feel the same one day. It was essentially true, but it made no sense to me who was experiencing it, so it made even less to him on the receiving end. I had fallen out of love, and all I wished for was a tablet I could take to change how I felt. I actually told him that numerous times. It was so shit, and the timing seemed extra bad as it was a Thursday evening, and Conor was out on a work night out the following day straight after work, and Michael had a friend coming over from England for the weekend. We were all going to be out on Saturday as well, and it didn't leave much discussion time, especially for a deep and upsetting conversation. The first thing in my mind was, I bet this will upset my Crohn's, and for once, I was right.

Conor had come home drunk on Friday, and I knew the following day would be horrible. He could barely stand, and Michael and his friend had returned to our flat with Michael's work friends. I had turned down going out but might as well have, as I was woken at 1 am when they all came back in, to the sound of Hanson – MMMBop. Before going downstairs to tell Michael and his mate, I was about to MMMBop them. I was then up until around 4 am between talking to Conor and the other ones downstairs, and then trying to help Conor stand and eat before passing out. Before we fell asleep, he had drunkenly tried asking me to talk about how I was feeling, but I said he was drunk and we'd leave it until the morning. Before passing out though, he managed to say, "You don't love me anymore". I replied, "Don't say that". It really hurt to hear and hurt even more it might be true. He passed out, and I cried myself to sleep.

The next day was equally as horrible, we were having a pre in our house, and quite a few were coming around. Conor and I had tried discussing how I was feeling, and he really wanted to try. We acknowledged that our date days and spending time together had really gone down the drain between me being ill and living with friends. We used to go out at least once a week for dinner and then have date days most weekends. Now we never went out by ourselves, anytime we were out it was always as a house or with friends. Or, a lot of times, if we had a date day, we headed out with friends that night, but now there was none of that. We were also extremely independent of each other when out and would spend our whole nights talking to others, and barely see each other until home time. I had been trying to spend more time with him before I vocalised these feelings by asking him to do stuff with me in the evening. Even something as stupid as watching TV and chatting or going for a walk, but he had kept saying he was busy. I would come downstairs and find him playing Xbox... I didn't have an issue with this, but it was counterproductive when I was trying to salvage a relationship. He said he didn't realise and would change, but I didn't want him to change; I just wanted things to go back to how they were, but knew deep down they wouldn't.

It was horrible trying to get ready as I couldn't stop crying. I hated crying so much and didn't want anyone to see either. My makeup was going to run, and it was becoming my biggest concern as I done my standard of smiling through the pain. It was very obvious something was up; apparently, we both had faces like thunder and couldn't hide it. We were also actively avoiding each other. There was a real divide in the group; the boys were firmly on Conor's "side", and the girls saw I needed support and helped me out. I had confided in a few of them previously about how I was feeling, and they had all been super supportive, which was continuing. The guys, on the other hand, not so much, and it really hurt. They were supposed to be my friends too. They had met Conor through me, but all they saw was a wounded guy whose long term girlfriend had dumped him, and Conor is emotionally explosive at the best of times. On the other hand, I keep it all in and put on a brave face, just getting on with it. I was known for being strong, and this probably seemed like no big deal to me, but in reality, my whole world was crashing down.

When we made it out, my Crohn's went insanely bad from the stress of the whole situation. I think I had fired about 3 imodems into me but was still shitting water. Katie had said she knew this would happen as she could visibly see how stressed I was, and it was only a matter of time. It felt like the undiagnosed days, where I sat in a toilet cubicle, shitting my lights out surrounded by friends. Not good. I had my radar key, what is a God send in places with the scheme, and good old Laverys did. Poor Katie, Caitrionia, and Sile stayed with me the whole night, and I apologised as I inflicted another Crohn's flare on them. They never seemed to be bothered, and anytime this happened, any of my friends with me never seemed fazed. It was nice and always made me more reassured in a horrible situation, but I still felt bad. Another joy of Crohn's is moments that are extremely private for most, can become a spectator's event if sharing a cubicle or your friends are with you making sure you're alright. My friends are all heroes, and it never bothered them, or if it did, they hid it well. I think they're well aware this isn't something anyone would inflict on another person if they had the choice.

The night was so terrible; anytime I walked past Conor and said hi, he couldn't even look at me, and it really hurt. At the end of the night, everyone ditched and left Katie and me as well; I actually got into a fight with Michael over it. They were all so concerned for Conor. It was also upsetting as I didn't want to be fighting with one of my best friends over this. Ryan had pulled me to the side and had been super understanding. He said we've been friends for so long and knows I wouldn't act out irrationally and had obviously been thinking about this for a long time. He was right, and he was concerned for me as I told him I didn't know what to do. There had been an after-party at ours, but I had spent most of the night in the toilet or corridor crying. As it began to die and everyone left, Conor and I started talking, and I had an emotional explosion at him. It must have been about 4 am, and I was tired of being treated differently already. I shouted at him in the kitchen as I hysterically cried, saying how I was sick of being the strong one and how people think things don't affect me just because I get on with it. I was so aware I was turning my life upside down just as my health was getting back on track and we should be finalising our travelling plans, but instead, this has happened, and it's so cruel. I had been trying to see if my feeling would change for ages, and nothing was happening, and I liter-ally couldn't fight it anymore. I wished they would change, but they wouldn't, and I had to accept that. He understood and said how upset he was and knew it was horrible for me too. I hadn't realised, but Ryan had been having a smoke on the balcony, so when he came back into the living room, he had heard it all. Be-fore going to bed, he came and gave me the biggest hug and told me he loved me. I know he does, and I told him I love him too. He could actually empathise with his good friend. I felt it was other "friends" who began showing their true colours during all of this.

The next day, emotional and hungover (never a good mix), Conor and I literally sat and cried until we physically couldn't anymore. It was really breaking both our hearts, but we had had a great 4 years, and I told him I'd do it all again, even as painful as this was. I knew I didn't want to be with him anymore romantic-ally, but it was really hard as I was literally losing my best friend. I had gone through breakups before and had my heartbroken, but this was the worst. I really felt for Conor too as he didn't want this, and he kept saying how he still loved me so much, and I was the funniest, kindest, most beautiful person he knew. It was hard to hear as I didn't feel like that at all, in fact, the complete opposite. I was hurting the one person I didn't want to. I felt more like a monster. I had texted Michael to apologise for the fight and explain why we hadn't left our room all day. Mick understood and said not to worry, he was just concerned for us.

As painful as it was, I moved home and was amazed I actually did it, as I was completely unwilling. I wasn't just giving up a relationship, I was giving up my home and freedom. It was a tough week, and Conor and I were on and off contact. By Thurs-day, however, I had got bored and wanted to go back to the flat; I also wanted to see how things would be with Conor after some space. He came and collected me, and I moved back in. I realise now a lot of it was FOMO with the boys and co-dependency. We had been going out for four years, and when I was single, I was the most independent person. I feel like going out with him for so long, and illness had taken some of that independence away. Although we hadn't been spending that much time together, we were still living together. He was also still leaving me to work when I was in the flat, and we were still planning our schedules around each other. This is all fine when in a happy, normal relationship, but these were now long formed habits I had to break. I've also realised I'm quite a loving and giving person with someone I like, whether it's evenly reciprocated or not and will make an effort based on how much I value the person. As I valued Conor so much, I continued to put him before myself and what I needed. It all had to change, and I had to start over. However, I done what most people do and tried to repress my feelings, continuing to ignore my shadow self.

It was all too painful to face the facts and, of course, was easier running away. I convinced myself I wanted to try and make it work, and I honestly did, but I knew deep down it wouldn't. The thought of being able to take a tablet and changing how I felt continued to haunt me, to the point it became a wish. One of the stupid impossible wishes like waking up and being a princess in a castle with loads of money and no worries. You know it will never happen, but no harm in wishing for it. He said he wished I had said something earlier, but another negative trait of mine is, depending on the situation, I won't say anything until I'm at a breaking point (when I react, people know it's bad). I tend to just brush it under the carpet and get on with it. It's not overly healthy, but it's what I had always done, especially when I was still trying to process my emotions. Conor said he wanted to work on the relationship and change and do more together. I was acutely aware that people tend not to change, and I didn't want to change him. I don't get those people who try to "change" their other halves. If you want to change them, then why are you with them? You're obviously not compatible, move on and find someone else. It was also me that had changed, not him. The last year's incidents had changed me as a person, and I had no choice but to adapt, change, and grow. It was tough, but I came out better and stronger for it. I was just resentful now, my health was getting better, and we were supposed to be travelling, but that was definitely not happening.

Conor and I both booked a day off work to spend together and try again. Of course, nothing was helping, and I was still trying to repress this. I also desperately needed a holiday, and he was making no effort towards this, something that was baffling me as we were supposed to be going travelling. But I again had to take a look at the relationship; every holiday we had ever been on, I had booked and planned from start to finish, he literally just had to be there. He actually sucked the joy out of holiday planning as when it came to something as simple as even planning the dates, or giving his opinion on the options I had lined up; he strangely went into meltdown mode and whinged. It usually resulted in a toddler-like tantrum of, "I can't do this, it's too much", because he couldn't be bothered or was irrationally stressed at having to make a decision. Since we have separated, he has whinged to me about not getting on any holidays, and I got on loads of class ones. I very honestly told him about the issue as I had also done when going out, to which he has agreed. Fair play to him for taking and acknowledging the criticism. You can't expect change if you don't change the problem.

I had seen my Crohn's consultant, Dr Turner, and he was happy with my progress and had encouraged me to book a holiday. Due to being on infliximab and having no immune system, I was warned against places like Thailand, as I was at higher risk of getting bit by a flesh-eating bug and dying. The joys. I took this as great news, though, and when back home later, I started pushing for a holiday. My thought process also being maybe a holiday will help our relationship. We always had the best time and were stress-free, just enjoying ourselves. Oh, how wrong was I.

When the subject was broached, I said as I had been saving for long-term travelling, money wasn't overly an issue, and I was happy to go away wherever and for at least 2 weeks. It turned out Conor had been lying about his savings. He didn't even have a grand put together. Excuses of how I was sick started coming up and not knowing what we were doing. Conor had always been terrible with money, and I on the other hand, was good with it. I was always helping him out or buying stuff, but this really fucked me off. It was like the final nail in the coffin, the one thing I felt I needed and wanted, and he couldn't even provide that. I was also so desperate for a holiday I didn't know what to do. I think if I was happy in the relationship, it wouldn't have bothered me as much, but I was massively fucked off now. I didn't know whether to walk again or what. I even tried compromising by saying we'd go somewhere in Europe, so it wasn't as expensive. I had decided then between Krakow or Croatia, but I wanted a longer holiday and to travel around a bit, so I leaned more towards Croatia to go to both Dubrovnik and Split. I suggested a week in each city, but that of course was too much money, and he didn't want to go away for that long. It was like pulling teeth.

I was really trying and coming to the edge, but my desire for a holiday was winning. I relooked at flights and accommodation saying we could go for 10 days, spending 5 in each, which was just about agreed to. Again, I was planning it all, and there was no help. All these things are so easily overlooked and forgiven when content, but now I was just grasping at straws. Conor was also now deciding last minute to do a part-time Master's degree, so all his money thoughts were going to this and how he would need a new laptop, books etc. I saw it all as an excuse at the time, and now, with hindsight, I also see it as selfish. If he loved me as much as he said he did, his actions would have spoken much louder than his words. Instead of doing the one thing I wanted/ needed, which should really have been enjoyable for the both of us (like really who whinges about a holiday, FFS), he was putting all his brand new spur of the moment plans in front of me. I was 100% for his progression and doing the Master's, but how the situation was handled was selfish and uncaring. The holiday was booked for September, so I was aware we would have to try to work on things at least until then.

Honestly, nothing changed; we continued to do our own thing and spend no time together. I'll not lie; it kind of suited me as it was just a reminder that staying in the relationship was wrong. However, I still had the longing to make it work or fix it, but I knew that wasn't going to happen. We also took each other massively for granted at this point. There was also a bigger worry on my mind now. I had started to come out in these weird rashes, and my scalp had been getting really itchy. I had been getting my scalp bleached at the hairdressers so would be used to the occasional blister or scab, but this was weeks and weeks after having it dyed, so I couldn't understand what the weird "cuts" on my head were. I asked Conor to look, and he said it looked like psoriasis.

WHATTTTTTT!!!!!!! Conor had psoriasis himself on his scalp and under his eyebrows but had always had it. How the fuck was I coming out in random rashes and psoriasis! I booked an appointment to see a GP, and they looked at my scalp and said it looked like psoriasis, but as I had long hair trying to show it was really difficult. He lifted a medical book and looked up what to prescribe me. It really filled me with confidence... I was prescribed a steroid ointment for my scalp and a shampoo called polytar, but I was so horrified I had developed it I was really reluctant to use it as that was admitting I had it.

The rashes began growing, and more and more were coming out all over my body. Of course, I started googling it at this point, and there was a link between TNF blockers (infliximab blocks the TNF in your body) and developing drug-induced psoriasis and dermatitis. I phoned the IBD nurses, who said when I was next in for my infusion, they would take my blood and sent it off for antibodies, as my body could also be rejecting the medication.

My joints, especially in my hands, had been really sore too, but it was a common side effect of infliximab. Sometimes the joints in my fingers would be so sore they swelled up, and I was concerned this was rheumatoid arthritis as my dad has it. How was this going from a dream drug to poisoning me? The shampoo I was using was doing fuck all as well, it maybe helped a bit the day I washed my hair, but it wasn't effective long term. It also smelled like actual tar, fucking gross man; perhaps that's where it got its name from.

They took my blood at the next infusion, and I had noticed that my symptoms started flaring worse again by about week 6 of 8. It then took a few weeks for the infusion to help again, so I was only really getting a few decent weeks of health. Yet again, I had been in denial about this as I was hoping it was just a long, slow process to remission, and how could I really have any more bad luck fs. The infusion was one week before we went to Croatia, and I had thought it would help keep me right for the holidays. How wrong I was yet again.

The following week we went to Croatia; I was soo excited to get away. I was used to having 3 holidays a year, not 3 hospital stays in a year. I was kind of concerned about how the holiday would go as my feelings still hadn't changed. I'm also bad for openly perving on fit wee boys, but Conor knew that it wasn't a worry. He knew I would never actually cheat on him (or anyone for that matter) and just had a flirty jokey personality, and usually found my comments funny. But he wasn't exactly feeling secure in the relationship at the moment, so I knew it was best to keep comments like "talent at 5 o clock" to a minimum. As it was a week post-infusion, I could tell my skin was reacting to infliximab. The weird skin things and psoriasis were getting worse, and I was actually paranoid wearing shorts and bikinis as my legs were beginning to be covered. When walking about Dubrovnik old town the first proper day, I became less paranoid as I saw people were covered in mosquito bites and my weird marks looked similar. So I hoped people would assume I was probably just covered in bites. The sweat from the 30-degree heat irritated the scalp psoriasis, though, and made it really itchy. Conor said he found after sports or sweating his would always be irritated too, so I guess that was normal.

The first few days of the holiday, I noticed how tired I was and couldn't understand. I was also a bit frustrated as I wanted to be enjoying my holiday but was wasting half the day because I felt so wrecked. I remember even saying to Conor I couldn't believe how tired I was and was forcing myself to get up. I also noticed my Crohn's wasn't that good but put it down to a different diet and tried to ignore it. However, it must have been noticeably getting worse, as Conor himself commented on it. Whenever he said, I brushed it off as I had literally had an infusion the week before; I was fine, it was just taking a while to kick in, although deep down I knew something was up. I wasn't going to acknowledge it on holiday, though, and continued to try to have the best time. However, my joints, especially in my hands, had also been playing up. They were painful, swelling, and even the skin was mildly blistering. One of the days, we went kayaking, thinking it was to explore Lokrum Island, but it was just a trip around the island unfortunately, and I thought my hands were going to die. I could barely move them by the end, and they were in so much pain throughout. Conor didn't appreciate this, as I was losing my patients being out at sea for over 4 hours, being tested both physically and now mentally, as we had started bickering when trying to paddle. I wasn't pulling my weight apparently, and I felt like shoving the paddle up his ass. Thankfully when it was over, there was some football match on that he wanted to watch. So we went to a bar and got pissed, and it all ended up ok. Dubrovnik was good, a real tourist trap, and I found the locals rude, but I couldn't really blame them. It was September which wasn't the height of the "season", and the place was still rammed. They definitely lived off tourism but hated tourists. I got it, they thought we were melters.

Apart from that, I really liked it, but a few more cracks were starting to show in the relationship. We were fighting over stupid stuff, and we rarely done that or even fought. I had bought Conor a watch he had wanted for part of his birthday present the previous year, but it was cheap shit and made of some metal wired material that frayed. I had actually asked him did he want me to buy another one for him because it was pure shite, but he declined. It did look nice, but the quality was terrible. When I had been released from hospital after my first-week long stint in the Royal, already covered in marks, cuts and bruises, his watch had sliced my hand and left it with a scar. I wasn't in a good place at the time and was raging when this happened. It felt like another unnecessary mark to add to the growing collection. I still have a mild scar on my hand to this day from it. But instead of taking the watch off as I asked, he kept it on, and I got more cuts from it.

On our last evening in Dubrovnik, I tried to make an effort before going to dinner and wanted to try and get nice pictures of us (pretending like everything was normal). I saw Conor putting on the watch, and I said to him, "Don't even think about putting that watch on." Well, apparently my "tone" was not acceptable. I think I mildly raised my voice, but I did say it sternly. I wasn't risking more fucking unnecessary scars because he didn't want me buying the more expensive watch like I had offered. He irrationally cracked up and took great umbrage at my request, and began shouting back, saying how dare I speak to him like that. It was a really stupid, irrational fight, and I couldn't understand why he was going off on one. I was starving at this point too, and we didn't know where we were going for dinner yet. As an eternal starvo, this was not ideal as it was getting late, and my concern was that we weren't going to get eating somewhere nice. He went so mad at how I had spoken to him and wouldn't take the watch off, and by the end of the fight, I was crying. This extra fucked me off as we hadn't even left the apartment yet, and my

SARAH DONNELLY

makeup was going to be ruined. He was also refusing to listen to why I obviously didn't want him wearing the stupid fucking watch. It was highlighting another reason why I needed to leave. He didn't listen to my point of view, and everything revolved around him and his oversensitive feelings. As we had left to try and go to dinner, I actually stormed back to the apartment and refused to go. I couldn't control the tears and was not going to be seen in public like that. I calmed myself and decided to be the bigger person.

I said again why I was fucked off, and I literally hadn't meant to say anything in a bad way, but him and that stupid fucking watch had left me with scars previously, so for obvious reasons, I did not want him wearing it. Again, I got it, I should've addressed him differently, but he needed to get out of his stupid ego. I also got that he was probably stressed due to our crumbling relationship, and all this was related to that. It was weird as we literally never fought before, and my life had come to fighting over a FUCKING WATCH ON HOLIDAYS. This was soo not me or any form of life I wanted to live. We made up, had a really nice dinner, and then when back at the apartment, I made him get a picture with me. I was literally trying to keep up appearances at this point.

By the time we got to Split, I was getting more and more tired, and the Crohn was still getting worse. I was still trying to have the best time, though, but it was also proving more difficult as the cracks continued growing relationship-wise. The last proper holiday I had been on with Conor was Greek island hopping with friends over a year before. I had forgotten how stingy he could be when he wanted to, and it was really starting to fuck me off. I had had a year from hell and had been saving for a long time (when I could), so I was happy to spend what I wanted. I kind of felt like I deserved it at this point. Conor's latest excuse of his Master's and needing to save for it kept being reiterated, but I thought back to previous holidays where he behaved the

210

same. He never had money. When we arrived in Split, we went for dinner that evening. I had forgotten he would purposely go into a huff, whinge about being out in a restaurant spending money, purposely order the most disgusting cheapest thing on the menu he wouldn't even like, and not even order a drink. I had flashbacks to Greece, where he had done the same on one of the first few days. Something about money then too and not having it and I had been telling my best friend Caitriona, as it had really fucked me off and I found the behaviour a bit embarrassing. He was sucking the joy out of dinner and, in turn, the holiday, so I simply said to him, "if you'll fuck up whinging about money, I'll pay for the whole holiday". Literally anything for an easy life. Of course, he refused as per, but I really wasn't having it. All I wanted was to enjoy my dinner and wine, and he was drinking tap water. He did get better after I said that, but pity it came to that.

The day we went to Krka waterfall was the earliest we had to get up in a while. Early mornings still kill me with Crohn's, but I should've really realised how bad this flare was or how badly I was digressing. I had eaten quite a lot the night before; even after dinner, I was still hungry. So when we went to a bar after dinner, and I knew we'd be there a while as there was more football on, I ordered more food. I was now really regretting it as even after taking imodem I still needed the toilet. Not a good sign. Before leaving on the over 2-hour long bus journey, I had to run into a café to use their bathroom. I asked the tour group if I could use their bathroom, but they said no as their cash was back there, so customers weren't allowed in for security reasons. I got it, but when at risk of shitting yourself, it also fucks you off. The woman, I'm sure, was unaware I have a hidden disability (like all randomers), and there was honestly more chance of me using the money as toilet paper than stealing it at this point. Thankfully the café was just next door though. The stress and anxiety of being stuck on this bus without a toilet was killing me, and as I fired more imodems into me, I knew this wasn't good. I felt the sickest and most nauseous I had in a while, so as I dragged myself away from the toilet to get the bus, I hoped for the best. I said to the tour guide was there any toilets on the bus as I had Crohn's and wasn't well, but although he had incredible English, I don't think he knew what that meant or, more specifically, the connotations. He told me not to worry, it would be fine, whilst I was thinking the polar opposite. He did say to the bus, if anyone was feeling unwell, please say, and they'd pull over, but that is something I just do not have in me to do until at the absolutely no choice stage. I would rather just suffer in silence and hope for the best.

The bus took off, and Conor had his tablet for us to watch stuff on that he had downloaded, as it was a full day trip. I done my standard and spent more time looking at how long the film had been on so I could count down how long it would be until we get there. My stomach was in so much pain, so I literally sat trying to talk myself down from anxiety, cradle my sore stomach, and also concentrate on not shitting myself. Conor was trying to reassure me too, but no amount of reassurance really eases the internal panic. It was thankfully fine, though, and I made it to the water-fall accident-free. My stomach was still in agony, and I was still panicking about that, as it usually meant flare up around that exact time. The disabled toilets were closed, and the queue for the ladies was crazy long. I thought about going into the guys as I usually do but never actually go through with it. A lady in front of me heard me talking to Conor and kindly offered for me to go in front of her, but I told her it was ok. I hate doing that to people unless it actually is an emergency, like I only use my radar key when I actually need it. Conor said I needed to stop doing that as it discredited my illness, and I should take the toilet. I saw where he was coming from, but I was already embarrassed enough in those situations without making more of a scene.

The rest of the holiday was great, despite there being obvious cracks in both the relationship and my health at this point. Our flight was in the evening on the last day, and my Crohns had been really bad that morning. I had left all packing to the last minute as per usual, so between running to the toilet and trying to pack, we were late leaving the air b&b. I didn't want to leave as my stomach was so bad, but I obviously had to, so I took 2 imodems (the first one wasn't working) and hoped for the best. I ended up really regretting this decision as my stomach was in absolute agony. I don't know if it was just Crohns pain or my body needing to have a flare-up and the imodem stopping this, but I could barely walk. I was in so much pain. Split old town isn't big and we had seen everything already, so just wanted to travel home at this point. It was the longest day trying to entertain ourselves, especially as Conor was supporting me anytime I walked. We sat in the sun most of the day as I held my stomach and whimpered in pain. Conor felt bad for me, and he could see by my face how sore my stomach was. We even left an hour earlier than we needed to get the airport bus as we couldn't sit around much longer come 5 pm. As soon as we arrived at the airport, we realised we probably shouldn't have left so hastily, the check-in was outside in a tent. It was quite the experience. The departures area was literally a big room with hundreds of people squished into it. There were no seats, and the majority of people were sitting on the floor. We soon joined them, and I really couldn't wait to get home. I sat cradling my stomach, waiting for our flight and to get out of this room that felt like hells waiting room. Eating had been so painful all day, so I hadn't really bothered but was getting starving now too.

By the time we got back to Belfast, it was the early hours of the morning, and Conor talked about getting the bus back. Absolutely fucking not. I told him I would pay for a taxi, and I was also ordering a dominos as it was the only place open. We would have been waiting closer to an hour for the bus, then it would have been over half an hour to Belfast City Centre, and then we would have needed a taxi back to the flat anyway. I was soo glad when we were in. I needed to eat and lie down. There was no way

I could eat with the stomach pain and now the hunger pains, so I had a smoke of some grass, and my stomach felt so much better. It was actually amazing the difference. The relief I got was insane, and it really highlights the need for medicinal marijuana. I was able to eat and fall asleep pain-free and could finally relax then. But little did I know that that was the start of permanent stomach pain again. I'm a huge advocate for medicinal marijuana and cannot understand why people will not take the benefits from a plant.

People sniff lavender to make them relax, which is a common non-judged practice. Yet smoking a planet that eases pain is frowned upon. Humans are fucking weird, man. The government also yet again proves how stupid and ignorant they are; if it was regulated and taxed, they'd make a fucking mint. Someone told me once something mental like three billion could be made in tax money. Stupid cunts. It would also be much safer when regulated and create jobs in a new field. Think idiots, think! But on a serious note, I don't actually know the ins and outs of getting it legalised and regulated. Apart from it seems to be working in other countries.

Infliximab to inflixibad

The next few weeks, my health really took a hit. Crohn's was flaring to the point I was off work again and coming in when I could. As I wasn't paid when off, it was my concern to obviously keep an income coming in, I had bills and rent to pay. I phoned the IBD nurses to see if my results were back, and they were. By the end of the 8 weeks, there was fuck all infliximab left in my blood; my body must have been eating it. They also read test results that showed I hadn't actually improved since April, and I was getting worse again. The nurse told me how it was and said the treatment isn't working. I told her how I was currently, and she said I was definitely in a flare and needed to get urgent bloods done. It was a Friday afternoon at this point, so it didn't seem likely. I felt so unwell too and couldn't have been bothered moving.

When I came off the phone, I burst out crying. How was this happening to me? I literally couldn't catch a break. I was trying to get on with my life, my relationship was in as big of tatters as my bowels, and I had no idea what was going to happen. I phoned my mum and was crying when I told her. She told me I needed to go to A&E for bloods, they'd do them quickly, and I'd have the information on the spot. I phoned my dad after too to let him know. Both were very concerned and wanted me to go to the hospital. I messaged Conor to let him know, and then I heard Michael downstairs. I went down to tell him and again burst out crying. He hugged me and asked how was it not working as he thought I was doing a lot better. I said I had been doing better compared to how unwell I previously was (anything's better than shitting 30 times a day), but I was starting to get worse again. I had also thought something was up for months but just kept ignoring it, hoping it would get better or was all in my head. Also, any form of improvement or temporary good health I was seeing as a much bigger improvement than it really was. I didn't know what was normal anymore or what my new normal should be, so I took every improvement as massive, even if it was just one good day. I unenthused, got ready to go to the hospital. I can't remember if Michael or my dad gave me a lift, but I went in by myself. I didn't want to be there and wanted to be in and out quickly, but that does not happen in hospital.

I sat for hours and hours, and they had moved the waiting area to a bit further back in the hospital. I chatted to a woman beside me who was there with her husband. He had one of those oxygen tanks he was carrying about and looked properly unwell. She told me about how he had been and about her family, and I told her about myself. We must have been chatting a while, but then he was called, and they were to head-on with the doctors. She was super lovely and said, "Aww, I don't want to go. I was enjoying chatting to you", and looked genuinely upset, then hugged me before she left. I hope her husband has returned to good health and she's good too. It was a long and boring wait, especially when wrecked, but I saw my friend Bebhinn who was working, so I also chatted with her a bit. When I was finally called into a room with a doctor to go over my bloods, it was confirmed inflammation levels were raised, and my liver function was off too. I was baffled at this, but he said it could be the medication I'm on; biologics can interfere with liver function.

Great, another thing to add to the list. He asked if I wanted to stay, and I strongly confirmed I did not, and there was no reason for me to be in hospital; I just needed the bloods done. He laughed and said it was better not to be here. Conor came up after work and got me. He had come into the hospital, and we chatted to Bebhinn before leaving. It was weird as we were talking about upcoming nights out, and I agreed to come along, but in reality, I had no idea if I'd make it or what the actual fuck was going on with my tragic life. I was just glad to get back home that day.

The following week, I had a phone call saying I had to get an emergency double dose of infliximab. I was nervous about this as my skin reactions were getting worse, and I was getting more of them, so it was definitely linked. I had hoped the sun might have helped or dried them up like it does with psoriasis, but this was not the case. In desperation, I had tried a few couple of minute sunbeds, but they were also useless. I had been in Boots pharmacy on my lunches and asked the pharmacists about my skin. They're always so nice and helpful in there, and they looked up side effects and confirmed the skin reactions were from infliximab. One of the pharmacists who I had talked to a few times had warned me about the possibility of my hair falling out or thinning from infliximab as well. I remembered someone else telling me this had happened to them. The person who had told me said, they were given all their infliximab starter doses close together and from this and being very unwell, their hair came out in bits and was all different lengths, so they got extensions to try and cover it. The pharmacist was lovely and said how she hoped it didn't happen to me, as she had told a colleague about a girl with amazing long silver hair that had been in. It was very kind of her to say. My hair had grown long after being on steroids, and I didn't want it to fall out either, but I didn't really think much more of it. Another day when talking to another pharmacist, I asked once off infliximab, will the psoriasis definitely go? He said it should, but there is a chance that it could stay due to that door being opened. Not what I wanted to hear, but I hoped massively for the former.

I went up to the Royal for my emergency infliximab. I was sceptical from my reactions, so I said to the nurses in the infusion suite. They're always so lovely in there, and the nurse agreed with me, so got one of the IBD nurses. One of them came around and reassured me about the unlikelihood of a reaction, but she was talking about the anaphylactic shock kind; it was my skin that was concerning me. I showed her pictures of my legs, and she looked alarmed but didn't say much more. I had the infusion anyway against my better judgement. It was back to being three hours as I had to be monitored for longer again due to the double dose. I think it had gone down to an hour and a half, as after so many doses, the time it takes to administer it lessens due to less chance of a reaction. I remember being really tired after. This wasn't a shock as it always made me sleepy, but I was long past the point of being accompanied to an infusion, so it was the standard two buses home afterwards. I was hoping for a miracle, but I knew even if the infliximab started working, my skin needed to be treated badly. As psoriasis isn't as serious as Crohn's, I knew they weighed up what needed to be treated more. I had been told this from another IBD nurse on the phone weeks previously. I understood that Crohn's was majorly the priority; it was just very annoying having both. I had also been told because psoriasis is autoimmune as well, they needed to figure out if I was getting it from a bad Crohns flare or a reaction. I had never had it before in my life, no matter how bad the Crohns was, so I knew myself it was a reaction. Infliximab is also used to treat psoriasis in extreme cases, so I think they thought it might potentially help.

Unsurprisingly however my skin started going even more mental. The already formed weird rashes were now turning into open sores. My skin was literally fluffing up and dying, leaving open wounds, as my Crohns doctor described it. It was so disgusting; they even oozed stuff that looked like pus. More of these also started appearing, along with more scalp psoriasis. Again, the already formed patches were getting worse and becoming thick layers of skin. I was told not to pick at it, but of course, I did. I hated it, and it was disgusting, so I used to rip the thick scales off my head, they'd then ooze or bleed, but I didn't care. The part that got me the most was when I pulled the skin off and how it flaked everywhere; it was so embarrassing and disgusting. I was used to an invisible illness where no one could see my bleeding inflamed intestines, or if I was unwell, it was in the privacy of a bathroom. But now, I felt like if I moved my head or hair, someone might be able to see it, or it would flake everywhere. I was purely horrified by the psoriasis as I knew it was a bad reaction to the medication and a reminder it wasn't working, but instead giving me another illness. It also wasn't like normal psoriasis I had seen on other people who naturally have it. The flaking skin this left behind was really thick and dense. Also, as my body was covered in these weird sores and rashes, it had got so bad I was even getting the equivalent of nappy rash around my bum. Was I 2 or 24 FFS. The palms of my hands also had holes forming in them now from the skin breaking, so of course, I referred to myself as Jesus.

The Crohns was also not improving, it was actually getting worse. That double dose infusion was only 4 weeks after my scheduled 8 week one, so I had a serious amount of the drug in my system. My consultant actually said that I should be doing really well for the amount of it in my body, and I was the opposite. I was feeling worse and worse and getting more and more tired. I was back to sleeping nearly all of the time, and when I was making it into work, I was always late from needing to jump off buses to get to a toilet or not being able to leave the house until a certain time. I had also just moved home at the end of September, spending half my time in the flat, half of it in my family house. It was really strange as Conor and I were like half broke up. The stress of this was also hanging over me as I still desperately wanted it to work whilst also knowing it wasn't going to, and I was just waiting for some kind of miracle. I was fighting the change. I had so much uncertainty in my life, and last time Conor had taken the breakup so bad, I really didn't want to hurt him again.

Shortly after the double dose, the inevitable happened, and my hair started falling out. It thinned massively and from the shoulders down was completely breaking off. It looked thin, straggly and absolutely rank. My mum kept telling me how badly it needed cut off, and I was well aware. I either have my hair in a long bob or grow it long, so cutting it doesn't annoy me. However, as the choice had been taken away from me and at the time did not want it short, this was not ideal, and I really begrudged it. Any GP who saw me said I needed to be seen urgently by a dermatologist and my Crohns consultant, and things were not good. I was growing more depressed and hopeless by the day and as the Crohns got worse, so did the anxiety, and I literally did not want to leave the house or be seen. My mood was never good, I could put on a brave face, but deep down I did not want to be alive. I was losing everything again, and after having a taste of semi-normal life for a few months, I was catapulted back into hell.

Things kept deteriorating, and I had hit a crisis point. It was now October and my birthday, and Conor had convinced me to do something for it. I had cut my hair off to my shoulders at this point and dyed it rose gold. It was nice, and I liked it, but I think it screamed: "I'm in a crisis and don't give a fuck". The skin things/open wounds were so bad that the worst ones on my shins had to be covered in bandages, as they oozed so much crap it would stick to my clothes and form a scab, meaning I would have to painfully rip them apart, causing more oozing and bleeding. Unfortunately, the bandages always moved even when taped on with medical tape, so some amount of pulling was always necessary. I was trying Sudocrem and all sorts on them, but nothing worked. My surgical wound from the summer was also getting really sore again, so I knew everything was flaring. We had a house party in the flat for my birthday as I said I wasn't going out. It was a good night, and I was surprised I kept going until 4 am. However, I've never really known when to stop when drinking/partying unless I pass out, so I shouldn't have been that shocked. It was good fun, and I was glad I did it, but I also massively wasn't in the mood.

The following day was my actual birthday, and I just wanted to hang and sleep. My mum, however, had different ideas and made me go to hospital. I was fucking raging. I was not happy to be 25; my life couldn't be anymore shitter, between my health and relationship. Happy quarter of a century bitch. My work I was so lucky had been nothing but understanding and supportive, but I needed to be in to earn, so this was added stress. When I was in, I was in a foul mood and couldn't have been bothered. My energy was drained, so I did not have the concentration most days. I, beyond reluctantly, after fighting with my mum for ages, went to the hospital. It was soo stupid they do fuck all on a Sunday, and it's only skeleton staff at the weekend. There's also every fucking moron there with nothing wrong with them or got too drunk the night before.

We were, of course, in A&E for hours, and I even had an unnecessary cannula put in as per usual for "pain relief" in case I stayed. It was stupid, though, I wasn't staying, and they're stingy fucking cunts with the good stuff. When we got to see the doctor, my bloods confirmed the same; inflammation was up, and liver function was off. The A&E doctors openly admitted they didn't have a clue what to do with me and they weren't specialists. It was really evident as they wanted to see my seton stitch, and the doctor had a nurse (there always has to be a female present when a guy is checking you out) swab the output to be sent off to check for infection and gave me antibiotics to take. The swabbing actually hurt as she put the swab inside the stitch, and it felt sharp. I must have flinched as the nurse apologised and said it would be over soon. The antibiotics I just did not take. I was told to come back the following day to see the GI team. It was weird as it was pretty much exactly a year since everything had started going really tits up, and I had been sent daily to see the GI team. I was so thankful to go home and chill out; the whole day had felt like an unnecessary waste. I already absolutely hate birthdays, so it really wasn't a great one.

The next day I went by myself to the Royal and waited around at the ambulatory care centre where I have my infusions, for the doctors to come around. I don't mind being by myself, and throughout this whole experience, I had done most of it by myself. But it was when I was unwell it was most inconvenient as if I needed the toilet when waiting and there was no one there with me, I had to ask a randomer if my name was called to please let them know I'm here but in the toilet. Cringy. I was raging at my mum, though, after fucking forcing me to go to the hospital the day before; she now wasn't taking me when they wanted to see me. The doctors came around, and it was strange as the junior doctors I could tell from one look were my age or younger. It didn't fill me with confidence, no offence. I was called around to a cubicle by some incompetent asshole with an attitude problem.

I'll assume he was a consultant, and he proceeded to tell me, "You don't look sick". This was beyond fucking me off; he wasn't the first doctor to say this to me, but he also had no idea how I looked normally, and I certainly didn't look well in comparison. I mean, I obviously didn't look like I was dying, but his comment was extremely unnecessary and unhelpful. I actually snapped back and told him I was regularly told this, including when admitted to hospital and just post-surgery. He tried to brush me off as he sensed the anger; the juniors could sense it too as I watched them shuffle their notes. He openly admitted he didn't know what to do as my consultant was on holiday, and it seemed I was having issues and frustrations with medication not working. No shit Sherlock. He got one of the IBD nurses, who I had been speaking to about 2 weeks before, and they thought I also had norovirus at that point on top of a Crohn's flare. Looking back, I think I did. Although all symptoms were only slightly worse, my eyes looked funny from being unwell. Conor had commented on how I really didn't look well, and it was mostly from my eyes going weird.

The IBD nurse said I needed to do a stool sample to test for bugs etc., and then get me into an emergency clinic to see a Crohn's specialist. They happened weekly, so I knew it wouldn't be too long a wait, but at the time, the thought of waiting even a week killed me. I went round to the IBD nurses office, and they got me stuff for the samples and said I could leave it in with my GP. They were saying I couldn't catch a break, and I agreed; 2018 had not been the one. I knew because the Crohns was so bad, I could definitely make myself go to the toilet while at the hospital instead of leaving it to the GP's in the morning. So me knowing the Royal so well, went up to where the clinics are held, knowing I would get private bathrooms, produced what I needed to and left it with the nurses on that floor to be sent off. I felt bad walking down to the unsuspecting nurses on that floor with a sample of my shit, but on a selfish note, it was a job done for me. I thought of the times I had to carry samples in my handbag to leave at the doctors, and even though the tube gets put inside a sealed plastic bag, I still always put it inside a container as well. Just in case. And often thought as I walked past unsuspecting members of the public, haha, you've no idea what's in my bag.

It was confirmed I had no bugs or other illnesses, and I got an emergency appointment to see another consultant. Mouth ulcers were starting to form, and all symptoms getting worse. I felt like shit both mentally and physically, and it was all getting a bit much. Going to the toilet over 10 times a day again was soul-destroying, and my stomach pain was so bad it felt like my insides were on fire. I actually asked my mum and dad to feel my stomach and see if it felt warm because it was burning on the inside but felt like it was radiating out. It was just the internal inflammation but annoying all the same. This and the numerous other types of stomach pain that comes with Crohn's were also keeping me up at night or waking me up for the toilet. I knew things were bad when it was back to having you up at night.

When I saw the consultant, I was in with her for over an hour, another consultant also came in, and I was showing them my skin. They said I needed to see a dermatologist immediately and emailed one then and there who specialised with Crohn's skin complaints.

The type of biologic infliximab is commonly gives people rashes, so it meant another medication, Humira, which is essentially an injection form on infliximab, I wouldn't be allowed to try. I was given 2 other options, Vedolizumab, an infusion or Ustekinumab, an injection. He said for me to research them when at home so I could decide, but I was already leaning towards the infusion. I didn't mind other people sticking needles in me but having to do it myself, I'd not be as ok with. My dad takes Humira for his arthritis, but he's had no reactions. Annoying I seemed to be the one that got bad ones from a similar drug. I was told I needed an emergency MRI and colonoscopy so they could see what was going on.

Surgery was also suggested depending on how diseased the area was. Potentially 4 surgeries in a year, unbelievable. However, I was getting desperate, and I really wanted a stoma bag at this point. I just wanted the problem solved, and if that solved it, I'd take an ileostomy for life. I knew because of the fistula and the nature of Crohn's spreading and it being incurable, I'd still need medication. But I felt so desperate I actually wanted to ask them for everything to be taken away, my whole colon and back passage and give me a "Barbie butt", as it was referred to. If it meant no more pain, suffering, and actually getting my life back, I'd absolutely take it. They were both really helpful and nice doctors. They went over everything and took down every symptom, including me being back to vomiting my stomach lining every morning. Oh, how I hadn't missed this, and it was back daily. They were super thorough and said I would be discussed in the weekly Friday meeting of urgent cases. I was most definitely a Royal celeb at this point. No papz plz x.

I waited for a phone call that Friday, and there was nothing come mid-day. My mum was getting impatient and embarrassing, and kept telling me to phone the hospital and was annoying me while I was at work. I know she was just really concerned, but I thought the hospital was dealing with it. I realised then she had phoned the IBD nurses, who then phoned me, to say the weekly meeting was cancelled due to a lot of staff being off with midterm. I was so gutted, I wanted something done and was still getting worse; the double dose had done absolutely nothing. I met Conor for lunch that day as he had moved jobs and was now situated in town. It was strange as when our relationship was good, we had said if he worked in town, we could go for lunch some days. Now it was ending and it felt weird going for lunch. When we were walking back to our works, my phone rang, and it was a "No caller ID", so I knew it was 99% the hospital phoning. It was the MRI department saying could I come in that Wednesday for a small bowel MRI. The doctors must have arranged this behind the scenes. I was delighted but also nervous as I knew that I had the contrast to drink for that MRI, and it was like a laxative. I could hardly wait...

Wednesday came, and I went for my MRI. I was now always getting taxis to and from the Royal, as I did not have the energy or trust my bowels to do 2 buses. It was weird, as I looked ok wrapped up in jumpers and makeup on, the taxi drivers would always ask was I going to work, assuming I was a nurse or something. When I told them no and what was happening, they were always amazed, or I had to explain what Crohn's is, as a lot of people still have no idea what it is. We had a really interesting chat. He told me about his nephew, who had a chronic illness and literally has a battery in his tail bone to try and stop him from being in permanent pain, but it wasn't working. He was housebound and could barely move. I really felt for the guy and could tell from our convo that his nephew was depressed and fed up as well without it being stated. I mean, it was pretty obvious, but I could empathise with the levels of depression as I had been there myself and at this point was pretty close to being back at that level.

When I arrived, I was given scrubs to wear again. I really enjoyed this and again contemplated taking them with me if they weren't so dirty. I was given the contrast and began drinking with the timer they gave me in front of me. The nurse had warned me it didn't taste great, but when thinking back to the last time, I didn't mind its taste, and the thought "sweet water" came to mind. I weirdly preferred it to actual water (again highlighting my dislike for the taste of water). It was the same sweet water taste, and it was fine. I was starving from having to fast, and all the liquid-filled me up a bit. As I started, a lady came in, and I assumed she was there for her chest as she was talking about her asthma and taking her inhaler. She was called in very shortly after. Just after this, a man came in, probably in his 50's but was moving at the speed of a 90-year-old with a walking cane. He looked at me, and I knew he thought I was a nurse due to the scrubs but also wondering why I had bare feet and was sitting there drinking. He asked me a question and a nurse heard and answered him. He apologised and said the obvious about my scrubs but lack of shoes, and I laughed and said not to worry, I think most people are thinking the same as him.

We began chatting, and he was in for a brain MRI as he had a brain injury, and explained it was why he walked and talked slowly. I was telling him about myself, and again he couldn't believe it because I didn't look sick. He said, "Without sounding like a creep or being weird, you're a very beautiful looking young girl, and you wouldn't have a clue." He wasn't being creepy at all, and I could tell he was embarrassed even saying it, but it was very nice of him. Especially as I certainly didn't feel beautiful in any way and had barely any makeup on. I had to, unfortunately, warn him that what I was drinking was a laxative, though, and if I ran off mid convo, he'd know why. Thankfully he was fine and completely understood and wasn't weird about it at all. We chatted away for ages before he got called in, and we wished each other the best of luck. He was a really nice man, and I hope he's doing well. The laxative began kicking in not long after, but as I had been to the toilet so many times already that day, I wasn't surprised it was just the contrast water passing through. I had forgotten how it burned, not as bad as colonoscopy prep but whatever is in it is not ass friendly.

I got called in for my cannula and had to do the standard, this vein is shit, this one works routine, but the woman looking after me was hilarious; I actually loved her. When I was pointing out I have an invisible vein that's a big one, but you need to feel for it because the visible ones are all overused and thin and shit, she joked and said I had a "grower, not a show-er". We both pissed ourselves laughing, and before I went in the MRI, I apologised and said I needed the toilet again because of the laxative. She was so kind and told me not to worry, you can't hold anything that's not in your hand. She had said she understood as well as she didn't have Crohn's but had issues, and she knew about the urgency, and when you gotta go, you gotta go. I hear ya sista. I also said to her, she was probably glad I said and went to the toilet before, instead of having some form of accident in a very expensive machine. She laughed and agreed saying it wasn't the first time that had happened. I thought of the sensation the laxative leaves you with and thought, oh fuck they definitely thought it was just a fart. Never risk that man. I also thought of the poor person who had to clean that up, gross. As we continued talking, before I got in the machine, I was saying how people always harp on about diet and what I should and shouldn't be eating when they've no idea what affects me or when it's bad it doesn't matter what you eat. She agreed and said she hates when people do that, as when people are on normal weight-loss diets, they hardly ever stick to them and go on about how hard it is, so how do they think it affects someone who's got a medical condition. She was absolutely right.

The MRI was about half an hour, and of course, I had to beep to get out at certain points. Panic really sets in when you're having all different layers of equipment put on you whilst being strapped in, so you really can't get out and know if you needed out in a hurry; it wasn't happening. Thankfully the MRI was fine, and when it was over, I had to wait for a bit as I had contrast and also needed the cannula taken out. I got chatting to another man who was also in for a brain MRI as he had brain tumours in the past and told me about passing out behind the wheel of a car. Scary stuff, but he was thankfully fine and just had been getting monitored regularly after he had surgery to remove it. When I told him about myself, he, like everyone else, was baffled due to how I looked, and we both laughed as he said he regularly got told the same. I agreed and said he looked really healthy, and you'd have no idea.

When I was allowed to go, I got changed and bumped into the woman who I had spoken briefly to earlier and had assumed she was up for her chest. We got talking, and I couldn't believe what was actually wrong with her; she had terminal brain cancer. Again, the woman looked the picture of health, but had to come up every 4 weeks for brain MRI's to check the tumour. She asked about myself, and I said I had Crohn's and what was going on. She said her brother had Crohn's and how serious an inflammatory disease it is. As we talked, I told her I'm sure many people don't realise she is ill at all based on how she looks. She completely agreed, and we empathised with each other. She also said she had stopped telling people, as most people don't know how to react or get weird, and she was fed up with it, especially people who had no experience with chronic ill health. I completely agreed; I don't think people realise what they're saying a lot of the time because it's something they can't personally comprehend. It does make you feel alien, though, especially when in a bad place. As we left, we wished each other all the best. I hope she's ok and still alive, as morbid as that sounds.

I got a taxi home and remember thinking, I hope he drives quick as this laxative is still running through me, and I do not want to shit out laxative water in his car (also do not want to pay the clean-up fee). Again, it was assumed I was coming home from work, but I told him I had been up for an MRI and got into that story. He used to be a personal trainer and began talking about diet and thought it stemmed from all the chemicals being put into our foods. He had a point, and it's probably a factor, but I didn't have the energy to explain I had read about my condition, and there are reported cases of Crohn's as far back as the ancient Egyptians, but they didn't have the medical knowledge to know what it was. Again, emphasising it is an autoimmune disease that no one actually knows the pinpointed cause of. He was nice, though, and tried recommending different things to eat or try, but at this point of the flare-up, diet didn't matter at all; it all produced the same result.

The running theme of taxi drivers assuming I was really healthy also happened on another trip home; I can't remember why I was at the Royal that day. As we were chatting, he was talking about his shift, and I asked how long he was on for. He then asked me about my work and if I was going to it after I go home. It must have been about mid-day, and I said if I really wanted to, I could probably drag myself in for the afternoon. I was, however, exhausted and ill and going home to lie down. He didn't realise what was wrong with me and began making a joke with a jab comments, like, I was lazy and scared of hard work. This bitch doesn't work in the legal industry for the fun of it, and I am certainly not lazy. Of course, I proceeded to defend myself and said, no, the reason why I'm not going in is because I am currently not well and told him what was wrong. The man was actually really nice and fully apologised, saying he was so sorry and that was entirely his own ignorance as I looked so well. I said not to worry, I get it all the time, and makeup works wonders. He began telling me his wife had been really unwell and he was her carer for a while. She actually had 2 stoma bags for her illness, and we began discussing. He actually sat for ages after leaving me outside my flat, chatting and trying to help by explaining about them. It was really lovely of him, and I wished him and his wife all the best before leaving.

I had an overall really positive experience with the MRI, though, to the point where it really interested me. There were leaflets about making radiography a career, and I lifted one. When I told Conor and the boys in the flat, they began picking holes in my idea by informing me that I would need to go back to education and do a science A-Level. "Fuck that", I believe was my response, and I let the dream go. They all burst out laughing and made jokes at my sudden lack of enthusiasm. I feel anyone would be unenthusiastic if they had to study a subject they had no interest in closer to 10 years after they last studied it. It was a nice thought and seemed an interesting career, but no science A-Level was worth it at my time of life.

Next, I had to wait for the colonoscopy but thankfully had the dermatologist appointment soon. Of course, when I phoned to book my appointment, the receptionist thought she was the doctor, and when I explained it was an emergency, she had a massive attitude and told me 6 weeks waiting was the standard. I explained I didn't have 6 weeks and suddenly managed to get an appointment for 3 weeks away. I then asked if there was anything even sooner, and it was just met with more attitude. My experience with the doctor's receptionists and secretaries was getting worse as they always seemed to have an attitude. They had no idea what was wrong with me or any other patient phoning, and when someone says their consultant said it was an emergency, I mean, they're probably not lying. You are not a doctor.

I was so excited to get to the dermatologist, but it was unfortunately a 9.30 am appointment, meaning I had to be up and in rush hour traffic. The whole journey was painful as I continually needed the toilet. My mum kept apologising, saying we would get there as soon as possible, but it wasn't her fault. We finally arrived at the Royal, and the girl's toilets were closed for cleaning, and someone was in the disabled toilet. A guy came out soon after, thankfully, but I wasn't sure if he was disabled or not. I am very aware that not all illnesses are visible, but I had nearly gone into the boy's toilets myself out of desperation. Undigested food was coming out again, which probably didn't help all the nausea, but I was now disgustingly finding it interesting to know what had extra fucked me off this time and how long it would take to appear again. I was long past the absolutely horrified stage and was now embracing it as a personal science experiment. When I left the disabled toilet, there was a woman outside waiting to use it who was carrying an oxygen tank and looked proper unwell. I could tell by how she looked at me she didn't think I was disabled and unnecessarily used the bathroom. When in reality, I was in much more dire need of it than her. I always felt really embarrassed after situations like this due to having an invisible illness and still feel guilty using a disabled bathroom when I know others may be judging. But it's something I need to get over, and the "not every disability is visible" signs some places put up are always great.

When I saw the dermatologist, I was in even more dire need. My skin was in bits, and I was struggling to find a bit of me that didn't have open sores, to the point the painful nappy rash kind of thing, also went right up my crack, and the skin was splitting open. It was starting to spread to my vag as well, and it was all very painful and gross. My dermatologist was super lovely, and I showed him my scalp and leg sores. I kept the more personal ones to myself. He said I was in a bad way and had seen infliximab give skin reactions before, but mine were really bad. He said I was never to go on it again. I hear ya bror.

I was prescribed steroids, prednisolone, and a lot of steroid creams and ointments for my skin and scalp. My first question was, "Will I get moon face?" I mean, I already felt like a fat mess, but this was the icing on the cake. He laughed and said no, the dose wasn't enough to get a proper one. I was put on 30mg for 12 days, then 15mg for the next 12 to taper down; I then had an appointment to see him again just after that. He was really lovely and had asked about the Crohns and previous history with it etc. Before I left, he said to me, "you've been through a lot, but you're a lovely girl and still smiling". I was trying. I didn't want people to see the pain I was really in. I also never wanted to lose myself to this horrible illness. It was never anyone else's fault I was suffering, just unfortunately my body seemed to hate me. It was funny he had said that though, as the following week I had been speaking to one of my aunties on the phone and after I had given the phone to my mum, she had said something similar as I heard my mum repeat what she said and say the dermatologist had said the same thing. I was suffering but would never take this out on another person, I was still myself, just a lesser depressed version. I was also trying to remember, I have Crohn's, it doesn't have me.

I had just found out about my colonoscopy as well, and it was in 2 weeks. I had phoned the IBD nurses previously to ask when it was, as I was to get an emergency one, and they said I would be waiting 8 weeks as that was the time frame for an emergency one. Luckily an hour later, though, I had a telephone call confirming it was in 2 weeks from the consultant's secretary, and it had been confirmed internally a few days prior. I had never waited for more than a week or 2 for an emergency colonoscopy. I was glad the doctors had realised Saza D is, in fact, VIP. As I was getting my prescription, I realised I would still be on steroids for my colonoscopy and wondered if they would interfere with my results. I phoned the consultant's secretary to ask what to do, and the consultant said due to how bad my Crohn's is, the steroid dose wouldn't be strong enough to make much of a difference. I was glad as I wanted to start treatment for my skin but also did not want a moon face. I had heard bad things about prednisolone as it apparently makes you mad, but that was all ahead of me.

Due to how unwell I was, I was back to sleeping approximately 15 hours a day/night. Systematic steroids on the other hand, means insomnia, and fuck it was real. Within an hour of taking the tablets in the morning, which I also had to take omeprazole for and take with breakfast as they were so hard on your stomach, this rage began building up in me. I knew it was all steroid-induced, but it was mad; it was almost exactly to the hour. My face began tingling and I was dizzy all the time. One day when trying to go to work, I fell into a bush and just lay there in the rain before calling my mum to ask her what I should do. Her obvious response was, go home and lie down, but even when trying to walk home, I was all over the place. I remember being annoyed because I had tried to go to work and had even done my makeup. I was so delirious I actually enjoyed just lying there in the rain for a minute before getting up. I didn't care if anyone saw either.

The Crohn's was so bad I was also back to doing my makeup whilst sitting on the toilet. So gross and unhygienic, but needs must. I was living half the time in the flat and half at home, but the mornings were so bad I was usually in work late as I couldn't be sitting in rush hour traffic. I also had to apply for PIP's for the THIRD time. This time I went to Ballinafeigh community centre to get help completing the form, to see if it would actually make a difference. The hunger pains on these steroids were intense as fuck as well. It was deep, aggressive hunger pains like I had never felt before, they were so distinct, and I was permanently hungry. I literally felt like I was losing my mind.

Between the aggressive mood swings, my head constantly spinning but feeling hyper-alert, insomnia, constant hunger, and my body retaining so much fucking water, I was the real-life Michelin man. My hands, feet, face, and stomach were all swollen. I was washing the dishes one evening, and Conor was standing beside me. I was looking at my own hands and noticing the swelling, then realised he was doing the same. I said to him, "Are my hands swollen?" And he laughed and said yes, it was what he was just looking at. He probably was afraid to say in case my mood swings kicked in, but I was never aggressive to other people. I would tell people about my mood and how irrationally angry I felt and explain it was the steroids; I was so aware of it.

My steroid moods left some friends hysterical as it changed my way of thinking. Normal emotions of pity when seeing a homeless person had now turned to anger. Not at the homeless person, of course, but the government. I went off on a foul-mouthed rant to Katie one day as I was walking to work and could feel the rage build inside me. I saw a poor homeless person begging in the freezing cold and rain and thought, "Why the fuck are you here?" It is fucking disgusting a person would be left begging in such conditions, yet we had a government that hadn't worked for years and were still on full pay. I was sick and dragging myself into work to get paid, yet they couldn't agree on a fucking Irish language act. THERE ARE PEOPLE DYING!!!!!!!!!!!!!! I was going to find Arlene Foster and Michelle always has a stupid look on her face bitch (I don't remember or care for her surname), and I was going to put their heads on spikes. After this, I was going to purchase a megaphone from somewhere (I hadn't figured out where yet) then parade their heads around City Hall as a warning. If I had got my hands on either of those stupid useless cunts, I would have been arrested. It was an anger I would have acted on. Katie was hysterical as I messaged her, and my good friend Jill who I worked with, I think was a bit scared as I told her about my plan in the office. I was aware it was the roids, but I genuinely couldn't understand how people didn't see it how I now did. These steroids had given me so much clarity. I also had the energy to actively campaign, with heads in tow, and lead a revolution at this point. I genuinely considered all of it and just needed people to back me. However, as no one else was on steroids, they failed to see my vision. I'd honestly make this country great again.

Another day when walking to work, I began pondering life and the concept of a God. It is mostly assumed a God is a man, and as I contemplated this, it hit me. They say that behind every great man there is a great woman, and surely God can be no different. I decided God was, in fact, the long-suffering husband to an emotionally reactive woman named Agatha. When tragedy struck her, the world knew about it. People question, "why God, why?" at natural disasters or illnesses such as child cancer. Little did people know Agatha had just had a fight with her gay bestie and decided to give the world AIDS. An uncontrollable woman when scorned and when God forgot their wedding anniversary, the 2004 Indian Ocean tsunami happened. My logic being I don't think men could get this creative when being vindictive. I imagined the words, "not again, Agatha", in a depleted tone, and thought, yes, God is a long-suffering husband just trying to have an easy life. She gave no fucks about the repercussions in her savage rampages, and God could not control this sassy bitch. Don't worry, this idea will be my next novel.

Out of all the side effects, though, it was the insomnia that was getting me the most. I had been sleeping 15 hours plus previously due to illness and fatigue, and sleep was a great escape. But now, I was getting no more than 3 or 4 hours of sleep a night. It would be 3 am or later, and I would be lying there insanely awake and angry, thinking about how I was supposed to be travelling the world right now. The long nights, anger, and hyper-alertness meant my brain was in overdrive. I lay there so angry about how life had turned out; why me? Was I a really bad person in a past life or something? Was I a really bad person now? Did I deserve all this and why was it happening? Would it ever end? Why was my relationship with Conor failing? Why couldn't I just love him like I used to? Would I ever get travelling? Would I ever get better? As I lay there every night for weeks thinking about it all, I got upset and angry. I was annoyed as I had no choice but to work through these horrible thoughts in the early hours. Everything I knew was crumbling around me, and I was scared and alone. I kept being told I was so brave by everyone, but I felt like a scared little girl who was sat rocking in a corner. It was the mental image of myself I kept seeing. Scared and isolated, I felt like no one understood me, but I'm aware to a very vast degree no one did; they couldn't totally empathise as they had never been through it. I was insanely jealous of this. I knew people felt sorry for me, but I also felt sorry for them. I felt like I couldn't relate to people my age anymore, and I was an isolated weirdo with a chronic shitting disease. I couldn't understand how perfectly healthy young people were wasting their lives stagnating, taking everything for granted, when if I was in their shoes, I'd be out of here. I was trapped by Crohn's due to infusions for the rest of my life, which were needed every 8 weeks. I felt trapped and couldn't understand why people didn't want to live.

It was the travelling aspect that was getting to me the most as it was all I wanted to do. At this point, I also knew it wouldn't be with Conor, especially as I was so angry that he hadn't saved any money. I felt unsupported and abandoned when I needed him most, and I knew I wanted to break up with him again but didn't know how. There was nothing certain in my life, and I was aware that I could be getting more surgery/a bag put in depending on what they found after the colonoscopy. At this point, I was beyond desperate for a bag and had every intention of begging my surgeon for one when I saw him. I couldn't believe how much had changed from when I was first faced with the possibility of one; I didn't want one but knew if I had to have one, I had to. When I told people I now wanted a bag, due to the strange stigma around them, I was usually responded to with, "OMG, no you don't" or "you wouldn't want a bag". People had no idea the suffering I was going through, and I don't think they could see past the vanity side of things. I was desperate for my life back and would take any measures for it. Nobody in an ideal world would get their insides cut open, parts removed, then have a bag attached to their stomach to collect their body waste out of choice. But if that was the surgery needed to get me and millions of others better, why is it such a strange taboo? I also wanted to be working properly again, especially as I wasn't paid when I wasn't in, so finances were stressing me out. People kept saying, "Yeah, but you're ill, so you probably don't need to spend as much." Yeah, you ignorant fucks, but I also have rent and bills to pay, on top of transport to and from constant hospital appointments and additional medical supplies, and I wasn't entitled to any benefits to help out. My work had always been beyond understanding/supportive, and I was able to come and go when needed, but I needed stability back.

I was so exhausted both mentally and physically from everything. My health was a never-ending waiting game, my finances were up and down, and my relationship was in tatters. It felt like a burden hanging over me that I still somehow couldn't let go of out of fear. Who else would ever love me? I literally felt and looked disgusting and thought of myself as nothing but a burden. Who the fuck would want to take all that there on? I was growing more and more depressed by the day, and I was struggling to find any light at the end of the tunnel. Little did I know, this extremely dark time I now believe to be a dark night of the soul. It was during this time I started these memoirs to try and move my energy and emotion into something productive. I hated my life and myself, and thought of the millions of others who probably felt the same. There was no one I could talk to as no one got it, and I was a 25-year-old woman. I thought of teenagers or younger experiencing the same, and it broke my heart. It kills me when I hear someone got Crohn's as a child or a teenager, and I think of the precious time it would have stolen from them. I thought of my own fond memories of going to festivals, and how if I had Crohn's then as a teenager, it would have been a very different story. If I could help even one person to know that how they felt was totally normal and there was someone out there they could relate to, I'd be happy.

Thankfully, my skin started healing quite quickly, and the numerous treatments were working. I was missing having normal hair and skin as it added so much more to my routine, especially after a shower having to put everything on. It was all much more maintenance than I was used to. When I saw the dermatologist again, he was really happy with the improvements and said I had been in a bad way previously, but I was healing nicely. He said the really bad sores that had been open wounds would scar/stain my skin like burns and would be there for a long time before they healed. He wasn't wrong, as to this day, the worst one on my shin still slightly lingers. The rest have now disappeared, but as he said, they took well over a year. When people saw the marks as they healed, they were always assumed to be a weird bruise/cut or something. I'm glad they're mostly gone, as they were daily reminders of all that went wrong for a long time.

Those few months felt like a lifetime, and I thought everything in my life was going to go wrong. I even had to go for my first smear test (which is not bad at all, it literally feels like it's described, a weird sweeping motion), but I was convinced those test results would come back bad as well, just another thing to worry about. But it thankfully came back all normal and got the standard letter saying, all is good, see you in a few years. Even during the smear, I thought something was going to go wrong, and as the nurse said she was finding my cervix with the clamp thingy, I had the mental thought, "oh God, I bet I don't even have a bloody cervix". I obviously did, and the test was over in probably 30 seconds or less. However, that night, the stomach pain was really bad, and I didn't know if it was Crohn's, cramping from the smear, or both. My insides were in constant pain and burning, and I had a bad hour or so of intense cramps in my lower stomach, which would suggest the smear, but I also get Crohn's pain there. My right-hand side was also sore, which was definitely Crohn's (terminal ileum and large intestine are there) and my stomach, as it tried to digest food, was making squealing sounds. It was actually quite funny as Conor and I laughed, whilst also being horrified. We could hear exactly where the sound was coming from in my stomach, and it literally sounded like a high-pitched squealing pig. We kept laughing and just waited for the noise to stop. Some seriously unhappy digestion was going on. I had said to my mum, and she told her friend at work who has Crohn's, and he laughed and said he knew exactly what sound it was. He said he normally just pushed on his stomach to try to pop it through. Kinda wish I had tried it to see what would happen, but would also be concerned about how sore that could be.

Crohns 1 – Sarah 0

On top of the Crohns, depression, lack of sleep and general shitness of life, the group chat with my best girlfriends from school was going mental. My friend Rhiannon had bumped into other girls from school on a night out over a month previously. One of them had asked how I was, and the other one, who we now realise has had serious mental health issues since school, took it upon herself to write about the interaction on her Instagram stories (yes, over a month later). Myself and Rhiannon were referred to as "Becky and Tiffany" in a foul-mouthed rant, including, why the fuck would she give a shit about my physical health condition, when mental health is just as important, and no one in school gave a fuck about her depression as she suffered in silence. Silence I found was the keyword here as it highlights the obvious. Nobody knew, so nobody could help. I have no issues with bad language at all; I have an unintentional, really bad mouth on me and don't even realise I'm swearing when I am most of the time. However, I take great umbrage at being personally attacked on a social media platform for absolutely no reason when extremely vulnerable. Rhiannon and I had been nothing but nice to her and had done absolutely nothing to her. But we were targeted, and after referring to Rhiannon as someone she barely knew, but she always melted her head and milked talking about my condition whilst not giving a fuck about hers or anyone else who silently suffered from depression in school. My 3 emergency Crohn's operations were also compared to a boob job. She is literally psychotic. I wish my scars were that aesthetically pleasing! Poor Rhiannon was as equally horrified especially as this ignorant bitch had no idea about her private life and how she has first-hand experience dealing with extreme depression with loved ones. In her self-absorbed, self-pitying, and self-victimising rant, she highlighted something I had always noticed about her at school, she was selfish, attention-seeking, and unintelligent.

Physical health conditions literally go hand in hand with mental health. All her attention-seeking brain could see was, "someone is getting more attention than me currently, and I need to find a way to get more and feel validated". She had issues for years and regularly posted about them. Basically everyone in her life, including immediate family, were "triggers", and she blocked and deleted everyone. So I also found this post cowardly, as she couldn't say it to Rhiannon or me directly but instead posted it, and other friends who had her social media account saw it and let us know. She was apparently going to some psychology student as a therapist, who we gathered was just validating her insanity (out of fear of being attacked themselves, no doubt). I was disgusted and soo angry, especially being on steroids; the rage was fucking real. I wanted to hunt the obese cunt down and kill her. She is the world's biggest hypocrite, regularly posting about self-love and care etc, but obviously is deeply unhappy and doesn't actually love herself. There was no care in what she did, and she did not think about the consequences of her actions, all in a desperate cry for attention.

I wasn't going to include this or give her air time as she is far more to be pitied. However, this toxic behaviour needs to be called out and highlighted for what it really is. She proclaimed being severely obese is "self-love" and caring for herself, whilst also posting videos of herself showing how she uses her herpes cream, dancing in lingerie, and sharing her Only Fans account. To each their own, but to me, self-love is looking after yourself and being that size is not healthy or "self-love", neither is that behaviour. I was so angry at the time I was going to message her, asking her what her problem was and how she had no idea how my mental health was, as I too was suicidally depressed and trying to keep it together. Every day I woke up wishing I was dead as I had to go through another day of both physical and mental suffering. I had read the expression, "You wake up every morning to fight the same demons that left you so tired the night before and that my love is true bravery." That was currently my life. I never wanted to be a victim or to be seen as one, I was just trying to keep fighting, but the will and want were getting smaller every day. I had told my mum as I was shaking with anger. She had said what the girls and I had said; she was always insane and needed a serious amount of help. I hope she gets the help she desperately needs, but at the same time, healing is on you. No one can fix you but yourself. It has taken time for me to learn and realise this but years into her insanity, I hoped she realises this herself. After her post about how triggered she was, I was so triggered and upset I didn't sleep that whole night.

I was close to breaking now. I think I was already broken and just a shell dandering about, but I could hold it together with my stiff upper lip for social situations. I felt too embarrassed to say how I was really feeling. I had tried breaking up with Conor again as well. I had said to him I needed his support the most at the moment, and when I needed it last time, he ran away, and that was after living together and going out closer to 4 years. Unfortunately, I had an explosive rant over WhatsApp whilst having a bit of a mental breakdown, and when he realised the direction of the conversation, he phoned me. I was hysterically crying and trying to stop. I told him I was facing the prospect of a life-changing surgery, and the relationship was becoming an extra burden when I needed to concentrate on myself, and he couldn't offer me the support I needed. He fought back and said he wasn't leaving me as I obviously needed him and was in a bad way. He done that thing where he reassured me, and I like the fool I am listened. He calmed me down, and we sorted it out, but there was only momentary relief as I knew this was going to happen again, and the burden still hung over me. It was killing me, I was losing my best friend on top of everything else, and it was the last thing I wanted, but I knew I was delaying the inevitable. There was no future.

It was finally time for my colonoscopy, and I wasn't scared this time around. The prep I was given was different, and I think it was called Klean prep this time and was 2 sachets. One to drink the night before and one in the morning, as I had an afternoon appointment. I was dreading the starvation more than anything, especially with steroids making me super hungry. This one tasted better than the Movi prep but had a real bite to it. It was apparently "orange" flavoured but tasted like undiluted Lemsip, like what I imagine tasting the actual powder is like, and the kick going down. I set up camp in my family house bathroom, laptop on the counter and began drinking. I managed to get it all down in the time recommendations they give and no projectile vomiting this time, which was a win. It was definitely easier to drink than the last one but still not something you would actively choose. I sat and watched Australian Love Island as the familiar unpleasant burn began. The hunger going to bed was annoying and made it harder to sleep. Also, the remaining clear liquid that was cutting through me meant I had to keep going to the toilet even when most of it was done. I wasn't looking forward to getting up at 6 am to start again as I knew I was clear, but needs must.

The 6 am wakeup call came and I began again. All I wanted was to fast forward to the afternoon for my actual procedure. My ass was raw as I knew it would be, but you always forget how painful it is. Especially as more and more burning water comes out of an already torn up delicate area. Showering even hurt as I got ready before going to the hospital, but I remembered this from the last time, the clean water still hurts the irritated skin. My mum came with me, and we waited in the Royal. I had definitely preferred the City, it looks brighter and cleaner; the Royal also seemed more basic. I felt like I was waiting for ages, but it was probably because I was so eager to have this over with and really hungry. I had a feeling ulcers were back due to the mouth ulcers returning, and after drinking all the laxatives, I was producing that familiar stomach lining looking stuff. I finally got called in for my pre-procedure questions and got asked to change into a hospital gown but keep my shoes on. The last time, I was in slippers, so I wasn't expecting this and was wearing biker boots. I was aware I looked like a dick as biker boots and a hospital gown are really not a lewk, but it was also strangely very me. I waited in the waiting area with another lady before being called, and we began chatting. Not long after, the nurse came around and called my name, and the lady I had been talking to told her, "You're taking my friend away from me". I found it nice and quite funny. I wished her the best of luck, and off I went with the nurse. The nurse said she recognised me and would I be in the ambulatory care centre. I said I was for infusions, and was a bit embarrassed as I seemed to be a big name on campus at the Royal. Not what every 25 year old aspires to, but here I was.

We went into the procedure room, and I still felt like such a dick with studded biker boots on. The room was tiny in comparison to the City's as well. It felt like there was barely any space to fit everyone and all the machinery in, like the screen was literally on top of me. It was also very dark and dingy looking. The City had bright lights, but this was a very different aesthetic. I was not vibing in comparison. I took the sedation through the cannula and wondered if it was a lower dose than last time as I didn't feel as out of it. I also wondered if my tolerance was just really high from all the pain relief I had been taking. The procedure began, and I said to the nurse, "I'm just gonna chat away to you, hope you don't mind", in my dopey state. She laughed and said that's what she liked to hear and loved talkers, and seemed genuinely happy at this. So, we chatted away, which I can only imagine was some incoherent shite, poor woman. We got to my small intestine and it was full of ulcers. They looked fresh and not as big as when I was first diagnosed, so I must have healed, then they came back. As the consultant was biopsying, he asked for silence to concentrate. It was really different from my first one where Dr Turner showed me the biospier and everything. I could feel the sensation of my insides being pulled at this time, so I knew exactly where in my stomach they were. It was a weird feeling, not painful, just more of a strange sensation. It was the bleeding as they biopsied bits that always weirded me out more, as they were just actively cutting bits out of you.

It was over shortly after, and it always didn't seem like that long. I told the consultant I had decided on vedolizumab as my new treatment, and he said he would arrange this. I got wheeled out of the room into recovery, and I remembered it from the year before when I had the emergency flexible sigmoidoscopy, and the nurse had been a cunt at the end. I really hoped she was here because if she was, I was going to give her a piece of my mind and tell her about the year I had had from Crohn's but sure, if it was up to her, I'd be with gynaecology. She wasn't there and instead had two really nice nurses. They were super attentive and friendly and straight away were telling me the standard, make sure to get all the wind out. I stayed with them, chatting until it was time to go. I really enjoyed my time with them as they were so lovely; it was such a different experience from last time and really put me in a good mood. I waited as I thought it would be like last time and I'd get my results on the spot, but instead got sent home, and the consultant told the nurses he would call me. It was kind of annoying, but I was glad to be going home. I also got tea and toast before I left, but it made me realise how hungry I was. One of the nurses actually got me extra biscuits, and of course, my mum shouted at me for taking them. Fuck off, Laura, I pay my taxes, I haven't eaten in closer to 24 hours, and I've just had a camera shoved up my ass whilst being blown up full of air and bits of my intestines cut out. I think I deserve the fucking biscuits. I left knowing I would just have to patiently wait for the call over the next few days for my results. If anything, the whole experience was teaching me I have now developed the patients of a saint.

I hit a real low over the next few days. I couldn't go to work, I was so depressed I could barely get out of bed. With how unwell I was feeling, I was used to that aspect physically, but this was also a depressed I can't get out of bed. My mum was going to my granny's in Tyrone, but she saw how down I was and wouldn't leave even though I kept telling her to. I was going to kill myself when she left, and it's why I needed her to go. No more fucking around with the idea of it or trying to come up with a master plan; I was going to just do it. I no longer feared death or the fear of the unknown, my whole world was unknown, so this wasn't much different. I welcomed the finalness of death as it meant no more suffering, and I couldn't cope with the ongoing unknowing. Fuck you Crohn's, you have won. The thing I said I wouldn't let you do, you have done. Unfortunately, my mum became aware of how low my mood was, and there wasn't much articulation happening. I kept telling her to go I'd be fine, but she kept saying she wouldn't leave me and I was the opposite of fine. I was a sobbing disgusting mess, and nothing was getting better; I couldn't do it anymore and had had enough. She forced me to come with her, and her and my granny arranged for my cousin, Danielle, who has her own beauty salon, to do my nails for me. I was dreading the journey as it was closer to an hour and a half, and that was currently a long time without the bathroom for me. I was thankfully fine and managed to hold it until my cousin's salon, with the bathroom being the first room I went to. I was glad I went in the end as I got to chat with Danielle, and it completely distracted me and put me in a better mood. I got acrylics done, so at least my nails looked fab, and I went to lunch with my mum, granny, and Danielle.

During lunch, a no caller ID phoned me, and I knew it would be the hospital. I answered in the café and spoke to the consultant. He told me the infliximab had been masking how severe the Crohns is, as with the amount of it in me, I should be very well, but it had worked to a point as my large intestine was actually in remission. I was absolutely shocked. However, my small intestine was causing the problems and was inflamed and ulcerated, like I had seen on the screen. He said the MRI results showed the same. He was emailing my surgeon as I needed to see him for surgery options, but they wanted to put me on the new infusion right away from a medical point of view and try it first. After the call ended, my mum shouted at me for pretending I was ok and going back to my bubbly self. I really didn't want the consultant to know how I was feeling, and it wasn't his business in my opinion. I would be going back to Dr Turner anyway, so that was my last interaction with him. I remember at the time being thankful for the day as it gave me the distraction I needed. I said to my mum on the way home, thanks for taking me, I think I needed it. She knew what I would have done if I was left alone, and it was acknowledged. Feelings are something I've never been good with and something so dark and personal, I especially wasn't good at talking about, especially to those closest.

I began getting phone calls that week from the ambulatory care centre arranging my infusion for vedolizumab that coming Tuesday. The nurse on the phone had said it seemed to work really well, and I was trying to be optimistic. I began researching it and reading about remission rates as apparently it is good at targeting ulcers. I did that annoying, stupid thing I do where I get my hopes up and began reading statistics about some people getting into remission in a matter of weeks. Remission seemed like a fairy tale, something that sounds amazing but isn't actually real. But I really wanted it. Most people wish for a nice house or a new car or something trivial and boring. I just wanted my health and life back. I had learned over the years that money doesn't buy happiness, and it was certainly a life lesson I was currently experiencing.

The Tuesday couldn't come soon enough, and as it was an afternoon appointment, I had intended to go to work then get the bus to the Royal as I normally did. However, that day I was so unwell I could barely leave bed; I was physically dragging my body about. I remember crawling on the floor and using units to support myself as the fatigue was so bad. I was dizzy and faint, and it wasn't from the steroids as I had now finished them. I felt so sick and tired, I just wanted to curl up into a ball. I was hoping for some kind of miracle, and sometimes infliximab gave me a surge of energy whilst getting it/just after and wondered if this one would be the same. I had to get a taxi to the hospital, but I was a bit nervous as I was by myself, and as this was a new infusion, there was a chance of a reaction etc. I arrived and was sent through to the infusion suite and began the standard process of checks. This one was different, it was the opposite of infliximab. Instead of it being made based on body weight, it was a standard 300mg dose over 30 minutes. The flush of saline after was the longest part and was going to be 2 hours. I was kind of raging; I had just mastered the pronunciation of infliximab and had to learn a whole new fancy word.

The hospital was short-staffed, and before my infusion began, myself and the others were brought around to a cubicle, and all piled into one with chairs. The infusion suite was being closed for the rest of the day as it didn't have the staff to cover it. The big armchairs with plenty of space between people were long gone, with about 5 people being crammed into this 1 cubicle. I was even more apprehensive in case something did go wrong. I had done the standard and borrowed Conor's tablet to watch Netflix's. The nurses made the medicine up, and this one takes about 20 minutes to dissolve, which feels like a long time, especially when apprehensively waiting. The infusion started, and I waited for the first half an hour to be up. When it was over, there were no reactions, and I was obviously super glad. The 2 hours for the flush seemed ridiculous when I saw the tiny bag; even the nurse said it seems ridiculous, but it's all about reactions, so can't risk it. The others who were in the cubicle with me were all new to Vedolizumab as well, or on their first few doses, so they had a long flush time. We all sat around waiting, and I was looking forward to getting home. A nice older gentleman worked there who I recognised from previous visits, and we were having a laugh when a psycho nurse came storming into the cubicle. The ward we were on was a place for those post-op or being discharged, and she came storming into the cubicle shouting, "I need a table!!! This patient needs their dinner!!!!" The rude bitch then began pulling my table, which had all my belonging on it, in her frantic look for one, as this patient was obviously in desperate need of a table before they died. I took my stuff and said I'm away soon and to take it. She frantically thanked me as she rushed away with it. The gentleman and I looked at each other, and he rolled his eyes and commented on how she thought she was an old school sister of the ward, and was actually technically retired but kept coming back. I laughed and commented that her behaviour was a bit extreme and rude. Myself and the others sitting there were also patients, likewise needing those tables. But this self-absorbed bitch only cared about what she was doing and accommodating the one patient she was looking after, not caring about how she spoke or treated other patients in the meantime. It was just yet another hit or miss experience with hospital staff. Some of them should really leave their profession as they clearly do not realise it is a vocation.

I had convinced myself I was feeling better already, but I wasn't. I was hoping for a miracle, but the next day, when I went back to work, I still wasn't good. I just felt disappointed and frustrated. It was 1 pm, and I had been to the toilet 11 times already that day. I had actually joked to workmates saying if I had to wipe my ass one more time, I was really going to lose it. They didn't know how I was doing it or how I was there, but needs must I had to get paid. I was so embarrassed anytime I was at work as I was usually late, and usually by a few hours as I couldn't get off the toilet from the moment I woke up. My anxiety was through the roof, so I had to fully talk myself into leaving the house. I was back to jumping on and off buses if I needed the toilet, or the first place I went to when I arrived in the office was the toilet. I kept thinking people probably just thought I was late or milking it, but when in reality, they had no idea how much it took for me to leave the house.

I wasn't social anymore and found most social interactions painful. I felt so far removed from normality, like this freak who couldn't fit in. My appetite was shit, so I could barely eat at lunch, and people's normal conversations about shite were not interesting to me, nor did I have the energy/attention span to follow. I would forget what I was saying mid-conversation with a person and get embarrassed. Conor had taken an interest, and from reading about Crohn's, said it was fatigue manifesting itself; my brain was too tired to function. I could barely concentrate on any work I did and did not want to be there, but had to. It was a horrible feeling as I really like my work and everyone in it, but I couldn't think of much else when feeling that unwell. I was also paranoid about how grim I must be coming across. When asked how I was, people roughly knew I wasn't well, but I felt like I was just whinging when telling them in more detail. This had been ongoing for a year now, so I was concerned that I sounded like a broken record. It was out of my hands but still not nice to have to repeatedly tell people more and more medical problems instead of getting better. I hate sounding or being the victim, which also contributed to me not wanting to socialise as much. Jaclyn, my work friend, had been so kind and was so concerned when talking to me. I told her that I must sound like a melter with never-ending problems, but she completely empathised and said anyone would be the same, especially with it going on for so long. It really helped when people listened and understood. This was not a life anyone would want or choose.

It was nearly Christmas now, and I was seeing both my surgeon and Crohns consultant the following week, which was the week before Christmas. I couldn't wait as I felt it would give me more clarity. Everything was still completely unknown and up in the air. I still wanted a bag or something to help, as the life I was living was no life. My mental health was also still in the shitter, and an emergency GP appointment had been arranged too. I did not want to go, but it was my mum who booked it and forced me. I had actually said if I was made to talk about my feelings, I would rather slit my wrists. I didn't want to admit I needed help as I thought that was embarrassing or showing weakness. I now realise I couldn't have been more wrong, it was a very brave thing for anyone who needs help to do.

When I saw Dr Tan, he did not want to perform any more surgery at the moment as I had just started a new medication. I said to him I was really at the point where I wanted a bag or at least surgery to cut bits out. He explained that having surgery now would be pointless as my MRI and biopsies showed how active the Crohn's still is. If he was to cut bits out now when not in remission, the Crohn's would just spread to new tissue around that area. The problem with this is that you can't keep cutting out bits of someone's bowel. I said to him, is that because it gives you short bowel syndrome (something I had read about and happens when too much of your intestines are taken away and then gives you the same symptoms as Crohn's)? He smiled and agreed, and said that if too much was cut out, it would be irreversible and result in a bag for life. He also said the last time a bag was talked about was because of how extremely poorly I was; my insides wouldn't be guaranteed they would knit back together again. He said I was at a point now where they should attach together, but the inflammation would come back, so he would only do surgery when I'm in remission as I would probably have scar tissue, and it would be to cut it out. It turns out inflammation, internal ulcers, some healing, and then repeating the cycle, fully scars you up. Apparently, its symptoms are mainly that of stomach pain, and there is no medication you can take for scar tissue, so it's only way for removal is surgery. He really wanted me to try the medications first and said if vedolizumab didn't work, there was a new drug being made and released in 2019 and to try it as well.

I felt hopeless, I couldn't wait to get my life back any longer. He examined my stitch and fistula and said what I already knew, it wasn't ready to come out. If infliximab hadn't worked, it certainly wasn't better. I was glad I didn't have another imminent surgery though. I had said as much as I wanted to be better, I couldn't have been bothered with it and the recovery.

I saw Dr Turner a few days later. I was in a bad place but trying to pretend I was fine. I think I had just had my second dose of vedolizumb as the starting doses are like infliximab, and you get the first 3 close together. First one, then next one 2 weeks later, then the next 4 weeks later. Up until the 5th or 6th dose, I think, you get it once a month, then it went on to every 8 weeks. The Crohns still wasn't settling, and I, of course, was now thinking this infusion was never going to work either. My recent bloods also showed my liver was still not functioning properly, great. As I was applying for PIPs again, he kindly said he had no problems at all with a letter and done one for me. When I read it after I was sent a copy, it was surreal.

"Sarah has developed extremely severe Crohn's disease", was the opening line. I knew it was true, but it was weird reading it from a medical professional. You get so used to it being your life, you don't think of yourself as being that bad. I was prescribed more steroids, the ones I had been put on pretty much exactly a year before, and also cholestagel for bile salts. The part that absorbed the bile salts was inflamed and ulcerated again. It was a year later, and I felt like I was worse off. It was really unfair and disheartening, it just didn't seem right. I had known people who had beaten cancer in this time. I was resenting them for having curable cancer and going back to their normal lives. Why couldn't I have had a curable cancer, my disease is incurable, and I was aware remission might not mean I was totally normal again. Imagine being 25 and wishing for cancer as an alternative illness. It evoked sadness and rage in me for the unfair cards I had been dealt. I had said this to a few people, not in a hateful way but in a matter-of-fact way, "I know people who have beat cancer before I can beat Crohn's". Yet half the world doesn't know what IBD is or realise the seriousness of it. Anyone I said to didn't argue either; they acknowledged the fact and didn't say much else. There wasn't really much else you could say to be fair.

I think Dr Turner saw a different side to me that day. My mum had outed my mental health and said she was worried sick with a suicidal daughter. He tried reassuring me it would get better, and as horrible as it was, it would get under control. It was just a horrible process, and he wasn't surprised about how I was feeling after everything I'd been through. He knew people who would have lost it at a lot less. This was probably strange for him as he was used to laughing at me and telling me I had a great way with words, as I swore and used words like "gooch" and "vag" in a medical setting. I didn't really know how I was still going either, I think it was just survival.

I was raging I was back on steroids again, and because they were the budesonide Crohn's specific ones, it took chemists ordering them in before I could get them and a lot of waiting around. They ended up taking a few days to be ready and had to go back to collect them. I didn't want to start them because of all the side effects, it was literally a waiting game before I'd have eyebrows starting from my mid-forehead and a 13-year-old boy moustache. Not to mention the weight gain when I already felt huge and was way bigger than my normal size. I was still in a healthy BMI and not overweight (never had been), but it was not my normal size. When I collected the steroids, I originally thought I had been given the wrong ones and googled them. They weren't the 3 little red heavy capsules like this time last year. They were sachets like you would get for readymade coffee or something. Apparently, they were the same, and when I opened the sachet, it was full of the little white balls that the pills were full of. I knew this as one day I had opened a spare pill to see why they were so heavy. Again, it had to be taken 30 minutes before food, and it actually tasted quite nice, like lemon. Basically, you had to neck the sachet of steroids and wash them down with a load of water. It kind of went a bit powdery and sometimes hard to get down, but after a few days, I could do it in max 1 or 2 goes.

I saw my GP lastly, and I did not want to go. My mum came in with me and began crying, saying how worried she was. I sat there with my head down thinking, don't speak, your voice will crack, and you'll cry. Do not cry, do not cry. I bit my tongue and tried keeping my best poker face. My GP tried reassuring me it would get better. She said she didn't know a person with Crohn's who didn't eventually get better, it was really rubbish and took a long time, but I would get there. I was fed up with hearing this as I did not think this would be my life. Tears, of course, came, and I was so embarrassed. I didn't want to be there talking about emotions; I just wanted to end it and not deal with it. I couldn't understand why people couldn't see where I was coming from. I thought their viewpoints were selfish as they weren't living this hell, hadn't experienced any of it ever, and most likely never would. I knew antidepressants could fuck you up more as well if not put on the right ones, and basically, that's what my GP said. She said I was on so much medication my body probably wouldn't handle this other stuff and could end up worse, so she wanted me to go to counselling instead. I think I was referred to the Samaritans or someone, I can't remember. I was also given numbers and sheets and was to phone them if I needed or feeling low. I permanently felt low, and I wasn't good with talking about my feelings, so I wasn't going to use it. She asked me if I was safe at the moment, and I said yes (I wasn't about to say no, I just wanted to die silently, no fuss). Before I left, she gave me a high 5 and told me it would get better. I hoped, but I just didn't know.

It was Christmas time, and I was so glad to be off for the holidays, but it was very bittersweet. Conor and I were getting on really well, but it wasn't right. It needed to end. A few weeks previously, he had come in from a night out, but I had been so unwell I had been simultaneously vomiting into a bag whilst also on the toilet. Just living my best Crohn's life, yano. He had told me ones were asking how I was, and he said he had told them I was sick, but I was so strong that I was fine and dealing with it all really well. WHAT. My face must have been a picture, as his dropped and he said, "oh, you didn't like that." What fucking planet was he on?!? Here I was trying not to kill myself on a daily basis, and he's out telling the world I'm coping 100%, no bother. It was at that moment I really knew I needed out. He was obviously in so much denial, and he wasn't coping himself.

Over Christmas, though, we had been doing nice things, like walking my dog on Boxing Day in Belvoir and had been out and about doing stuff together, whilst also having time by ourselves to chill. Halfway through the Christmas break, when we came in from a night out drinking with mates, he asked me was I going to break up with him again. I didn't lie; I told him the truth and said yes, my feelings still hadn't changed. It broke my heart saying it and even more so as I watched him burst out crying and say, "How could you blindside me like that again." I couldn't make sense of my own fucking brain, never mind try to articulate it to him, and I just didn't want to hurt him. I apologised and said I didn't want to break up but knew we had to, and I would have told him, but I just didn't know how. He said he knew it was coming as I had already tried breaking up with him twice before and knew this time would be it. He was right. It was soo fucking sad, I was literally losing my best mate. We discussed it, and I was moving all my stuff out after the Christmas break.

We had a really nice last week together, but the upcoming events were lingering and hanging over us. Both of us ignoring what was actually happening just to have a nice time together. It was the definition of an elephant in the room. We went to our friend's house party on NYE, and I, unfortunately, had a 10 glass of vodka to myself. I was really drowning the sorrows and saying fuck you to 2018. We ended up fighting as he thought I was behaving badly. I think I was flirting with other friends which I always did as a joke, but it didn't go down well with drink involved and a break-up going on. I was also so blocked I couldn't actually remember.

New Year's came, and we were into 2019. I began moving out on the 2nd. It was heart-breaking, and I didn't want to leave the flat. It took a few days, but I moved back into my old room in the attic. I felt like I had gone back in time. My mum had got units from IKEA for all my stuff, and building flat packed furniture with her was not the one. I hate that shit, and she loves it, and we were not gelling well. As I began unpacking my stuff and sorting my room, there were so many memories of Conor or joined things we had owned. It was overwhelming, and I was trying to stay calm. My life felt like a shambles. I was moving back home where I didn't want to be, I had lost my boyfriend and best friend, I still wasn't in remission and didn't know when I would be or if any of this new medication would work. I wanted to get on with my life but didn't know what to do or where to start, or what was happening.

My heart started racing, and my chest felt tight and sore. I felt dizzy, and like I couldn't breathe properly; sweats had even started. I didn't know what was wrong. I told Katie, and she told me I was having an anxiety attack. Fucking hell. She said it was really good that as the panic raised, I could talk myself down, as it would go into a panic attack if I didn't. She would suffer from them, so she knew what was going on. It was mad my body was actually doing this with everything going on. I kept getting them for weeks but did always manage to talk myself down. I was really struggling with not talking to Conor every day, so by the end of the first week, I reached out to see if he was ok, as I really wasn't. He was a bit cold understandably, but made it out he was better than he was. This wasn't my first break up, but this was the first break up where I didn't really want it to happen or to cut ties completely. We had such a solid friendship, and I was so scared it was going to get ruined during all of this. There was still that high level of care.

Finding the light

The next few months were weird. I very slowly started improving and was only going to the toilet in the morning now. Although what was coming out was not normal, it was all slow, steady improvements. My skin open wounds were all improving and healing, and some of them had completely disappeared. The biggest one on my left shin kept causing issues though and kept randomly flaring up. It would be nearly healed, and then it would go bad again. I was aware all the steroid creams I was using weren't for long term use too, as they thin your skin. The scalp psoriasis was the same, sometimes it was completely gone, and then other times it would randomly but mildly come back. This happened until about April, and then it never came back again. Of course, I also got moon face again but thankfully milder than before. I also grew more hair, but likewise, it wasn't as bad as before. However, there was one new steroid side effect I was NOT prepared for.

One day near the end of January, I must have been back on the roids about a month, and as energy levels and general health had thankfully greatly improved, I was back to exercising. I had been such an active person and was usually toned, so the weight gain and lack of routine or movement had really got to me, but it was all coming back. I'm not sure how I even noticed it, but there were two big purple marks up the inside of my left leg. They looked like burns, and I thought I maybe burned myself with the straighteners when holding them between my legs. But also, hadn't felt anything and was wearing clothes, so I couldn't understand how I wouldn't notice. I showed my mum, and she was also like, WTF is that. When going up for my next infusion, she told me to take a picture and show the nurses to see if they knew. I had shown a few people, and no one could understand what it was. I showed the nurses as well, and they too didn't know what it was. I worried it was stretch marks as they scar (more scars yay...), but I also hadn't suddenly lost or gained a lot of weight. Everyone I showed had said no, they didn't look like stretch marks, but I was unsure. What could they actually be? Of course, I started googling what it looked like, and stretch marks appeared. No. Fucking. Way. I went to my steroid box and got the information sheet out. There it was listed in top most common side effects, "red stripes on skin (stretch marks)". Unbelievable. I then googled steroid-induced stretch marks, and mine matched exactly. They were big, thick, purple, burn looking things, like proper gashes, and I understood the term "tiger stripe". I looked like a tiger had scratched its paw down me. Funnily though, a few of my mates I showed a picture to and said it looked like a tiger had scratched me, had all said they'd like to see how the tiger ended up.

Over the next few weeks, another gash formed on the top of my right leg. It was weird, I literally watched as it formed and got a bit worse every day until it stopped. I wouldn't have minded if they were natural as I had stretch marks on the side of my hips from a teenager, but these were huge and medically induced, yet again!! I hated them soo much and was soo conscious, even though they were in a place no one was going to see without my permission. When I saw my consultant, I said to him, and he apologised and said, yes, it's a side effect and would be from the steroids. When I saw the dermatologist again, I asked about having them lasered off, but apparently it doesn't really work. Also, it was the NHS; they weren't going to offer that. He told me to make sure they were really moisturised, and I had already been using Bio-Oil as soon as I noticed them. Not that I think it worked or overly helped. They were more scars that needed to heal in their own time. I even tried retinol and a derma roller, no miracle workers. My mum told me to lay off the exercise as I had hit it hard, and my body was probably in shock. No time Laura, I was trying to control this steroid weight as I was back at work full time and regularly saw in public. I did not want to look fat.

I received a letter with a telephone appointment from a suicide hotline place. It was who I had been referred to and basically was a telephone call with questions to triage where I should go for counselling. I nipped into a private room at work and took the call the day of the appointment. The questions asked were personal and intense; I can't remember them in detail, but it included questions like how I had tried to hurt myself and why etc. I ended up embarrassingly crying on the phone all whilst thinking, oh fuck I've to go back to my desk, I better not look like I've been crying. When I was asked about my situation and story by the woman on the phone, she said to me it sounded like I had been traumatised by all my experiences and how I felt was completely understandable, but it's also not normal to want to kill yourself, so I was to be referred to Wave Trauma Centre for counselling. There was, of course, a backlog and a long wait, so it would be a while before I heard. I remember thinking, I probably won't need it by the time it comes around and thought of ways to cancel or not go, but I also knew I probably should. It was embarrassing to admit I was so mentally unwell due to my circumstances that I had to go to counselling. Now upon re-flection, it was a bad mindset I was in. Your brain is your most vital organ, requiring 20% of your energy, and like all organs, it can get sick. Just like my Crohn's, my brain needed treatment. I remember being shocked when they said about trauma as well. I had never thought about it like that and never thought I had been traumatised.

However, the more I thought about it though, the more I became not surprised. It kind of all started making sense. I've since chat-ted to one of my friends who has had Ulcerative Colitis since she was a teenager. She said how she went to counselling years ago and just cried and cried for hours, and how there is no support for young people diagnosed with life-long incurable illnesses. She is 100% right. IBD is a "young person's disease", and we are expected to just be diagnosed with a brutal, debilitating, taboo illness and get on with it. It's not an easy thing to deal with at any age, never mind as a child, teenager or young adult, and more needs to be done in this area.

I went back to my desk but made sure I looked ok before I went back. I pretended it was all good and just a few stupid questions to my friend Jill who I sat beside. We're really good friends now but were more work friends at the time and didn't want to embarrass myself or make a scene at the time. I was paranoid since we had started working together, I had been nothing but sick and depressing, and that's obviously not something you want to be thought of as. I hate people who play the victim, and I really didn't want to be doing that at any point. I never wanted people pitying me; I'm not a pity party. I think all anyone with a chronic illness wants is a bit of empathy and compassion. As I got better though, Jill said my personality and mood had completely lifted, and could tell I was doing a lot better. All the people who had told me how well I looked when unwell also got a shock. As I got better, they said you could now tell I wasn't previously well at all. I'm very naturally pale, and apparently, sickness had made me more of a grey colour. Now I was being told I was pale but looked healthy, not grey. I was finally becoming myself again.

The process of getting better was slow, and I still wasn't mentally or physically in the best of places for a good few months. I was much better than I was but still not back to my full self. I hadn't realised, but there was a lot of healing to be done. I hated myself and how I looked. I wanted to blow all my savings and get my whole face injected so I could look like a different person. Massively trying to fill a hole I now realise, but I felt like it was a serious option at the time. I had actually booked to get my lips injected and underneath my eyes filled. I always hated the dark circles under my eyes (which I've since been told is because I'm so pale it's blood vessels/pigmentation...thank you, genetics) and wanted them gone. I was newly single as well and did not feel attractive. The person I was going to though because she was a doctor, said I needed a doctor's letter from my Crohn's consultant AND dermatologist, both of which were absolutely baffled. Crohn's and its medications do not interact with facial fillers, maybe a higher risk of infection from immune suppressors, but that's it. She made me feel like a freak as she refused to treat me if I didn't have the letters, also commenting on not wanting to touch me because of the seriousness of the medication I'm on. I got it, but it reminded me that I'm not normal when already feeling fragile. The appointment had to be cancelled as I couldn't get consent letters in time and actually had a mini fight with Dr Turner and his secretary. I was actually extremely upset about this as I really am very lucky and love my consultant; he's really good and super nice. I also rarely fight with anyone and found the whole situation really upsetting. Now with hindsight, I'm glad it was cancelled. When feeling gross after surgery in the summer, I had got 0.5ml of filler in my top lip, but no consent was needed. I was so desperate now in March, nearly a year later, I went somewhere else consent was not needed. I had just tried booking in with a "Doctor" as I thought she'd be well trained with needles, and I had learned the place I had went to in the summer was not actually that great, and she wasn't properly trained (dodgy). I desperately booked in with a proper clinic and got another 0.5ml in my top lip a week later. They wouldn't touch my eyes and said I didn't need it. The sad thing was, it was all down to how I felt in myself. I felt I needed these changes made to me. Between the stretch marks, moon face, facial and body hair, weight gain, all of which were out of my control, I hated myself. I could barely look in a mirror. The saddest fact of all is for a good while, I cried myself to sleep every night, mentally repeating the line from Beauty and the Beast, "who could ever love a beast."

I was scared about dating again. I mentally had it in my head no one would want me because I have Crohn's and all the baggage that came with it, and who could actually be bothered with that. A few of my friends I had said this to, including the guys, were absolutely baffled. When on a night out, I had been talking to Conor and had said this. He laughed and joked saying, he can think of a lot of other reasons why not to date me other than having Crohn's and what came with it, and began listing tardiness, sassiness etc., amongst other undesirable qualities. We laughed, and he said to wise up and that people would be lucky to date me. I didn't feel it at the time, but I was learning to re-love myself.

Dr Turner had been concerned about my liver. I had a lot of hospital appointments in early 2019 to see if I was on the right track, and he was most concerned at the blood result taken on my birthday when my mum had forced me to go to hospital, and the GI doctor I saw had no idea what to do with me. He said that whatever result or function was off was really bad, and I asked him would it have been from drink, as I had been drinking a lot the night before. He said no, if it was alcohol, it would be another function that was off and showed me what one it would have been on the computer screen, and it was normal. I said to him what had happened with the other doctor and that those bloods were taken in the hospital, and he was horrified. I could see the visible annoyance on his face as I should have been admitted or dealt with and just wasn't. My liver function had improved a bit but still wasn't normal. He said I needed to go for a liver scan just to make sure there was no permanent damage. Him and Dr Tan were always so good with me, they knew I was interested in test results and always showed/explained things in depth. Dr Tan had previously asked me if I had seen my MRIs before and was going to show me them, but didn't have a copy of the video available at the time. I absorbed everything they told me, went away, and done my own research, trying to understand everything the best I could.

When I went for the liver scan one afternoon, I remember thinking it was probably going to be fine and have healed itself. The ultrasound bit where I went to in the Royal was quiet, and although I was like 40 minutes early for my appointment, I was seen straight away. The nurse who took it was really lovely, and we chatted away. She warned me about the cool gel as it was rubbed all over the scanner thing, but I had had ultrasounds before, so I knew what it was like. I wondered why they put the gel on though, and she explained if any oxygen is present, the machine can't pick up the image, so it is to block out any air. Interesting. My whole stomach was scanned, and when in different areas of my abdomen, the machine said on the screen what organ it was. A lot of it was blurry, and I couldn't make it out, or the organ was a lot bigger or not in the place I thought it was. I guess my medical knowledge of the anatomy is not what I thought it was. Quite a lot of pressure was applied throughout, and I remember thinking, this isn't sore, but I can really feel it.

When the scan was over, the nurse said she would be back in a minute, she just needed to get the doctor. I thought nothing of this as I was used to nurses grabbing doctors for me from hospital admissions, but this was a hospital appointment, I should've known better. The doctor that came in was also really lovely, and he repeated the scan over my liver. Throughout the scan, constant pictures and videos were taken. He then brought them up and confirmed the liver damage. He showed me on the screen, a large white area and shadows and explained your liver should be clear, with no white areas or shadows at all. I couldn't believe it. He said from how it was disbursed, it was most likely from medication, but all results were to be sent to my consultant for him to review. I was diagnosed with fatty liver, which was described on the scale of liver disease from lowest to a full-blown alcoholic who needs a transplant, the starting step. He was confident it would get better and at the early stages, but my consultant needed to review it. I got my standard 2 buses from the Royal home and phoned my mum to let her know. We couldn't believe it, but with my medical luck, we really should not have been surprised.

I saw Dr Turner again, and he sent me for a liver MRI. I asked was the damage from medication, and he said no. He had reviewed the videos and images, and if it were from medication, my liver would have healed really quickly, like within a month. Mine was damaged from my body being so sick. What the actual fuck. I was a 25-year-old. Yes, I had been binge drinking when out for about 10 years, but no more than the average young adult. I knew alcoholics/drug addicts who had abused their bodies for years and were also a lot older than me, who had full body scans done that showed not a single thing was wrong with their bodies and, most importantly, livers. Again, I wasn't sure how this was fair or just, but it was the cards I had been dealt. I knew the liver healed itself, but mine had been damaged for at least 6 months by this point and was still trying to heal. I had also been told the constant weight gain and loss would have also been a factor and enough to give some people fatty liver. My weight gain/loss had of course come from illness, so it was all linked in. It needed to be monitored until it was better, and my hope was no more surgeries, or any permanent damage shown on the MRI. I also learned my hair had thinned/fallen out due to ill health as well as infliximab. When you're sick, your body stops concentrating on normal functions like hair growth and tries repairing itself instead; therefore, leading to hair loss as it temporarily stops that function.

I received my letter for the liver MRI, and it was in the Royal on a Saturday. There was a backlog, and now a Saturday service had been set up. My dad took me over for it, and it was by far the easiest MRI I had been for. A 12-minute scan with no prep, just a cannula in my vein. I was given the standard form to fill out, if I had any metal in my body, been shot etc., then went through the questions again with the radiographer. I was a pro at this now. I was given my scrubs and was waiting to get my cannula put in, telling them the standard of what veins worked and what one's didn't. There was a wee boy maybe in his early teens there with his mum, and he obviously and rightly so wasn't used to all this. But no offence to him, he was coming across like a little bitch. I could tell the radiographer, although being super nice and accommodating, was also thinking the same. He needed to get the cannula in, and before any needles were even produced, he was complaining about the thing they put around your arm to make your veins come up. I call them a heroin belt, but I don't think that's the medical terminology. They're tight (they're supposed to be) and sometimes made of plastic, meaning they can tug uncomfortably at your skin, but they're on for no more than a minute. He was told if he found it really bad, they could give him numbing cream that they give to kids, but it takes a long time to kick in, and he would be waiting a long time. I remember sarcastically thinking, "They've never offered ME numbing cream before", as I thought of all my punctured veins.

At one of my infusions, one of the nurses pointed out to me my arms are scarred from all the puncture wounds. She was right, and now I can see all the little holes in my arms where I've previously been stabbed. His mum then asked if she could be in the MRI room with him when he was getting his scan. She was obviously told no. They got the needle in after a load of fuss and whining, and his mum said she was treating him to lunch and shopping after. Fair play to ya kid, it was probably an ordeal, and your mum was treating you after, but I personally thought he could've manned up a bit. I realised; however, I was probably becoming desensitised, and it was nothing personal against him. But I had also had my first surgery at his age, if not younger, and there was no getting on like that.

Like all people, when I initially see a cannula or needle, I do get the fear as I'm well aware it can be sore. One day, a nurse told me the pain varies as it depends on what nerve endings are hit with the needle. It's not a pleasant experience, but it's over quickly, and it's for the benefit of your health. I thought back to a day after seeing Dr Turner, and I was getting my post-appointment bloods done (you usually get bloods done every time you see your consultant, so they know how you're doing). I walked into the room where they were doing them, and an old lady who was having hers done, was literally screaming and squirming in the chair as the nurse tried to get her blood. I thankfully got moved to another room as that one was so busy, but I had started laughing and was biting my tongue. I genuinely couldn't believe how she was getting on, it was very comical. She was easily in her 60's, grow up. The nurse I was walking out with saw me, and her face went as well, as we both walked out, trying not to laugh. She just went to me "I know" on the way out as I said, "that's what you's are up against."

Shortly after, it was time for my MRI, and I was put in the machine with some layers of the stuff they usually put on top of you. The music on the headphones they always give had started, and the radiographer spoke through the microphone, saying the scan was starting now. A poor-quality version of Ed Sheeran – Castle on the Hill started playing, but from all my MRI experience, I knew the scan hadn't started just yet; there were no loud noises. Moments later, I saw through the slight gap between the layers placed on top of me and the top of the MRI machine, the radiographer come into the room and pull me out of the machine. She laughed and said, "You're so slim the machine can't pick up your image". WHATTTTTTT. This super-expensive machine has just given me the best compliment ever!!! Feeling like I had eternally resembled a large sack of potatoes and was extraordinarily single (I had been single a few months and was not in the place of wanting to meet anyone or dating), this was phenomenal! She put more layers of the foamy pillowy stuff on top of me, and I was put back in the machine, delighted with myself.

There were so many layers on top of me I could barely see out of the machine now and had always thought about a generally big/ tall person most likely struggling to fit inside, never mind having the extra layers. But they probs weren't as much of a stunner as me, who needed extra equipment for their image to be picked up yano. The scan started soon after, but they forgot to put the music back on, so it was 12 minutes of the loud beeping. Every MRI I had had all made different types of beeping noises. Some were generic loud prolonged BEEEEEEEP's whilst others were like BEEP BEEP BEEP continuously. All loud, but I always amazed myself at how well I settled into them. The noise and lack of space didn't annoy me. I always concentrated on a space where I could see out or some form of light and just zoned out. Not long after, it was over, and I got to go home straight away, absolutely delighted with myself and my new bae MRI. Until next time boo x.

I was contacted by Wave Trauma Centre around March and was invited up for the 6 sessions every Friday. I was really apprehensive and felt like I was in a much better place as both my mental and physical health were improving, and again was concerned I was wasting a space. My friends who had been to counselling had really encouraged it though, and said it was really helpful. So, I bit the bullet, and I went. My counsellor was really lovely, and the first session was mostly figuring out why I was there and what to do. It was emotional, and I cried during most of it, talking about the past and what had happened. It was weird, I never felt these emotions at the time; it was all as I processed them upon reflection I got upset. Again, I panicked about how I'd look when I went back to work but had mastered the skill of wiping away a tear before it destroys your makeup. She said I had been through a serious amount and didn't know how I had coped so well as most others wouldn't have. It really validated how I felt, and she said what most people said to me, "How did you do it? I couldn't have." People don't realise their strength until they have to, no one would choose a difficult life, but you gotta play the hand you've been dealt, and that's all I did. I was really glad I went to the counselling, and it was really helpful. It was Cognitive Behaviour Therapy, more commonly known as CBT. Every week I'd have a new task and have to put it into action, which I actually surprised myself by doing. She kept telling me each week she was really proud and impressed with me. One of the tasks was about what gives you value in your life, something with being chronically ill, I hadn't been getting in the areas I wanted. I said travel, so I booked to go to Australia that October. My friends were going to Lisbon in the summer for a week for a festival, Nos Alive, and then a few days seeing the city. Scared about my health etc., I didn't let it stop me, and I went.

One of the weeks, the counselling was postponed to the following week, and I had that Friday off work. So, I pushed myself out of my comfort zone and done something simple I hadn't done by myself in years. I took my dog to the park. The overwhelming fear and anxiety of needing a toilet meant anytime I had been to the park in recent years, I was with someone, and we usually drove to and from it. But that day, I got up, worked out, got ready, then walked my dog to the park, done a couple of laps with him, and walked back home. It sounds ridiculous, but I was so fucking proud of myself. I had used another technique CBT had taught me to talk myself down and rationalise things. Like what happens if I do flare, how to work through the negative thought processes. I was so glad I done it and had a really nice day. The simple things people take for granted I no longer took for granted. I'm still thankful it doesn't hurt when I cough, sneeze, walk etc., but of course, like all humans, I have got used to this again and forget how bad it really was. I completed my 6 weeks and was happy I did. I would honestly recommend it to anyone. I had a joke with one of my friends who had also been to counselling, and they had called them their loopy meetings. I pissed myself laughing and affectionately referred to my meetings as that as well. There's still so much stigma around mental health, which is probably due to the invisible nature of it, just like all invisible illnesses. People can't see it, so they don't understand.

If someone has a cold or cough, it's obvious, and there are outward visible signs. There is no stigma around seeking treatment either. However, when your most vital organ needs a little help, people seem not to seek it.

Around that time, I received my 3rd pips decision back. This time, I had professionals help me fill out the form, along with medical evidence, purposely didn't shower or brush/wash my hair before the interview, and gave minimal answers, also confirming yes when asked if I was suicidal. The woman's response was horrifying but to be expected from PIP assessors. She responded basically saying, yeah, we don't care, and there's nothing we can do if you are suicidal, but we just have to ask so we can inform someone else. Cool. Overall, she was horrible and cold, and I really wanted her out of my house. Of course, the decision was another no, and the letter yet again reduced me to such rage I actually cried. She had stated that I "came across intelligent", therefore meaning I do not need PIP as one of the reasons... pretty sure Stephen fucking Hawking's was one of the smartest people in the world and also incredibly disabled due to illness, you fucking idiots. She also "noted" my mental health, but I seemed in a good mood, so disregarded my medical evidence. I can't even remember half the fucking shite they yet again spewed out on the beyond insulting letter. The system is beyond disgusting, and their appalling decisions coincide with the number of deaths and suicides that are happening post-decision. The government quite literally has blood on their hands. These wrongly established systems have been set in place by those in authority, living privileged lives, who have no fucking clue about illness in general. Pieces of shit. Probably Tory shit at that too. Something needs to change, and in recent light of the coronavirus pandemic, I hope people open their eyes to the thousands of debilitated people stuck in their houses (if they're lucky enough to have accommodation) every day. Living with the constant unknown/uncertainty that is life, asking for that tiny bit of help from the government to survive and cover medical costs that are outside of their control.

Time to go and love myself

I spent 2019 getting my life back. I had brought my mum to Edinburgh for a few days for her Christmas present in January as a massive thank you. I'm eternally grateful for everything her and my dad did and continue to do for me. The few days away with my mum was actually class and we had great fun. She was up for drinking loads, which she normally isn't, so I encouraged this and took full advantage. She enjoyed the trip so much it's now a yearly thing where I take her away as her Christmas present. What have I done... only joking. In early 2020 I took her to London to visit my sister for a few days, and again was good fun. My mum went above and beyond for me as all good mums do, and it's the least I can do to repay her. Thanks for everything, Laza D, you the real MVP.

I went to Lisbon with my friends, a group of 11 of us and had a great time. I was initially scared, of course; what if something happened or I needed the toilet, and there were 10 others there and someone in it. Thankfully I was absolutely fine but always have spare imodem just in case. I can't quite kick the habit. I thought I might be in remission, but of course, remission didn't mean what I thought it did. I was about 80% a normal person but still had good and bad days or the odd flare-up. I also continually got the "sure you were only 80% normal anyway" joke one too many times, but it's fine; they were right. At this time, my Crohn's was closest to what I would consider "remission" and was mostly symptom-free.

After Lisbon, I really pushed myself out of my comfort zone and booked to go to Bali by myself, 5 or 6 weeks after I had booked it. The mental stress of this did cause a mini flare up for a few weeks, but it went back to normal again. I had always wanted to go and was supposed to go with Conor, but that didn't happen. So I took it upon myself to go. I booked with STA travel and done one of those G Adventure groups. I'm so glad I did it as I was paired with Holly, who I've made a friend for life with. We booked to go away together again to the Philippines, but the Coronavirus (Covid-19) happened, so that is currently postponed. Bali was beyond amazing, but before heading, I was also scared as I had never travelled by myself before, and here I was going across the world. As I am late for everything, I was worried I'd miss my bus to Dublin as I had left packing so late (standard), but I made it in the nick of time. I had a serious nervous tummy too but was thankfully fine and took my standard precautionary imodem. As I talked to the taxi driver on the way down to the bus station, he said a really good expression when I told him where I was off to and why, "if you knew what was around every corner, you would never go." He was 100% right. If I had known anything that was going to happen to me in 2018, I would never have believed it and would not have done it, well, at least tried not to.

The tour took us around Bali, Lombok, and the Gili islands, which I would highly recommend. Everyone's stomach was a bit funny with the foods and drinks, but compared to some, I actually think my Crohn's behaved better than their normal bowels from what people had been saying. Or maybe I was just used to it, I don't know. It was the drinks that got me the most, not the food. Holly and I were always drinking cocktails, and her stomach was the same as mine afterwards, so we knew it was the cheap drink and the ice. I was mostly eating stir fry dishes, so there was nothing too offensive food-wise. In the Gili islands, we were offered to try street food for dinner one night. It was a unanimous no, thankfully. Fuck knows what that would do to your insides. The hygiene levels were not good, and I unfortunately got a skin infection when out there and had to go on antibiotics for a week when home. All round though, Bali was amazing, and I was literally depressed coming home. Holly and I hadn't left each other's sides for 2 weeks and missed each other like mad when home. Everyone in the tour group was lovely as well, and there was a complete mix of people from all over the world.

When I was in Bali, I received a hospital letter to see my consultant, but as I was away, my mum rearranged it for when I was back. The only appointment available then was with another doctor in an overflow clinic. I attended this and realised months later I still didn't know my liver results, and as I thought I was in remission, could the doctor check. On 7th October 2019, I had my best doctor's appointment ever. I went to this one by myself, as my mum said she couldn't get it off work, and of course it was the one I got good news in. My bloods showed that I was in a stable and normal range. Not "normal for Crohn's" normal but ACTUAL NORMAL PERSON NORMAL. My last faecal calprotein test taken in the summer when I had a mini flare, showed my internal inflammation levels were sitting at 200 and something, which is considered "normal/remission" for a person with IBD (I mean 0 is the dream, but I doubt I will ever get that and it was stress that triggered that mini flare, not ill health). Also, my liver had fully healed itself, and blood results were all back to normal, and no permanent damage confirmed from the MRI. FUCKING YEOOOOOOOOOOOOOO!!!!! I was delighted! FINALLY!!! After all this time!! I could say that magical 9 lettered word, remission. Again, it confirmed that I was only about 80% normal, but I absolutely took it compared to what I had been. I done stupid happy dances for days, and I couldn't wipe the smile off my face. I think I told everyone I knew. It was really nice that everyone I spoke to seemed genuinely happy for me. It was mad that nearly 2 years after diagnosis, I was getting this good news. I was in such a different place from the previous year as well. I had finally got my life back and was doing what I wanted. Of course, I want to go travelling long term/move countries but getting infusions every 8 weeks for potentially the rest of my life has put a spanner in the works with that. I'm not annoyed though, I'm eternally thankful and just have to plan trips differently. It's just adapting and thinking about things in new ways.

I had Australia upcoming a few weeks later, and it was great going with that news; it was also a great holiday. For Bali, we were on a schedule, so a lot of travelling and early starts that were starting to take their toll on the group. Oz was much better in this regard as I done loads, but on my own schedule, so it was very relaxing in comparison. Both trips felt like a really long time as well, and yet again, I nearly cried the day before leaving Melbourne as I didn't want to go home. It was such a nice holiday doing family things with my mum, Auntie Annie and some of her friends, then meeting my friends for drinking or lunch/dinner. It was great seeing my best friend Katie, even though she had just moved out there a few weeks before and I had last saw her just before she went. Anna-Marie lives in Preston, so I just got a 20-minute train into the City or to another burrow to meet friends. I kept being told to stop doing my Australian accent by Katie though, as she said I was at risk of being punched by a local. I begged to differ, it's pure class, in my opinion, "BLIMEY MATE ANOTHER BLOODY SCORCHAAA."

The journey I have been on the last few years I think was a catapult into some form of spiritual awakening, being forced to look at my shadow side, reflect and grow. Thinking back, it was probably traumatic at the time, but I didn't realise as I was just rolling with the punches. I wouldn't wish anything I went through on anybody, no matter how much I hated them (I don't actually hate anyone, so maybe that's also why, but I wouldn't wish it on a single person). I would never EVER want to go through it again, but at the same time, I have grown so much as a person, and I never would have if I didn't go through the suffering. In a time where nothing good seemed to happen, I was transforming like a lotus in the mud. In the thick of the mud, I just couldn't see the light at the top yet. What I have been through may also seem like absolute child's play for some compared to their life experiences. But we all experience different things for different reasons, and we all have our own life to live.

I think about myself and life so differently now; I don't take the little things for granted most people do. I try to find joy and love in everything I do. The expression money can't buy you happiness I was always aware of, but I truly believe now. And most importantly, your health is your wealth. But of course, with time and healing like everyone, I forget how bad things truly were and don't like to dwell on the past. I've learned, grown, strengthened, and took the life lessons. It's all you can do. In light of Coronavirus and the pandemic, I hope it gives people a moment to reflect and change their consciousness to what is important. But of course, when it all goes back to normal, over time, "normal" life will be taken for granted again, but there will be a remembrance. The stress of the Coronavirus situation actually caused another mini flare for a few weeks but thankfully calmed down again. I heard this also happened to a lot of people with Crohn's and various other illnesses as well. I would like people to remember though, when life goes back to normal for them, there are millions worldwide due to chronic illness, or other situations who cannot ever go back to normal, whilst the world is going on for everyone else.

Also, the government manages to fork out 80% of wages for people unable to work due to circumstances out of their control. Yet, pitiful allowances are given as benefits for those genuinely unable to work with medical evidence to back it up. The word "BENEFIT" in these circumstances needs to change. An offensive living allowance per week when unable to work due to illness or disability should not be called a BENEFIT. It is basic fucking SURVIVAL. There are obviously assholes who abuse the system and have ruined it for those actually in need, who should be shot the lazy fucking assholes. My Crohny bowels produce better quality shit than the piece of shit those fuckers are, but hey, it takes all sorts. I'm also not sure why money isn't put into getting people better or helping them recover, as in turn, most when better can return to work and therefore put back into the economy. Another thing people are massively freaking out about, the "crashing economy". Personally, my inner hippy says the economy is a social construct, and if it crashes, why not make a new one. But then again, I'm no economist.

What I have noticed, and the rest of the UK is now noticing, the cunt's that abuse the NHS. From some of my stories, I have shown how people are coming to A&E with no real medical emergency and completely ruining it for those in need. I have met women who have nearly died when admitted and could barely get the services they needed, due to stupid assholes who think having mild pain in your side for a few weeks warrants you going to the hospital on a Sunday because you're bored, then getting bored waiting so leave before being seen. WTF is that about!! For anyone who has been to A&E for themselves or with a loved one will know the wait is insanely long. Now we're in coronavirus season; imagine that wait whilst not being able to breathe or knowing there are too many people there, and you probably won't get the ventilator you or a loved one needs. It's scary the vast majority of the public (luckily) have absolutely no idea. It again makes me eternally thankful and grateful for everything my doctors, nurses, porters, auxiliary staff, radiographers, etc., have all done for me over the years. Bar the few who, as I've said, were assholes, but again you get all sorts in all workplaces. I'm not annoyed or angry at any of those situations anymore, it was a bigger reflection on the people who behaved that way, and I hope they someday find inner peace. I wouldn't be here today if it wasn't for the NHS, and I hope people wise up and realise along with Tory cuts, it is people abusing it that has it on its knees and ruining it for those genuinely in need. Thank you to the NHS from the bottom of my heart.

The Tory government having the absolute audacity to think they deserve pay rises whilst not protecting the UK adequately is beyond shocking and shows how out of touch they really are. I'm not arguing that they don't have hard jobs, not at all and in fact, don't envy them in the slightest. I don't think anyone really knows how to deal with a global pandemic, especially so unexpectedly. Like it wasn't initially in the job description. However, I can't imagine going to work knowing that both my life and my patient's lives are genuinely on the line, breaking news to families of their loved ones passing, having strangers body fluids sprayed on me, and knowing every decision I make directly impacts a human's life, all whilst working at least 12 hours a day in an extremely high stress and fast-paced environments. But sure, a patronising clap from the general public is enough. The government has the cheek to call our NHS "superheroes" (they are), yet if you think about it, every superhero had help. Batman has his Batmobile and his wee butler to help him out, Spiderman has his Spidey suit, and even Superman can be killed by kryptonite. Yet, our superheroes can't even get adequate PPE equipment.

The scars on my skin from the bad reactions have all disappeared except one. As the dermatologist said, my skin would stain, and the worst open wound on my left shin has a very faint pink mark still. Like all the others, it will go eventually, but for now it's a subtle reminder. I realise now I hated all my scars and stretch marks as they were reminders of everything going wrong and a bad time in my life. Scars run deep, they say, and that's exactly what it was. They were triggering, but now I don't mind them. They actually don't annoy me at all, and due to time, they have faded. Just like my internal scars, they have healed and faded over time. I realise now I was also mourning the loss of the person I would have been if I never had Crohn's disease/the life I would have had. I will never know that Sarah and I'm alright with that. I'm jealous she would probably be living in another country or have travelled the world already, but everything I went through made me who I am and got me to where I am today, and I wouldn't change that for the world. I've become a better, stronger person for it, and I'm proud to say I have learned to love myself unconditionally. Of course, there are flaws like all people, I mean, wouldn't it be great to be a bit skinnier or have bigger tits, but really, I don't care.

I'm totally cool with myself as a person, how I look, and how I am personality-wise, and it's really great. I never got any more fillers/injections and regretted my decisions as I healed (the "filler" was not filling the hole in me), although at 27 and with the incoming wrinkles, I should probably consider botox. Embrace your flaws and who you are. Your scars tell a story of what you survived, whether it be aesthetically pleasing or not. Be proud and unapologetic. You've fucking earned it! I think back to how I was and how badly I thought of myself, and I am now horrified. I was going through so much and as per usual was far too hard on myself, expecting perfection all the time. We're all only human and learn and grow from our mistakes and actions. I gave myself a second chance at life and loving myself, and beyond happy I did.

Mental health wise I am a different person and can safely say I am so happy I didn't kill myself. I'm honestly just happy to be here, taking the unexpected of life one day at a time. I have no fear of the unknown, and if anything, it excites me. It's a reminder I am alive, and yeah, things can be shit, but it's all about embracing it and growing as a person. It's so great to be able to reflect on my life now and see how far I've come out the other side. Times when I thought that was it and there was no future, also planning on ending any form of future as I couldn't see past the now due to pain. Caroline Flack's death I found particularly poignant as that poor woman couldn't see a way out or any end to her pain. I actually shed a tear upon her death, not just for her but for everyone in the world suffering. I could feel their pain, and when I was in that much pain, I couldn't see a way out, especially when being told by people there was. All I thought was that they couldn't empathise, and they had no idea what I was going through, so they could hardly understand. I also thought they were just saying it to stop me from doing anything but didn't really mean it. I was so far into a depression I thought no one could see the light and were just telling me lies to keep me going. But it wasn't true, they were right, and there is ALWAYS light at the end of the tunnel. It mightn't be today, it mightn't be tomorrow, but it WILL happen. It might feel like forever and that you can't get any lower, then you get a shock of something that brings you even lower, and you couldn't imagine that even being possible. But there is a way out, and you will get there. Good things come to those who wait, they say, and I thought I couldn't wait any longer. But I did, and it was all worth it.

I witnessed this first hand one day when getting an infusion whilst in remission, and a gentleman sat beside me who was in a bad colitis flare and facing the prospect of a bag. He had just been moved onto vedolizumab and was asking how it was as he was on the intro doses. I witnessed the anxiety as he went to the toilet before being attached to the pole, just in case. It was all so familiar. I told him it worked really well thankfully, and I thought I was in remission (it hadn't been confirmed yet, but it was about the summertime when I was doing well). We talked the whole time, and he told me about how upsetting he had found being unwell recently. He had missed school plays and a lot of other stuff of his kids due to illness and was obviously very upset. I could see it on his face, and it broke my heart. It made me think of my future, and this was a worry I already had thought about. What if I have kids one day and miss out because I'm sick. Or what if I pass it to them. I've been asked before if I could have a lab baby to ensure my kids don't have Crohn's, would I? Of course the answer is yes. It reminded me of my dad, who has arthritis which is autoimmune as well, and my mum had joked before saying he's the reason I have Crohn's.

The pain on his face was visible as she said this. Nobody wants to give anyone an incurable lifelong illness, especially not a loved one. If I were to have a child who unfortunately inherited Crohn's, the only positive would be they would have a mother who would understand them like nobody else. The gentleman I was speaking to I could tell was at breaking point. He had had years of good health before his colitis came out of remission, and he couldn't get out of this flare. I tried reassuring him and told him about myself and how I was the same, but this actually worked slowly but surely. He asked loads of questions, and I related to him a lot. I wished him all the best before going and hoped it all worked out, just keep sticking to it. I really hope it worked for him and he got his life back. It is all about weathering the long horrible storm.

Believe it or not, I have dated people/went back to my standard of pulling (kissing) on nights out. This time last year, I would not have believed that. But it's all been fun and nothing serious, which has been great as I'm really enjoying living my own life doing my own thing. It would take a king to be allowed to properly enter my queendom. Meeting someone really isn't something I'm fussed about at the moment. Not in a bad way, I just know what I want, and I'm not going to settle for less, like really, what is the point. I'm completely happy in and with myself, so any person I do meet, and something serious does happen will only be a bonus as I will have met someone great that I want to be a part of my already fabulous life. I mean don't get me wrong, I'm not where I want to be career-wise etc., but that all comes with the flow of life. I'm just so happy with where I am and excited for where the future will take me. My only priority is to be happy in life. Life's too short not to be.

Conor and I have got to a really good place and are good friends. It took a while, but we got there, and both have nothing but the highest things to say about each other. We both didn't want to lose each other's friendships, and as hard as it was at the start, we are now friendly enough to have even talked about dates we've been on with other people and laughed. We also have agreed we work much better as friends. We have been through so much together, and I'm forever thankful for Conor and the time we spent together, also the friendship we have established now. I wish him nothing but infinite love and happiness, and whoever he ends up with is an extremely lucky person. He's one of the kindest people I know, and he knows I will be eternally grateful for him. I'm forever sorry for the shit show I dragged him into; it wasn't fair, expected, or in any way normal, but he was amazing. Thank you for everything.

At the start of March 2020, I moved out of my parents. It has honestly been the best of fun, and it is so great having independence back after living back at home for over a year. My quarantine was extremely lucky and now I live with my friend Nicole, which has also been great. So here is where I leave you, 2020, a 27-year-old woman who is a different person than the scared, lost, little girl who started these memoirs. I didn't know where they were going to go when I started them, but I am so glad it has ended how it has. Being in remission, means I actually enjoyed lockdown and furlough. The isolation reminded me of being sick and unable to go out; however, as I am in good health, I was doing daily meditation, yoga, pilates, other workouts, hoping to come out of a quaranTEN lol. It is also a lot easier when the whole world is affected, not just you. I learned from being sick and unable to do anything, it's really not great for you, so I like to keep as active as possible. Obviously, with lazy rest days in between and listening to your body but I like being active. I always had been super active, and I'm back to that now. I also forgot I could cook and really enjoy it.

Understandably, the world isn't coping, and all underlying health conditions are flaring a bit due to the stress and fear of the unknown of a pandemic. I can testify this from recent personal experience as well. I hope the world is learning what myself and others who have had no choice but to learn, what is actually important in life. A lot of my friends have said to me that my priorities and life choices/goals are different to people my age, but they're great priorities. I just want to be happy, and everything else is a bonus—good health and happiness for me and the world. Life is far too short and you never know what is around the corner. There is no point in having regrets. I put myself in situations where I may get hurt or be vulnerable, as I have grown and learned how to express my feelings and validate them. It may be painful but guess what, so is life, and it is a reminder that I am alive and so thankful for it. I am so genuinely happy and thankful for everything and everyone in my life that as I type this, I am very cringely shedding a tear. I am by no means in an ideal life situation, but my story isn't over, and I am so excited for the future. I hope this Coronavirus pandemic is shedding this light onto others. As no lesson worth learning is ever easy, but the outcome makes it that much better. We will get through this, and it will become a memory we learn, reflect, and heal from. But hey, it Crohn-ly get better!

Printed in Great Britain
by Amazon